Thinking Well

An Introduction to Critical Thinking

D0218234

Thinking Well

An Introduction to Critical Thinking

STEWART E. KELLY

Minot State University

Boston   Burr Ridge, IL   Dubuque, IA   Madison, WI   New York
San Francisco   St. Louis   Bangkok   Bogotá   Caracas   Kuala Lumpur
Lisbon   London   Madrid   Mexico City   Milan   Montreal   New Delhi
Santiago   Seoul   Singapore   Sydney   Taipei   Toronto

McGraw-Hill Higher Education

A Division of The **McGraw-Hill** Companies

THINKING WELL

Published by McGraw-Hill, a business unit of The McGraw-Hill Companies, Inc., 1221 Avenue of the Americas, New York, NY, 10020. Copyright © 2001 by The McGraw-Hill Companies, Inc. All rights reserved. No part of this publication may be reproduced or distributed in any form or by any means, or stored in a database or retrieval system, without the prior consent of The McGraw-Hill Companies, Inc., including, but not limited to, in any network or other electronic storage or transmission, or broadcast for distance learning.
Some ancillaries, including electronic and print components, may not be available to customers outside the United States.

This book is printed on acid-free paper.

6 7 8 9 0 QSR/QSR 0 9 8 7

ISBN-13: 978-0-7674-1848-5
ISBN-10: 0-7674-1848-4

All rights reserved. No portion of this book may be reproduced in any form or by any means without written permission of the publisher.

Library of Congress Cataloging-in-Publication Data
Kelly, Stewart E. (Stewart Emmett),
   Thinking well : an introduction to critical thinking / Stewart E. Kelly.
      p. cm.
   Includes bibliographical references and index.
   ISBN 0-7674-1848-4
      1. Critical thinking. I. Title.

BF442.K45 2000
160—dc21   00-032908

Sponsoring editor, Kenneth King; production editor, Julianna Scott Fein; manuscript editor, Thomas L. Briggs; design manager and cover designer, Jean Mailander; text designer, Claire Seng-Niemoeller; cover illustrator, David Wink; art manager, Robin Mouat; illustrator, Emma Ghiselli; manufacturing manager, Randy Hurst. The text was set in 9.5/12.5 Stone Serif by Thompson Type and printed on acid-free 60# Finch Opaque by Malloy Lithographing, Inc.

Acknowledgments and copyrights are at the back of the book on page 270, which constitutes an extension of the copyright page.

www.mhhe.com

To Jane, the love of my life, and to
John Lachs, teacher, mentor, and friend

Preface

This book arises out of my experience teaching critical thinking over the past fourteen years. Over time it became evident that many critical thinking texts were logically rigorous yet lacking in user-friendliness. Other texts emphasized clarity and student accessibility but were deficient regarding logical rigor. Unable to find a text that emphasized both elements, I decided to write my own, one that would capture both of these crucial ingredients.

The text is informal and conversational, and the prose is clear and straightforward. I explain a wide range of challenging concepts in clear, nontechnical language, and I keep academic jargon to a minimum. In addition to being user-friendly, however, the text retains logical rigor. I challenge students to carefully develop the skills necessary for thinking well, and I emphasize both the precise use of language and the right application of critical thinking skills.

Although the primary goal of this book is not to entertain students, I believe that learning good thinking skills and having fun are not mutually exclusive. With that in mind, I include liberal doses of humor as a reminder that none of us should take ourselves too seriously. The result is that students are challenged to learn good thinking skills while enjoying themselves at the same time. Students who work their way through this book should greatly improve their thinking skills, enjoy themselves along the way, and become more aware of the considerable practical benefits of thinking well.

OVERVIEW OF THE TEXT

The text covers a wide range of topics, and the chapters are arranged so that each chapter builds on the ones preceding it. Chapter 1 introduces students to critical thinking and its benefits. Chapter 2 briefly examines the contributions of Socrates and Descartes to thinking well and looks at common obstacles to good thinking. Chapter 3 focuses on the role of language and emphasizes the importance of using language carefully and precisely. Before arguments can be evaluated, they must be identified and labeled, and Chapter 4 presents the tools to do these tasks.

Chapter 5 tackles the central ideas of validity and soundness, helping students learn how to distinguish between good and bad arguments. Needless to say, there are many ways to reason in a poor or improper fashion, and Chapter 6 presents twenty-two fallacies with the goal of helping students better identify and respond to these flawed types of reasoning. People do not reason in a vacuum but are significantly influenced by a wide range of factors. In light of this fact, Chapter 7 examines the idea of worldview and shows how people with divergent worldviews may approach controversial topics differently. Students are challenged to see how a worldview influences how we think about important issues. The problem of evil in the world and the recent legal and political challenges encountered by President Clinton are examined so that students might see concrete examples of the influence of worldview.

Like almost everyone else, students struggle when asked to evaluate issues involving values. Chapter 8 discusses matters of taste and aesthetic judgments and surveys some of the most common approaches to moral issues. This chapter also examines the popular view known as ethical relativism and questions whether the common understanding of this view is a reasonable one. Chapter 9 models the various skills that students have learned over the course of the first eight chapters. The issue of capital punishment is explored in depth, with the main arguments, pro and con, carefully evaluated. Finally, in Chapter 10, students have an opportunity to apply all they have learned to date. The essays in this chapter cover a wide range of thought-provoking issues, including starvation, the existence of evil, and capital punishment.

There are exercises throughout the book. Questions marked with a star are answered in the answer section in the back of the book.

DISTINCTIVE FEATURES

One objective of this text is to appeal to a broad range of students by introducing a number of features not found elsewhere. The seven distinctive features in this text can be summarized as follows:

- Students often ask, "Why should I study this stuff?" Chapter 1 challenges students to consider five benefits of learning to think more critically.

- Chapter 1 also introduces students to the characteristics of critical thinkers, thus giving them goals to strive toward.

- Chapter 2 focuses on the importance of leading an examined life and on obstacles to critical thinking. Students are challenged to carefully examine their own lives.

- Though it is widely believed that our worldview plays a significant role in shaping our thinking, this belief is rarely discussed in critical thinking texts. Chapter 7 explores this important idea.

- Judgments involving matters of beauty in music and the arts—aesthetic judgments—are discussed in Chapter 8, where it is argued that claims such as "Bach is better than Brahms" are not entirely subjective, as is sometimes thought.

- One of the benefits of thinking well is learning how to think more clearly about moral issues. Chapter 8 introduces students to the domain of ethics and includes an examination of ethical relativism and three other approaches to ethical theory.

- Finally, Chapters 9 and 10 present students with a number of interesting and challenging essays on which to practice their newfound critical thinking skills.

SUGGESTIONS FOR USING THE TEXT

The text covers aspects of both informal logic (critical thinking) and formal logic. Chapters 4 and 5 focus on the formal elements, while the remaining chapters are either introductory (Chapters 1 and 2) or more on the informal side of the spectrum (Chapter 6 especially). Chapter 3 (on language) and Chapters 7 and 8 (on worldview and values respectively) can be profitably used with either an informal or formal emphasis, and Chapters 9 and 10 tie together the entire book. The text is designed so that most or all of it can be covered in a one-semester course.

ACKNOWLEDGMENTS

Many individuals have helped me along the way. I have used a number of critical thinking/logic texts over the years, and a number of them have been of value in preparing this book. These include Brooke Moore and Richard Parker, *Critical Thinking;* Trudy Govier, *A Practical Study of Arguments;* Jerry Cederblom and David Paulsen, *Critical Reasoning;* and C. Stephen Layman, *The Power of Logic.*

The people at Mayfield demonstrated wisdom, patience, and encouragement in helping me move from first draft to the final product. I would like to thank Ken King, Senior Editor, for his many valuable suggestions and doing much to make the book better, and Julianna Scott Fein, Senior Production Editor, for her advice and encouragement along the way. Also, thanks to Marty Granahan, Permissions Editor; Katherine Bates, Marketing Communications Specialist; Jean Mailander, Design Manager; and the rest of the staff at Mayfield. My copyeditor, Tom Briggs, also deserves many thanks for carefully reading and polishing the sometimes rough text before him.

I am significantly indebted to a number of reviewers, who made many constructive suggestions. They include Richard Botkin, Avila College; Gordon

Brown, Grossmont Community College; Alberto Carrillo, Rio Hondo College; C. Lynne Fulmer, Southwest Texas State University; Cynthia Gobatie, Riverside Community College; Anthony Hanson, DeAnza College; Henry Liem, San Jose City College; Janet Madden, Ph.D., El Camino College; and Julio Torres, Los Angeles City College.

I would like to thank Minot State University for granting me release time to work on the book. I also wish to thank two good friends for their support and encouragement along the way: Jay Wahlund and Greg Strand, who modeled the virtue of friendship. Finally, I would like to express my deep gratitude to my wife, Jane, and to my daughters, Anne and Katie, for patiently enduring my frequent absences as I worked on the book. Their love and support helped make it all possible.

Contents

6   *Fallacies*   134

7   *Knowledge and Worldview*   176

8   *Thinking about Values*   202

9   **Putting It All Together**   224

10   **Essays for Analysis**   238

CHAPTER 1

Introduction to Critical Thinking

FIRST THOUGHTS

All think what other people think. —W. B. Yeats, "The Scholars"

In recent years Americans have been challenged to consider a host of issues— for example, (1) Should the tobacco industry be more heavily regulated? and (2) Should same-sex marriages be legally recognized? and (3) Should abortions be legally permitted? Many of us have an opinion on some or all of these matters. But what is more important is whether our opinion is an *informed* one. This involves having reasons (especially good ones) for our beliefs.

How can we tell the difference between a good reason, a mediocre reason, and a poor reason? This is not an easy question to answer. One goal of this book is to help you learn how to tell the difference between a good (well-reasoned) argument and a bad (poorly reasoned) argument. An **argument** is a group of claims in which one or more claims are offered in support of another claim. Each supporting claim is called a **premise**, while the main claim is called the **conclusion**. A **claim**, by contrast, is simply a sentence that is either true or false.

Here are some examples of claims:

Sacramento is in California.

Millard Fillmore was our greatest president.

The Minnesota Vikings are a good football team.

The economy is booming.

Santayana was a philosopher.

Other people may disagree with us about one or more of these claims. The question then becomes, How do we settle disagreements? Merely exchanging opinions is not very satisfactory. Suppose I say that X is true and you respond that it is false. Unless some reason(s) is given for either supporting or rejecting the claim, what we have is **mere** (or **factual**) **disagreement.** Many of us grew up hearing disagreements of this sort. A classic example would go something like the following: "Is not!" "Is too!" "Is not!" "Is too!" and so on. Obviously very little is accomplished other than the people involved getting more and more frustrated.

One goal of critical thinking is to move beyond mere disagreement to **reasoned disagreement.** Here both sides offer reasons (other claims) in support of their point of view and are willing to discuss the strengths and weaknesses of those various supporting reasons. This process is both civilized and constructive. It is civilized in that certain rules are observed (such as no name calling), and it is constructive in that both parties may hope to learn from and benefit from the exchange of ideas.

Critical thinking is the careful and reflective process of evaluating claims and arguments. One goal of critical thinking is **rationality,** or having a reasonable belief. A claim is rational when there is more evidence in favor of the claim than against it. But rationality also is a matter of degree, in that some claims are more (or less) reasonable than others. Consider these examples:

1. Today it will rain.
2. Elvis Presley is alive and well.
3. 2 plus 2 equals 4.

Claim 1 is *more* reasonable than claim 2 but *less* reasonable than claim 3.

Even if all this is true, you may be wondering, "Why should I bother?" Indeed, why should anyone care whether they know anything about critical thinking? A course in critical thinking may involve all of the following:

Getting three college credits

Meeting nice people

Preparing for the LSAT

But if none of these benefits strike you as particularly compelling, the question remains, Why bother?

BENEFITS OF CRITICAL THINKING

There are a number of benefits of knowing something about critical thinking. They include, but are not limited to, the following:

1. **Autonomy.** This involves being self-directed and in control. We need to know who we are and what we are doing (and why) if we are to be truly self-directed. Specifically, critical thinking helps us figure out these things with regard to autonomy:

BORN LOSER® by Art and Chip Sansom

Good thinking skills help us separate truth from falsehood. THE BORN LOSER reprinted by permission of Newspaper Enterprise Association, Inc.

a. Who we are (a sense of self). This is a difficult and lifelong process.

b. What we believe, and why. The "what" part is relatively easy, but the "why" part is another matter.

c. Why we do what we do. (This involves knowing the motives for our various actions.)

d. What our goals are.

e. How we can best attain these goals. Knowing what we are doing at a given time may improve our chances of being happy, something all of us are interested in.

f. How we should live our lives. Philosophers and others have debated this matter for thousands of years; there is broad consensus only that it is an important question, worthy of everyone's attention.

Autonomy is not an all-or-nothing thing but a matter of degree. Although autonomy cannot be achieved overnight, learning to think critically can help get us started along the road to self-direction.

2. **Political literacy.** This refers to when citizens are well informed and reflective concerning the important issues of the day. For democracies and representative republics (like the United States) to survive and prosper, citizens should have some idea of what they are doing— and why—when they vote. Thomas Jefferson and many others viewed a politically illiterate public as the death knell of any truly democratic society.[1] Only as educated and informed citizens can we hold our government accountable for its policies and actions.

3. **Social values.** This is the "glue" that holds a society together. Societies require a shared set of values, traditions, and practices if there is

---

[1] Contrary to popular belief, colonial America was not a collection of people with only a limited number having the ability to read and write. Thomas Paine's *Common Sense* (1776), an intellectually challenging call to revolution, sold more than 100,000 copies within three months of its publication—despite a vastly smaller population than today's and the rather academic tone of the book.

> ### Five Benefits of Critical Thinking
>
> 1. **Autonomy.** This involves being self-directed and in control, so we know who we are and what we are doing, and why.
>
> 2. **Political literacy.** This refers to voters being well informed and reflective concerning the important issues of the day, so we can hold the government accountable for its policies and actions.
>
> 3. **Social values.** We require a shared set of values, traditions, and practices if there is to be social cohesion and stability and if we are to identify and respond to major social problems.
>
> 4. **Career considerations.** Many jobs require the ability to solve problems and to think creatively and independently.
>
> 5. **Practical considerations.** Critical thinking skills can greatly enhance the wisdom of our everyday choices.

to be social cohesion and stability. Such values can also help us identify and respond to social problems such as racism, sexism, and poverty.

4. **Career considerations.** Many jobs require the ability to solve problems and to think critically, creatively, and independently. The ability to think well should also help us figure out both what we are good at and what we might like to pursue as a career. So, if learning critical thinking helps us get a better job, and getting a better job improves our chances of leading a fulfilling life, then learning critical thinking can actually contribute to our leading a better life! It is hard to think of a better reason to do something than that it makes our life better.

5. **Practical considerations.** Critical thinking skills can greatly enhance the wisdom of our everyday choices. Here are some typical dilemmas you might face:
    a. Which car to buy. Clearly not all cars are of equal value, but which cars are better, and according to what standard?
    b. What is important to do today? Obviously some of the things we might do are more important than others.
    c. Whom, if anyone, to marry.
    d. How to handle money.
    e. What to look for and value in friends.
    f. How to connect current activities to long-term goals.
    g. What to eat.

Many of our conversations focus on controversial issues—for example, the abortion issue or the gay rights issue or the capital punishment issue. One of the realities of everyday conversations is that key issues often are not identified, and the resulting disagreements are not very profitable.

Consider the issue of capital punishment. This broad issue involves a number of different questions, including the following: Is capital punishment an appropriate punishment for some crimes? Should the electric chair be used to execute offenders? Is capital punishment applied fairly? Are innocent people ever put to death? Should capital punishment be applied if absolute certainty about a person's guilt is lacking? Is mandatory life in prison an acceptable alternative to capital punishment? These questions all revolve around the central issue of capital punishment, but each focuses on a different aspect. This suggests that when disagreements occur it's important to identify the main issue (or issues) at hand. Only then can we have a rational discussion.

Disagreements often occur because people are not even addressing the same issue. Consider the following:

Bill: We need to have tighter gun controls so violence won't occur in our schools.

Lisa: You know that the right to own guns is guaranteed by the Second Amendment.

Notice that Bill is suggesting a way to limit gun-related violence, while Lisa is focused on an amendment to the Constitution. The two issues may be related, but Lisa has said nothing about the main issue that Bill is focusing on, namely, the problem of gun-related violence in schools. In short, critical thinking skills help us identify issues, think about them clearly and rationally, and interact with others who are attempting to do the same thing.

COMMON MISCONCEPTIONS ABOUT CRITICAL THINKING

It is important to note that we can think poorly about critical thinking itself. For example, people sometimes view critical thinking as a bad or undesirable kind of thinking. But practicing critical thinking does *not* mean being a negative or "critical" person. Critical thinking might be more accurately called "reflective" or "evaluative" thinking, for it involves thinking about an argument and evaluating it in light of certain standards.

Critical thinking also has been wrongly accused of promoting intolerance. **Tolerance**—respecting other people's lifestyles and opinions—is a good thing, and some claim that critical thinking promotes intolerance by suggesting that some claims are more reasonable than others. Tolerance is indeed a good thing, but there is nothing about critical thinking, properly applied, that undermines tolerance. We can think that our view is more reasonable than someone else's while still fully respecting that individual as a human being. By participating in a civilized discussion with someone about, say, capital punishment, we can demonstrate that, though we may disagree with that person's views, we still respect him or her as a person and still take his or her views seriously.

Calvin and Hobbes

by Bill Watterson

People tend to think they're always right. CALVIN AND HOBBES © Watterson. Reprinted with permission of UNIVERSAL PRESS SYNDICATE. All rights reserved.

Finally, most philosophers believe that we can know little with complete certainty. If this is true, does it mean that our beliefs in general are merely guesses? Not necessarily. Though perhaps we can know little with certainty, we can still know that many things *probably* are true. This means that the evidence supports one belief as opposed to another and that our commitment should not be to certainty (rarely attained by humans) but to probability and reasonableness. Damon Runyon, an American writer and journalist, once wrote that "the race is not always to the swift nor the battle to the strong, but that's the way to bet." In other words, as creatures capable of reason, we should believe ("bet") according to what is probable or likely.

COMMON CHARACTERISTICS OF CRITICAL THINKERS

Though thinking well is a matter of degree, all critical thinkers have some characteristics in common.

Honesty

One of Socrates' virtues was that he knew how little he knew.[2] Critical thinkers are honest with themselves—they know what their areas of expertise are and what their limitations are. Unfortunately we generally have many more areas of limited knowledge than we do areas of expertise!

Humility

Knowledge of our own limitations promotes intellectual humility. We need to be able to admit that we may not have all the answers. The fact that on any given issue many thoughtful and intelligent people will fundamentally dis-

---

[2] Socrates was a Greek philosopher (470–399 B.C.) who is famous both for being a great thinker and for teaching Plato, another of the great thinkers in Western civilization.

Five Characteristics of Critical Thinkers

1. **Honesty.** Critical thinkers are honest with themselves—they know what their areas of expertise are and what their limitations are.

2. **Humility.** Knowledge of our own limitations promotes intellectual humility, which involves keeping an open mind and being aware of the possibility that we could be wrong.

3. **Patience.** Critical thinking, like most important things in life, involves hard work over a period of time if the appropriate skills are to be acquired and maintained.

4. **Self-awareness.** We all have "lenses" through which we view reality, and we need to know what our individual lens is composed of and how it influences our perception of reality.

5. **Social interaction.** We need to interact with others and to be genuinely interested in the ideas of others, especially since it is highly unlikely that all of our beliefs are reasonable.

agree with our view should encourage a sense of modesty rather than arrogance or a "know-it-all" attitude. Also, the more we do know, the more we realize how little we *really* know. Humility, then, involves keeping an open mind and being aware that we could be mistaken in our beliefs, even on matters that are important to us.

Patience

A lack of patience is one of the main reasons people jump to conclusions, and jumping to conclusions is one of the major roadblocks to developing good critical thinking skills. Also, many of us are daunted by long-term tasks that involve hard work. But critical thinking, like most important things in life, involves hard work over a period of time if the appropriate skills are to be acquired and maintained. Skills, by their very nature, do not come easily and cannot be developed quickly. Our goal should be to get a little better, a little more proficient, each day and each week. No one learns how to play the cello or to be a top golfer without practicing long and hard, and learning to think well is no different. If you want to become good at it, you have to work at it.

Self-Awareness

We all approach life from a unique point of view. It is not possible, contrary to what some claim, to approach reality with complete "objectivity." To accomplish this we would have to abandon all of our assumptions and biases and anything else about ourselves that is the product of culture. For example, the fact that I am an East Coast, middle-class, college-educated American has a lot to do with how I look at the world. We all have "lenses" through which we view reality. These lenses not only help us see reality but also play a part in shaping our understanding of that reality. We need to know what our individual lens is composed of and how it influences our perception of reality. Learning how to think critically can be thought of in terms of "polishing the lens" through which we view reality. The more we polish it, the more clearly we see and understand the world.

The fact that we all have our own unique lenses does not mean that all knowledge is entirely a matter of perspective—that is, how we look at it. Although we cannot be completely objective, it does not follow that all human knowledge is completely subjective. (We will return to this important matter in Chapter 7.)

Social Interaction

We need to interact with others, and we need to be genuinely interested in the ideas of others, especially since it is highly unlikely that all of our beliefs are reasonable. Plato, Aristotle, and many other great thinkers believed that humans are social creatures who do best in the context of community. We need other people not only for companionship but also as sounding boards for our own ideas and as sources of new ideas.

SUMMARY

Critical thinking is an important skill in interpreting both everyday matters and issues of greater significance. Critical thinking promotes autonomy, political literacy, and social values; it helps us vocationally; and it aids us in making everyday decisions. Critical thinking also is compatible with tolerance of and respect for other people. And even though we can know little with certainty, as critical thinkers we can still have many beliefs that are probably true. Critical thinkers are honest with themselves and have intellectual humility, patience, self-awareness, and a need for interaction with and feedback from others. Learning to think critically can benefit us all in many ways.

EXERCISE 1.1

Answer each of the following.

★ 1. What is an informed opinion?

2. What is the meaning of the word *conclusion* in the statement "That is the conclusion of the argument"?

3. What is the difference between mere disagreement and reasoned disagreement?

★ 4. Define critical thinking in your own words. How does your definition compare to the one in the text?

5. What is autonomy, and why should people pursue it?

6. Is political literacy important for a society in which citizens have a significant say in government? Defend your answer.

★ 7. For what decisions in life will it be especially important that you make wise and careful choices?

8. Does critical thinking promote intolerance? Why or why not?

9. Why is it important for critical thinkers to practice humility?

★ 10. How aware are you of the influences on your outlook on life? For example, how much have each of the following influenced you?
   a. Your parent(s)
   b. Your friends
   c. Your siblings
   d. Your neighborhood (or the area where you grew up)
   e. Your school/education
   f. Television
   g. The Internet
   h. Movies
   i. Music
   j. Your gender

EXERCISE 1.2

For each exchange, determine which of the following is present: (1) mere agreement, (2) reasoned agreement, (3) mere disagreement, or (4) reasoned disagreement.

★ 1. *Reggie:* My school is the best.
   Tanisha: Is not.

2. *Victor:* Lincoln was a great president.
   Danny: Yeah, right.

3. *Lili:* Affirmative action is a good policy.
   Camilla: I think you're right—it helps make up for past injustices.

★ 4. *Dawei:* If you work hard in life, then you will probably be successful.
   Sarah: I think you're right.

5. *Marcus:* I don't think you should go out with her. She treats guys like dirt.
   Grant: Yeah, I know. I saw how she dumped on poor Allan.

6. *Nannan:* I think it's pretty clear that God exists.
   Arthur: Oh, gimme a break, will you?!

★   7. *Cheryl:* I think being a doctor would be rewarding and fulfilling.
       Dave: Yeah, especially with all that money they make.

   8. *Colleen:* I think same-sex marriages should be legally recognized.
       Nikki: It's pretty obvious you're right.

   9. *Charlie:* The summers in the South are hot and humid.
       Amy: I don't think so.

★ 10. *Adrian:* It's OK to speed as long as you don't get caught.
       Semeka: I disagree. Is it OK to commit murder as long as you don't get caught?

EXERCISE 1.3

For each of the following, indicate whether you think it is a rational belief. Be prepared to give at least one reason for each answer.

1. Sacramento is in California.

2. Sex education should be taught in the public schools.

3. The police should not shoot unarmed criminals.

4. Potato chips taste better than dirt.

5. Schools should not have a dress code.

6. Free speech means we should be able to say anything we want at any time we want, with no penalty.

7. Human life has value.

8. Mosquitoes have less value than humans.

9. Elvis is alive and well and living in Encino.

10. It is stupid to commit suicide.

11. The United States is a great country.

12. Racism is a problem in the United States today.

13. Women should wear makeup so they look better.

14. Children should not be spanked for any reason.

15. Parents should never say "no" to children but should always give them what they want.

16. There is too much violence on TV.

17. Life is full of obstacles.

18. We should treat others as we ourselves would want to be treated.

19. Physical objects exist.

20. I am currently awake and not dreaming.

EXERCISE 1.4

For each of the following, identify the point the first speaker is making, and then determine whether the second speaker is addressing the same issue.

★ 1. *Female student:* All you guys are interested in is sex.

   Male student: And all you women are interested in is fashion and malls.

   2. *Pro:* If people are allowed to own handguns, then crime will definitely go down.

   Con: That's not true. Studies show that areas with high handgun ownership rates have no less crime than areas with low rates.

   3. *Joe Winter:* Snow is what makes winter great.

   Jane Summer: Yeah, if you're a penguin or a walrus!

★ 4. *Raylene:* If we study hard, our chances of passing the math test will increase.

   Desiree: But I hate studying!

   5. *Marshall:* We shouldn't allow Third World countries to get nuclear bombs.

   Ron: I think you're wrong. We handle that kind of thing responsibly, and they will too.

   6. *Hans:* She's a maniac!

   Steffi: And your momma wears army boots!

★ 7. *Citizen 1:* In 2004 it will be Al Gore versus John McCain in the presidential election.

   Citizen 2: I don't like either one of them.

   8. *Antoine:* Michael Jordan is the best basketball player ever.

   Mark: Nope—Magic Johnson could do more things well than Jordan.

   9. *Peter:* You should never intentionally kill any living creature.

   Kim: Come over to my yard this summer when the mosquitoes are out in full force. Then we'll see if your approach is realistic.

★ 10. *Metalhead:* Metallica is the best group ever, of any kind, period.

   Non-metalhead: Have you ever heard of the Beatles? They had many more top-40 hits than Metallica ever did.

EXERCISE 1.5

For each of the following, identify the main issue being presented.

★ 1. "Christine Craft . . . was fired in August 1981 because research indicated that her appearance hampered viewer acceptance." (Neil Postman, *Amusing Ourselves to Death*)

   a. Whether Christine Craft was a woman
   b. Whether "hampered viewer acceptance" is valid grounds for dismissal
   c. Whether she was fired
   d. Whether she was fired for bad reasons

2. "In a study released today, the Cato Institute in Washington cites last year's 41-bullet police slaying of Amadou Diallo, an unarmed Bronx immigrant, as evidence that the department's practice of stopping and frisking mostly black and Hispanic men is lethal." (Hans Chen, "NYPD Is a Threat to the Public, Study Says")

   a. Whether the NYPD killed a man
   b. Whether Amadou Diallo was killed
   c. Whether the Cato Institute issued a report
   d. Whether the NYPD policy of stopping and frisking blacks and Hispanics is flawed

3. "An incapacity to have children cannot, any more than an unwillingness to have children, establish ineligibility; otherwise sterile men, post-menopausal women, and couples uninterested in child rearing would be ineligible." (George Will, "Judges and the Definition of Marriage," on whether homosexual couples should be allowed to legally marry)

   a. Whether only some couples should have children
   b. Whether not being able to have children should make a couple ineligible for marriage
   c. Whether it is good to have children
   d. Whether homosexual couples should be allowed to adopt children

★ 4. "The way cops perceive blacks—and how those perceptions shape and mis-shape crime fighting—is now the most charged racial issue in America. The systematic harassment of black drivers in New Jersey, the shooting of Amadou Diallo, an unarmed African immigrant, by New York City police officers earlier this year, and other incidents in other states have brought the relationship between blacks and cops to a level of seemingly irreversible toxicity." (Jeffrey Goldberg, "The Color of Suspicion")

   a. Whether police have a difficult job
   b. Whether racism exists in the United States today
   c. Whether the relationship between cops and blacks is an especially bad one
   d. Whether New Jersey is a bad place for blacks to live

5. "Smokers' attorney Stanley Rosenblatt argued all three plaintiffs became addicted in the 1950s, long before they became aware of the health dangers of smoking, even though the industry was discovering links to disease and addiction at the same time." (*USA Today*, "Jury Orders Big Tobacco to Pay Up")

   a. Whether some people smoke too much
   b. Whether smoking is addictive
   c. Whether tobacco companies care about the health of smokers
   d. Whether some smokers started smoking before there was public knowledge of smoking's dangers

EXERCISE 1.6

In a paragraph or two, state your position on two of the following issues, and offer one good reason in support of your position.

1. Should abortion be legal?

2. Was O. J. Simpson guilty? Focus here on the evidence, and not the verdict, in the criminal trial.

3. Should same-sex marriages be legally recognized? Note that the question focuses on the *legal* aspects of the controversy, and not necessarily the *moral* ones.

4. Is affirmative action a good thing?

5. Should the lyrics of hard rock or rap groups be censored?

6. Does God exist?

7. Is human nature fundamentally good? What might be meant by "good" here?

EXERCISE 1.7

1. For each of the following statements, identify the main point being made.
★ a. "You ain't nothin' but a hound dog, cryin' all the time." (Jerry Leiber and Mike Stoller, "Hound Dog")
   b. "Life is like a sewer. What you get out of it depends on what you put into it." (Tom Lehrer, "We Will All Go Together When We Go")
   c. "Will you still need me, will you still feed me, when I'm sixty-four?" (John Lennon and Paul McCartney, "When I'm Sixty-Four")
★ d. Whether President Clinton had an extramarital affair has nothing to do with whether he was a good president.
   e. The important thing in sports is to play your best, so it doesn't really matter that the Boston Red Sox haven't won the World Series since 1918.
   f. "The proper study of mankind is books." (Aldous Huxley, *Chrome Yellow*)
★ g. "Despair is the price one pays for setting oneself an impossible aim." (Graham Greene, *Heart of the Matter*)
   h. "Don't look back, someone may be gaining on you." (Satchel Paige)

2. For each of the following statements, identify the main point, and indicate what support, if any, is offered for the main claim.
★ a. Dr. Jack Kevorkian[3] is aiding in the premature death of human beings, and this is morally wrong. It violates both the Hippocratic oath and the dignity of the patient.
   b. Capital punishment does not deter murder so it should not be practiced.
   c. Women are treated better than men. We know this because women are paid more than men for the same kind of work.
★ d. The biggest problem in the United States today is violent crime. It is the biggest problem because it impacts the most people.
   e. Polygamy is morally right if each spouse is loved.
   f. The finals of the World Cup soccer tournament should not be decided by penalty kicks because there is too much luck involved. Rather, the teams should keep playing until someone scores a goal.
★ g. Animals should have as many rights as human beings because there is nothing special about human beings.
   h. Consumers have confidence in the economy, so the economy must be doing well.

---

[3] Kevorkian, a medical doctor in Michigan, has helped a number of terminally ill patients end their life by means of a lethal injection of drugs.

GLOSSARY

argument   When a claim is presented and one or more reasons are given in support of it.

premise   A supporting claim in an argument.

conclusion   The main claim in an argument.

claim   Any sentence that is true or false.

mere (or **factual**) **disagreement**   When two or more people disagree about a claim but fail to support their views.

reasoned disagreement   When two or more people disagree and reasons are offered in support of their views.

critical thinking   The careful and reflective process of evaluating claims and arguments.

rationality   The state of being reasonable; not to be confused with the word *rationalize,* which means "to make excuses for."

autonomy   Self-direction or independence; it involves being in control of one's life to the extent that such a thing is possible.

political literacy   When the citizens of a country know what the key issues are and have some idea of what they believe (on these issues), and why.

tolerance   Allowing others the freedom to live as they please as long as they are not harming you; to live and let live.

CHAPTER 2

Obstacles to Thinking Well

The easiest person to deceive is one's self.
—*Edward Bulwer-Lytton,* The Disowned

The unexamined life is not worth living.   —*Plato,* Apology

SOCRATES AND THE EXAMINED LIFE

Socrates (470–399 B.C.) is one of the key figures in the history of Western thought. He is worth studying for many reasons, but here our concern is his emphasis on the importance of the examined life. Specifically, what did Socrates mean when he claimed that the unexamined life is not worth living?

Before we discuss the relative merits of the examined life, we should say a few words about Socrates' views on human beings in general. He believed that each of us has both a body and a soul (psyche). In this view, often called "mind-body dualism," humans have two basic components: a physical body and a nonphysical soul. Our soul gives us the ability to reason and to reflect on who we are and what life is about. The person leading an unexamined (unreflective) life simply is not living up to his or her potential as a human being, so the unexamined life is a life of wasted potential. Put another way, the unexamined life is a life contrary to our basic (thinking) nature as human beings. To have some idea as to what life is about and how we fit in as individuals, we must regularly use our ability to ask probing questions. Examples of such questions include (1) What is most important in life? (2) What is happiness? and (3) How should I live my life?

We all know of individuals who had significant talents in some arena but who never worked at developing those talents, thus allowing those talents to go untapped and unrealized. And we regard this as a waste. What Socrates claimed about the unexamined life is analogous. We all have the ability to

15

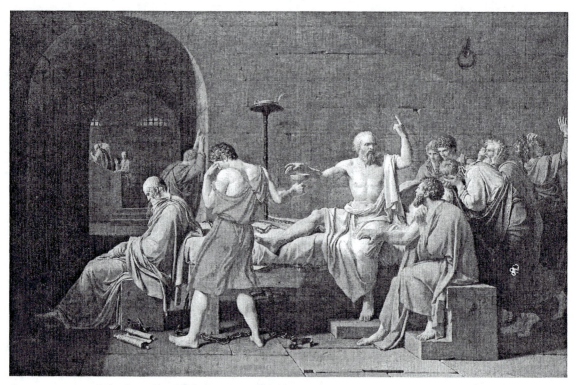

Socrates promoted the "examined life" as an ongoing process involving reflection on important issues. Jacques-Louis David, *The Death of Socrates.* The Metropolitan Museum of Art, Catherine Lorillard Wolfe Collection, Wolfe Fund, 1931. (31.45) Photograph © 1995 The Metropolitan Museum of Art.

think and reflect about what is most important, and the life of mindless conformity and "couch-potatohood" is a wasted life, a life of squandered potential and opportunities.

It is not necessarily a bad thing to do as our parents do or to believe as they believe. But it is a bad thing to do this *unreflectively.* If we unreflectively believe what our parents believe, then our beliefs are not our own. When we reflect on a specific belief that our parents hold and decide that it is a reasonable belief, then we make it our own belief; in a sense we make it a genuine part of ourselves. Just because our parents or friends or culture believes X to be true is no guarantee that it is in fact true. Thus we must carefully examine each belief.

To begin leading the **examined life,** you need answers to the following:

1. What do you believe? To answer this, begin by listing your most important beliefs. For example, ask yourself this:

   a. What are the best things in life (the things that make life meaningful)? Here are some possibilities:

      1. Happiness

The Best Things in Life

Things that make life meaningful include the following:

Happiness	Beauty
Love	Peace of mind
Material possessions	Living in harmony with all life
Sex	Liberty
Physical pleasure	Equality
Friendship	Wisdom
God	Moral virtue
Music	Autonomy

Which of these are most important to you? Is there anything you might add to this list?

2. Love
3. Material possessions
4. Sex
5. Friendship
6. Moral virtue
7. Belief in God (or a supreme being of some sort)
8. Music
9. Beauty
10. Peace of mind
11. Living in harmony with all life
12. Liberty
13. Wisdom
14. Autonomy
15. Marx Brothers' movies
16. Nothing

b. Does God exist? Here you must first define what "God" means before you can try to answer the question.

c. What is happiness? How do you get from where you are (for example, moderately happy or unhappy) to where you want to be?

d. Is there an afterlife of any kind? After you die, will you come back as a houseplant, live on through your soul, or simply stay in the ground?

e. What is a human being? What characteristics do you share with all other humans? B. F. Skinner, a well-known American psychologist, and others believe that humans are not qualitatively different from higher animals. Is Skinner correct?

Calvin and Hobbes

by Bill Watterson

Television is one of the pillars of modern American culture, but it may be an impediment to the examined life. CALVIN AND HOBBES © Watterson. Reprinted with permission of UNIVERSAL PRESS SYNDICATE. All rights reserved.

    f. What are your personal goals in life? How do you plan to achieve them?

    g. Who are you? What does it mean to have a sense of "self"?

2. Why do you believe what you do?

3. What are some possible reasons for believing contrary to what you believe?

4. Do you have a good reason for rejecting each of the contrary beliefs?

5. In light of your response to question 4, does your belief need to be either modified or rejected? Why or why not?

Some people complain that the examined life is for intellectuals and the highly intelligent, but not for average folks like themselves. But everyone has the ability to reflect on life and everyday human existence. The fact that we may not be geniuses does not get us off the hook so easily. Most of us have the ability to think long and hard about the questions just listed. So the examined life is an equal opportunity kind of thing, and not some sort of elitist trip reserved for the very intelligent.

Not only is the examined life an equal opportunity matter; it is also a long-term thing. For example, we do not, at age 18 or 21 or 30, go away for a weekend, nail down all the answers to the questions, and then end up with it for life. The examined life is a lifelong process and thus requires a lifelong commitment. Besides, as we get older, we often find that the views of our youth were simplistic, naive, or uninformed. How many times have you said, "If I had only known then what I know now"? So, just as we now know more than we did ten years ago, we may also reasonably assume that we will continue to learn and understand more as we go through life.

DEVELOPING A SENSE OF SELF

Socrates emphasized the importance of knowing ourselves, but this kind of knowledge is not easily gained. To illustrate, imagine that you are at a party and someone you do not know (Kate) comes up to you and asks, "Who are you?" You respond that your name is Anne, and the following dialogue ensues:

Kate: I'm glad to know that your name is Anne, but who exactly is Anne?

Anne: What do you mean?

Kate: Well, for example, you could change your name [as many married women do], but you would still be the same person ["who"], wouldn't you?

Anne: I think I get it. A name is a label for a person ["who"], but it's not the same thing as a person.

Kate: Yes, that's my point. I want to know what the name "Anne" refers to.

Anne: How about if I change my answer to "I am a medical doctor, specializing in orthopedics"?

Kate: That's interesting, too, but there is still a problem. You now have told me what you *do*, but I still want to know who you *are*. Even when you are not practicing medicine, you are the same person. And I'm asking who that person is. Also, you could change profession but still be the same person, couldn't you?[1]

Anne: I guess you're right. But if it's not my name or what I do, then how does one go about answering your question?

Kate: Well, I'm not an all-knowing sort of guru here, but I think it involves, among other things, something like the following:
1. Having an idea of what your personality is. This involves knowing what your basic tendencies, habits, dispositions, and the like are.[2]
2. Knowing what your beliefs are and the various reasons you have for those beliefs.
3. Being familiar with your values—what you think is important and why. There's more to it than this, but this would be a decent start.

Anne: OK, I think I'm beginning to get the picture, though it doesn't sound too easy to figure out who we are.

Kate: You're right. But I think if we make an informed commitment to doing it, we can get started on it as a sort of lifelong project. It also helps to have other people around who know you pretty well. It's always helpful to have other people to bounce ideas off of and to get feedback from on a number of issues.

---

[1] Kate is introducing the issue of personal identity, one that philosophers have struggled with for years. Here the central question is, What, if anything, keeps us the same person over the course of time?

[2] For a helpful overview of personality theory, see Nicholas S. DiCaprio, *Personality Theories: A Guide to Human Nature* (New York: Holt, Rinehart & Winston, 1983).

DESCARTES'S CONTRIBUTION

Another famous philosopher is **René Descartes** (1596–1650), one of the great thinkers of modern times. Like Socrates before him, Descartes was searching for knowledge of both himself and the world around him. He lived at a time when, in many senses, the intellectual world was in turmoil. He realized that many of the beliefs he had held since childhood were either entirely false or in need of modification. Descartes was searching for a method that would give him certain knowledge concerning the world around him. Writing in the 1600s, Descartes suggested that at least three prominent groups were vying for people's loyalties:

1. **The Catholic Church.** This was the most influential institution in Europe during the Middle Ages and after. As a serious Catholic, Descartes had no desire to say or believe anything contrary to the teachings of the Church.

2. **The scientific community.** Copernicus, Galileo, and other scientists had made discoveries, based on observation of great significance (such as the fact that the earth is not the center of our solar system), including some that appeared to be contrary to the official teachings of the Church.

3. **The rationalists.** Descartes and other **rationalists,** who emphasize that knowledge can best be attained by using our ability to reason, thought that many important truths could be discovered without appealing to the five senses, as the **empiricists** would have us believe.

Descartes made many contributions to Western thought, but two in particular merit our attention. First, for us to have a decent grasp of the world, we need to ascertain both what knowledge is and how we can attain it. Second, we need to recognize that environment and culture play a prominent role in shaping what we believe and how we look at the world. Being unaware of our own lenses and how they shape our outlook on life is but one obstacle to good critical thinking. Let's look at some other common obstacles.

EXERCISE 2.1

Write a one- to two-page essay describing who you are. Be sure to keep Socrates and his idea of the examined life in mind. The following questions should be of some help here.

1. What is the most important thing in your life? (See the list early in the chapter for some possibilities.) Now think about why you chose what you chose. How well can you support your first choice?

2. What are your goals in life? In other words, what do you most want to accomplish, and why? Does it matter what your goals are? For example, would watching TV and eating junk food be worthwhile goals? Why or why not?

3. What must you do to be happy? Be careful about arguing that happiness is entirely different from person to person, as there is evidence to suggest that humans have, for example, a number of basic needs in common.

4. What are you passionate about in life? What really matters to you the most?

5. Are you more inclined to be an optimist or a pessimist? Why do you think you tend more toward one than the other?

6. Do you have a basic need to interact with others? That is, can a person be truly happy without having any friends?

7. How important to you is it that your views be accepted by your peers, family, schoolmates, and/or co-workers? Given that most of us would answer, "Fairly important," how might this fact come into conflict with the pursuit of truth?

8. How would you rank the following in order of importance?
   a. Physical health
   b. Mental health
   c. Friends
   d. Money
   e. Peace of mind
   f. Luck
   g. Moral virtue
   h. Job
   i. Pleasure
   j. Knowledge

9. What reasons can you give for your rankings in question 8?

10. What skills, talents, and abilities do you have?

11. What skills, talents, and abilities would you like to develop or improve on?

OBSTACLES TO THINKING WELL

Hidden Assumptions

To assume something is to take it for granted or to accept it unconsciously. In many discussions and arguments, participants have what might be called **hidden assumptions**—beliefs that are unstated because they are taken for granted or assumed to be true. Consider the following:

> If your wife is Norwegian, she must be blond.
> **Hidden assumption:** All Norwegians are blond.

> If he is black, he must be a good basketball player.
> **Hidden assumption:** All black males are good basketball players.

If she is Asian American, then she must be a good student.
Hidden assumption: All Asian American girls are good students.

You must be liberal if you voted for Senator Muckraker.
Hidden assumption: Only liberals would vote for Senator Muckraker.

Hidden assumptions are not necessarily bad things, because many assumptions are perfectly reasonable. For example, when we pick up the phone and dial a number, we expect to hear the other phone ringing or to get a busy signal. Given how likely it is that this will happen, we can reasonably assume that it will happen. But hidden assumptions need to be made explicit—to be clearly stated—so that we can better evaluate what is being claimed.

Emotions

Another important obstacle to thinking well involves human emotions. Emotions are an important component of being human. We experience emotions (anger, pity, fear, and so on) on a daily basis, and whether we are aware of it or not, they often significantly affect how we look at the world. Strong emotions can hinder our ability to think rationally about many issues, from capital punishment, to abortion, to sexuality, and to musical tastes. And they can hinder our ability to see situations with clarity and objectivity. Consider the following scenarios:

Scenario 1: A close friend suggests that you seek professional counseling to help you deal with some of the stresses and problems that make your daily life less than ideal. If you react with anger, your ability to rationally evaluate the suggestion will be seriously impaired.

Scenario 2: You find a lump in your body. The emotion of fear (at possibly having cancer) is very strong, and you allow this fear to prevent you from immediately going to the doctor and getting the lump examined.

Being in touch with our emotions is important not only for understanding ourselves but also for helping us maximize our ability to think carefully about important matters.

Stereotypes

A **stereotype** is a judgment, usually negative, about a group of people (or places or things) based on a limited or distorted sample. Here are some common stereotypes about groups of people:

All people of Irish descent are heavy drinkers.

Jews are good with money and are stingy.

All blacks are good basketball players.

Poles are stupid.

All Italians are highly emotional.

People from New Jersey can't speak English properly.

All Philadelphia sports fans are very demanding.

Native Americans drink too much.

All women are short.

Asians are good at math.

All men don't do their fair share of household chores.

Brazilians love soccer.

People who resort to stereotyping do not willingly take new facts into account but rather ignore them or make the silly claim that the exception proves the rule. This, of course, is nonsense. An exception is evidence *contrary to* the stereotype, not evidence in its favor.

But can a stereotype turn out to be substantially true? To illustrate, think about what might separate these two claims:

1. The Asians are taking over our schools.
2. Asian students are good at math.

There is an important distinction here that cuts to the heart of what stereotypes involve. The first claim is based on little, if any, evidence and is thus an uninformed claim. But suppose the second claim is based on evidence about the actual performance of Asians in the American school system. It would then be not a stereotype, but rather a belief based on evidence.

Note that there are at least two types of stereotypes:

1. **Strong stereotypes** typically include the word "all" or "every" and are meant to apply to everyone in the group in question (see the list beginning on p. 22).
2. **Weak stereotypes** are merely broad generalizations about a particular group of people and are intended to apply only to the majority of the members of the group in question (again, see the list beginning on p. 22).

When people make claims that can be categorized as strong stereotypes, coming up with one exception is sufficient to show that their claim is mistaken. Consider this claim:

All people of Irish descent are heavy drinkers.

We can show this claim to be false simply by coming up with *one* example of an Irish person who is not a heavy drinker. People who tend to resort to stereotypes are often guilty of being closed-minded and not open to the possibility that their claim is mistaken. Indeed, the worst kind of stereotype is the strong stereotype with little or no supporting evidence—and this is the kind of stereotype we often encounter in life.

NON SEQUITUR WILEY

People tend to blame others for the bad things in life but to take credit for the good things. © 1994 The Washington Post Writers Group. Reprinted with permission.

Stereotyping not only undermines rational thinking but also does not allow individual humans to be treated with respect and dignity. If we immediately lump all members of a group together into a negative stereotype, we do not allow individuals to show us that they (and perhaps the other members of their group) do not exhibit the negative trait ascribed to them in the act of stereotyping. It should be noted that, even if that person had the quality in question, the stereotype would fail to consider the many other good qualities that such a person might have.

Closed-Mindedness

If individuals are **closed-minded,** their ability to think critically is seriously impaired. Closed-minded people are not open to the real possibility that they may be mistaken about one or more of their beliefs. Religion, sex, and politics are three areas in which we are often reluctant to consider the possibility that we might be mistaken. Most of us are afraid of the unknown and insecure about the less familiar; we become emotionally attached to the familiar and the habitual. For example, over the years many Americans have felt threatened by one or more of the following:

Racial integration (in some southern states, until recently racial intermarriages were illegal)

Homosexuality and the gay rights movement

Anything smacking of Marx, communism, or the political left (a remnant of the Cold War)

Much of the problem can be ascribed to ignorance. Many of the issues that people felt most strongly about were issues about which they knew little, and what they did "know" was often a caricature or distortion of reality.

The Will to Be Right

Many of us have the will to be right, which has to do with the human ego and our tendency to want to come out ahead in discussions, arguments, and the like. Just as many of us like to believe that our country, our lifestyle, and our ethnic group are better, so we also like to believe that our beliefs are better. It is almost as if our own views have a better chance of being correct *merely by virtue of being ours*. We need to commit ourselves to the pursuit of truth and rationality (being reasonable), rather than maintaining a win-at-all-costs mentality.

To illustrate, imagine that Jana is discussing abortion with Vijay, and they find they are in significant disagreement on the issue. After a long and civilized discussion, suppose Vijay realizes that Jana has made some excellent points and that his view is not rationally defensible as it stands. He could bring his ego into play and nicely tell Jana to take a hike, or he could admit that his view needs modification and thank her for her input. If someone courteously points out problems with your view, why not see this as an opportunity for learning and growth, rather than treating it as an occasion for anger or hostility?

Laziness

Many of us admit that at times we are lazy. We would rather relax or do nothing than engage in vigorous physical exercise—as the large number of overweight Americans suggests. Critical thinking, much like physical exercise, can be hard work. It takes time, energy, patience, and sometimes perseverance to think long and hard about complex issues. Popular culture, and especially television, is part of the problem here. As Neil Postman says, "Television offers viewers a variety of subject matter, requires minimal skills to comprehend it, and is largely aimed at emotional gratification."[3] Too many people, when given the choice between instant TV entertainment and long, hard thought about a new and unfamiliar topic, choose television. However, nothing worthwhile ever comes easily, and being well informed on a given topic is no exception.

Worldview

All of us have a **worldview**—a personal map of the world and all it contains. It is "a conceptual scheme by which we consciously or unconsciously place or fit everything we believe and by which we interpret and judge reality."[4] Our worldview includes our perception of what exists (metaphysics), what and how we know (epistemology), how we should live (ethics), and how humans in general live (anthropology). These perceptions are often deeply ingrained and so are not easily modified or rejected. These beliefs, as well as our personality and values, are all components of the lens through which we look at the world. We need to be familiar with both our worldview and the way it shapes our perception of the reality we experience. Other people have different lenses, and the fact that, say, Juan's lens is different from Lili's is not a valid reason for claiming that Juan's beliefs are mistaken or inferior. Lili and

---

[3] Neil Postman, *Amusing Ourselves to Death* (New York: Penguin Books, 1985), p. 86.
[4] Ronald Nash, *Faith and Reason* (Grand Rapids, MI: Zondervan, 1988), p. 24.

Juan would need to identify their worldviews, note their differences, and engage in a rational and civilized discussion about the various strengths and weaknesses of their views. Assuming that one's worldview is correct is therefore a major stumbling block to thinking critically. (The idea of worldview will be examined in some detail in Chapter 7.)

Enculturation

All human beings are, to a large extent, the product of **enculturation.** This refers to the idea that our values are, to a significant extent, the result of the conditioning and shaping influences of our particular culture. For example, if I had grown up in India in the twentieth century, there is a good chance that I would be a Hindu and worship gods such as Shiva and Vishnu. If I had grown up in France in the 1400s, there is a good chance that I would have been taught to distrust and dislike the English. And if I had grown up in many parts of modern-day Africa, I might well view clitoridectomies (euphemistically called "female circumcision") as either something for the woman's own good or something worth little or no attention on my part.

The following list gives some examples of how enculturation can lead to vastly different perceptions of laws, customs, beliefs, and so on.

1. The U.S. Constitution provides for the separation of Church and state. This means that the federal government cannot do anything either to promote or to prohibit a given religion. Most Iranians would see the Western emphasis on Church-state separation as a clear sign of a decadent culture. Indeed, for many conservative Muslims the government has a moral obligation to promote the faith of Islam. Many Muslims, for example, would be puzzled by the U.S. Supreme Court case of *Lynch v. Donnelly* (1984), which focused on whether a town in Rhode Island should be allowed to have a nativity scene in the town square.

2. Most people in the United States are meat eaters. But members of some cultures, such as the Jains in India, view meat eating as morally repugnant and are strict vegetarians.

3. People in the United States are generally turned off by the idea of eating dogs or horses. But in many Asian cultures, such as China, eating dog meat is commonplace.

4. The sports of choice in the United States are baseball, football, and basketball. But in Europe and many other parts of the world, the number one sport would likely be soccer.

5. Polls show that the majority of Americans believe in God. But Europeans are less likely to believe in God, and in some Eastern cultures polytheism, animism, or pantheism is the norm.

6. In the United States people generally get married only if love is involved. But in other cultures marriages are arranged or are made

Elements of Enculturation

Key elements in or influences on enculturation include the following:

Parents	Material possessions
Peers	Music
Politics	Dress
Religion	Values
Education	

How important are they to you? Are there any items that you would add to the list?

for social and/or professional reasons, with love often not a consideration.

7. The Bible is widely respected in the United States as a source of moral principles. But in the Middle and Far East, the Koran and the Bhagavad Gita are sacred scriptures more revered than the Bible.

8. The amount of space between an individual and another person that an individual requires to be comfortable varies from culture to culture and even within a culture. Growing up on the East Coast, I was used to more distance between people than is customarily granted in North Dakota, where I now live.

9. Guns are an important part of American culture, and many Americans rank gun ownership as one of the fundamental rights in a civilized society. But in many other cultures gun ownership is widely seen as neither a right nor generally desirable.

10. Pro wrestling and soap operas are immensely popular in the United States. But that popularity is hardly universal.

Given the reality of enculturation, Americans might consider doing the following:

1. Identifying their distinctively American or Western beliefs, which would not be particularly difficult for many.

2. Identifying at least one argument in favor of and one argument contrary to each belief.

3. Being able to offer rational support for their beliefs, as well as list reasons for beliefs contrary to their own.

Many Americans would not fare particularly well. Number 2 and especially number 3 would be daunting challenges that relatively few would be able to meet (although many more could rise to the challenge by developing their critical thinking skills).

The Myth of Objectivity

Pride is therefore pleasure arising from a man's thinking too highly of himself. —Benedict de Spinoza, Ethics

Some people claim that as humans we have the ability to look at the world "objectively." This **myth of objectivity** encourages many students to pursue an unattainable goal, a practice that is neither profitable nor practical. Factors that contribute to making us who we are include these:

1. **Genetics.** Humans clearly have certain inborn abilities and dispositions. The fact that I look somewhat like my father is hardly accidental.

2. **Upbringing.** Our parents, siblings, and immediate environment did much to shape us and our worldview. The simple fact that I grew up in a home where the *New York Times* was read helped shape my view of things.

3. **Historical situation.** The fact that I am a twenty-first-century American raised in middle-class, suburban New Jersey has a lot to do with my general outlook on things.

4. **Education.** Where we went to school, what was taught, and how it was taught all are significant influences on us.

5. **The human condition.** We are limited and finite creatures. We do not know very much compared to the total body of possible knowledge, and what we do know is significantly shaped and conditioned by the factors just mentioned.

This does not mean that complete subjectivity is something we should embrace, but it does indicate that we should be skeptical of anyone claiming complete objectivity. It is a false dichotomy to believe that either we have complete objectivity or we are left with complete subjectivity. There is another option, called either partial or moderate objectivity, available to us. Complete objectivity would only be possible if we could somehow step outside of or rise above the five factors listed here. Most thinkers consider this to be a silly, if not ludicrous, venture.

God, if there is a God, might be able to look at things objectively, but since none of us is God, we must be content to have a far more limited perspective. From the fact that we cannot be totally objective, it does not logically follow that we are left with complete subjectivity. By leading an examined life and seeking to overcome the obstacles to thinking well, we can attain a degree of objectivity that we may not currently have. This degree of objectivity must be tempered with the sort of intellectual humility and open-mindedness that

Nine Obstacles to Thinking Well

1. **Hidden assumptions.** Knowing what people are assuming when they argue in a particular situation helps us assess their arguments.

2. **Emotions.** Being overly emotional makes it difficult to think clearly and reason well.

3. **Stereotypes.** Believing that an entire group of people is guilty of something that only one or two of its members do reflects a failure to reason carefully.

4. **Closed-mindedness.** Consistently refusing to admit that we might be mistaken, especially on controversial matters, blinds us to the truth.

5. **The will to be right.** Failing to recognize that most of us prefer to win rather than lose arguments prevents us from recognizing better arguments by those with whom we disagree.

6. **Laziness.** Developing an informed and reasonable view on an important issue can be hard work.

7. **Worldview.** Becoming aware of what we believe and why makes it easier to evaluate whether our beliefs are reasonable.

8. **Enculturation.** Understanding that society plays a huge role in shaping how we look at the world around us helps us understand our worldview.

9. **The myth of objectivity.** Knowing something about how genetics, parents, peers, society, and so on shape us suggests that it is unreasonable to think that we can look at the world objectively.

make possible genuine exchanges of ideas. Otherwise, we merely turn a blind eye to many of the obstacles to clear thinking discussed in this chapter.

SUMMARY

A fulfilling and productive life requires that we make the most of our abilities, including the ability to lead an examined life and think reflectively about life's important matters. We also need to live an examined life so as to develop a sense of self, a sense of "who-ness." From Descartes we learned the importance of carefully defining what we are seeking and carefully developing a plan of how to get from here to there. There are many obstacles to thinking well, and we must both identify and understand these obstacles if we are to overcome them. Although we cannot attain pure objectivity, we can still make progress toward that ideal by practicing humility and open-mindedness and by seeking to surmount the many obstacles to thinking well. And if we are committed to thinking well, we can try to identify our biases and worldview and carefully evaluate them. Our goal should be to have *reasonable* biases, or ways of looking at things, and not to have no biases whatsoever.

EXERCISE 2.2

1. With the obstacles to thinking well in mind, consider these questions:
   a. What stereotypes are common in your part of the country? How might they differ from those in other regions of the country?
   b. How have your parents influenced your values? What values did they attempt to instill in you?
   c. What emotions sometimes cloud your ability to think well?
   d. How often do you admit that you made a mistake or held an incorrect belief? Have you been wrong about something of importance in the past five years?
   e. Does it matter to you whether you "win" an argument? Why or why not?
   f. Why is thinking about the existence of God hard work?
   g. What is your worldview? How well can you defend it?
   h. Do you agree with your friends on most matters of importance?
   i. Why is it difficult to be an independent thinker?

      1. How does peer pressure figure in here?
      2. Do most humans have a desire to fit in?
      3. What makes going into intellectually uncharted territory so challenging?

   j. If you had grown up in England in the 1800s, in what sense would you be the same person and have the same worldview?
   k. Is it possible to "step outside of" one's culture and look at the world "objectively"? Why or why not?

2. Write a one-page essay describing what the "objective" point of view involves.

EXERCISE 2.3

1. Identify the hidden assumption in each of the following.
   ★ a. If she is a doctor, then she is happy.
   b. If we live in an age of electricity and atomic energy, then it is no longer possible to believe in miracles.
   c. "Condom distribution sanctions, even encourages, sexual activity." (Rush Limbaugh, *The Way Things Ought to Be*)
   ★ d. If capital punishment were immediately enforced, then it would act as a general deterrent to crime.
   e. Belief in God is not reasonable, as it is a matter of faith (common belief).
   f. If we spend more on that social program, then things will get better.

2. Identify how a particular emotion may affect the reasoning process in the following scenarios.
   ★ a. Taylor gets a phone call offering her a good job in a different state. You, as her best friend, know this is a very important decision. You also know she

is currently sick with the flu and feeling a little down. Given all this, would it be wise to advise her to take a few days before making a decision? Why or why not?

b. Yolanda has just had a heated argument with Jamal concerning abortion, and she is upset that he disagrees with her. Would it be wise for her to begin work on her ethics paper on abortion now or to wait a few days? It is due in three weeks.

3. Identify the stereotypes in each of the following statements.

★ a. People on welfare just want a handout.
  b. He's a used car dealer and so can't be trusted.
  c. He's an Ivy League graduate, so he must be well educated.
★ d. She is a feminist, so she hates men.
  e. He is black, so he must like fried chicken.
  f. He's from New Jersey, so he must have an accent.
★ g. It's a country music song . . . how deep can it be?
  h. She is Asian; of course she did well on the exam.
  i. He's got lots of money; after all, he's Jewish.
★ j. What do you mean "honest"? He is a politician.
  k. She changed her mind, but then, she is a woman.
  l. He's a jock, so why expect him to do well in school?
★ m. Rhonda is blonde, so she must be stupid.
  n. Vito is Italian, so he must have mob connections.
  o. Hispanics just take one long siesta every day.
★ p. Faith in God cannot be reasonable.
  q. She's his mother! How could she be in touch with his generation?

4. Identify the closed-mindedness in each of the following.

★ a. This is the gist of a discussion I once had:

  Friend: Kennedy was a great president.

  Me: What about his handling of the Cuban missile crisis?

  Friend: I don't care what you say, he was a great president.

  Me: What about his increasing the number of military advisors in Vietnam?

  Friend: I don't care what you say, he was a great president.

  Me: What about the botched Bay of Pigs invasion and his desire to have Castro assassinated?

  Friend: I don't care what you say, he was a great man.

  Me: And what about his womanizing?

  Friend: Now don't get started on that, and he was still a great president.

b. In the Senate hearings concerning whether President Clinton should be convicted and removed from office, the Senate voted almost exclusively along partisan (party) lines. The Republicans (with a few exceptions) voted to convict Clinton, while the Democrats voted en masse not to convict. What conclusions might we reasonably draw in this matter? Why might the party line vote be discouraged?

c. Consider the topics of abortion, political preference, and religion. Is it true that the more emotional one is about a particular issue, the more likely one is to be closed-minded about that issue? If it is true, then what does this tell us about human nature? Also, if it is true, then what does it tell us about the difficulty of thinking clearly and even-handedly about controversial matters and/or matters that mean a lot to us?

EXERCISE 2.4

1. Consider these two questions:

   a. How many times have you gotten into an argument or disagreement and, a few minutes into it, you were not entirely sure why or how it got started in the first place. But didn't you still want to "win" the argument, even though you were not entirely clear as to what it was about? What obstacle to critical thinking does this suggest?

   b. How many issues are there about which you are neither an expert nor completely in the dark? How many of these are issues of real importance. We generally know that if we read up on the topic we can become better informed and give our beliefs a firmer foundation (or make changes if necessary). We also know that if we do such research we will probably be glad we made the effort—at least after the research is completed. So why is it that so many times we choose not to learn more about a particular topic or issue that is worth learning more about? A lack of time and a busy schedule may well be part of the answer, but aren't there other factors at work here? Carefully consider what obstacles to critical thinking may also play a significant role here.

2. Answer the following questions as best you can. Also try to determine what the point of the questions might be.

   ★ a. If you had been a male adult in the United States in 1890, would you have been more likely to have facial hair than a male in the United States in 2000?

   b. If you had lived in France in the 1300s, what would likely have been your attitude toward the English?[5]

   c. If you had lived in England in the 1300s, what would likely have been your attitude toward the French?

   ★ d. If you had been an American teenager in the late 1960s or early 1970s, what kind of pants would you likely have worn at some point in time?

   e. If you had been an American teenager in the early 1950s, what kind of music might you have listened to?

   f. If you had been an American teenager in the late 1950s, what kind of music might you have listened to?

   ★ g. If you had lived in Europe in the 900s, what would you have believed about the shape of the earth?

   h. If you had lived in the United States in the late 1700s, what would you probably have believed was a good way of helping sick people get better?

---

[5] See Barbara Tuchman's excellent book on the Middle Ages, *A Distant Mirror* (New York: Ballantine Books, 1978), for some insight into this.

    i. If you had been an adult in the United States in the early 1960s, what would likely have been your attitude about the need for a U.S. military presence in Vietnam?

★ j. If you had been a young adult in the late 1970s, what kind of music might you have listened to (but may no longer admit!)?

    k. If you had been an American in the mid-1930s, what would have been your attitude about having a job that paid only enough to cover the bare necessities of life?

    l. If you had been an adult between 1865 and 1900, what attitude might you have had toward human nature and your hopes for the twentieth century?

★ m. If you had lived in Brooklyn (New York) in the fall of 1957, what might have been your attitude toward Walter O'Malley, the owner of the Brooklyn—soon to be Los Angeles—Dodgers?[6]

    n. If you had been an American in the early 1950s, what would likely have been your attitude toward communism?[7]

    o. As a teenager in the late 1960s, would you have been more or less likely to try drugs like marijuana than a teenager in the late 1950s?

★ p. Would an American in 1970 have been more or less likely to believe in some form of evolution than someone in 1870?

    q. In the 1920s, in the United States, what would likely have been your favorite sport?

Did you figure out what obstacle(s) to critical thinking were lurking in the background? The importance of understanding enculturation is one of them. Clearly the time and place in which we live play a huge role in shaping how we look at ourselves and the world around us. These questions also show just how difficult it would be to completely escape the influence of culture and to achieve total objectivity.

GLOSSARY

Socrates (470–399 B.C.)   Greek philosopher and teacher of Plato, best known for claiming that the unexamined (unreflective) life is not worth living.

examined life   The lifelong process of reflecting on our views on important issues.

René Descartes (1596–1650)   French philosopher who was searching for certain knowledge and a way (method) to attain it.

rationalists   A group of philosophers (including Descartes) who believe that reason is the primary source of knowledge.

empiricists   A group of philosophers who believe that knowledge is gained primarily through the five senses.

hidden assumption   An assumption, or a belief that is taken for granted, that is left unstated rather than made explicit.

---

[6] Dodger fans were famous for their zealous loyalty to their team. It is also worth noting that the Dodgers were a profitable team. By most accounts they left for greater profits than were potentially available in Brooklyn.

[7] The Supreme Court decision in *Dennis v. United States* (1951) is instructive here. The Court ruled that it was unconstitutional to be a Communist, whether one was nonviolent or not!

stereotype A generalization, usually negative, about a group of people, places, or things and based on little, if any, evidence.

strong stereotype A universal generalization.

weak stereotype A broad generalization.

closed-minded Not being open to the possibility that one could be mistaken; a form of arrogance.

worldview A comprehensive outlook on life and reality that includes one's views on metaphysics, knowledge, ethics, and anthropology. Marxism, Christianity, and Hinduism are three examples of worldviews.

enculturation The process of a culture (one's environment and all that it includes) shaping and influencing who we are and how we look at the world.

myth of objectivity The false belief that it is humanly possible to look at the world from a point of view free from all bias and enculturation. Even though complete human objectivity may not be possible, this does not mean we are left with a complete subjectivity such that every belief and view is equally reasonable.

CHAPTER 3

Definitions and the Importance of Language

Then you should say what you mean.
— The March Hare, in Lewis Carroll, Alice's Adventures in Wonderland

SOCRATES AND THE SEARCH FOR GOOD DEFINITIONS

We use words to communicate with other people. But if we are asked to define a word, we often find it to be surprisingly difficult. When we properly define a word, we present its essential, or core, characteristics or qualities. In other words, we spell out what the word means. Consider something that most adults think they know something about, namely, love. But what exactly is love? It is widely accepted that there are different kinds of love. For example, the Greeks believed that there were four such kinds:

1. Romantic love (*eros*)
2. Friendship love (*philos*)
3. Unconditional love (*agape*)
4. Acquaintance love (*storge*)

Of course, even here we need more information if we are to know what each of these kinds of love entails. For example, what does it mean for love to be unconditional? Other questions we might ask about love include these:

Is romantic love *merely* a feeling?

Is it *both* a feeling and something else, such as commitment?

Is it primarily *not* a feeling?

35

Calvin **and** Hobbes

by Bill Watterson

Choosing our words carefully reduces the chances of miscommunication. CALVIN AND HOBBES © Watterson. Reprinted with permission of UNIVERSAL PRESS SYNDICATE. All rights reserved.

How do we know when we are "in love"?

Can we *choose* to love someone romantically? Or is it something that just "happens" to us? Or is it a little of both?

Many other questions are relevant here, but as the ones just listed indicate, defining love may not be as easy as we first thought. So the next time you hear someone say, "Jay loves Carla," you might ask, "What do you mean by 'love' here? Are there good reasons for thinking this to be true?"

Socrates spent a considerable amount of time searching for knowledge—about beauty, justice, moral goodness, and many other matters. And since he knew he did not possess full knowledge in these areas, he decided to ask others who professed to have some deeper understanding. One of the people he talked to was Euthyphro, who viewed himself as a "righteous" man (Euthyphro was prosecuting his own father for murder!). Socrates, understandably, asked Euthyphro, "What is righteousness?" Socrates assumed that, if someone claims to be righteous, then he must (or at least should) have some idea of what righteousness is. But Euthyphro had a very difficult time answering Socrates' questions, suggesting that his own grasp of certain concepts was not as firm as he thought.

So what exactly does a good definition involve? There are six requirements:

1. **A definition must be clear.** A good definition should be clearer than the word it defines. For example, suppose someone defines the verb *obscure* as "the act of obfuscating." The problem is that many more people know what *obscure* means than know what *obfuscate* means. Thus this definition is, ironically, an obscure one, as it fails to make clear what the word means.

2. **A definition must not be circular.** The definition should not include a form of the word it is defining; otherwise, we have a circular definition. For example, defining a square as "a squarelike figure" is clearly, well, circular, in that the word *square* is used in the definition.

Six Requirements for Good Definitions

1. The definition must be clear.
2. The definition must not be circular.
3. The definition must not be negative.
4. The definition must focus on *essential* rather than *accidental* characteristics.
5. The definition must not be too broad.
6. The definition must not be too narrow.

---

3. A definition must not be negative. To define *cat* as "something that is not a dog" is not particularly helpful. After all, there are millions of things that are not dogs, while there is only one thing that is a cat, and that is what we want to know about. On rare occasions a negative definition may be the best we can come up with, but generally a decent positive definition is possible.

4. A definition must focus on *essential* rather than *accidental* characteristics. Suppose we define *human* as a "two-legged thinking creature from Hungary." The ability to think may well be an essential human characteristic, but the other two characteristics do not seem to be. For example, a baby born with one leg is still a human, even if disabled. Similarly one does not have to be from Hungary in order to be a human. Countless individuals born in other countries are every bit as human as the person born in Hungary. Good definitions, then, focus on qualities that are **essential** (crucial) to the thing being defined and should not include **accidental** (secondary) characteristics.

5. A definition must not be too broad. In the modern, environmentally sensitive, world, many fishermen try to catch tuna without also catching dolphins, as dolphins are highly valued as intelligent and social creatures. Framing a good definition is much like fishing for tuna—the fishermen want to catch all the tuna they can, but no nontuna. Similarly, when a definition "casts its net" too wide, it "catches" more than it is supposed to. For example, the definition of a human as a "featherless biped" is too broad in that it includes creatures that are nonhuman. For example, gorillas and bears are both featherless and capable of walking on two legs, but they are clearly not human beings. So the "featherless biped" definition is too broad, gathering too many other creatures in its net.

6. A definition must not be too narrow. A definition is too narrow when it leaves out or excludes something it should not. For example, the "featherless biped" definition is both too narrow and too wide. It is too narrow in that it excludes creatures that are rightly viewed as being human. Any person with only one leg, whether from birth or due to injury or disease, is still a human. But the "featherless biped" definition would exclude all one-legged creatures from membership in the human race, thus indicating that this is not a suitable definition of *human*. In fact the "featherless biped" definition is especially weak in that it is simultaneously too broad and too narrow.

NECESSARY AND SUFFICIENT CONDITIONS

Suppose a friend asks you what the word *bachelor* means. You respond by saying that the correct definition is "an unmarried male." Your friend points out that baby boys are unmarried males, but we don't refer to them as bachelors! So you modify your definition to "an unmarried adult male." But your friend notes there is still a problem here. His neighbor Fred is an unmarried adult male, but he is not a bachelor, since he was once married and is now divorced. You again modify your definition to "a never-married adult male." This, then, is a good definition, as it refers to all real bachelors and to no nonbachelors.

What you have done in this process is spell out the *necessary* conditions for being a bachelor:

Never married

Adult

Male

All three of these conditions are necessary, or required, for bachelorhood. The three conditions combined also are *sufficient* for bachelorhood. Individually they are necessary (you cannot be a bachelor if you lack any of the conditions listed), and jointly they are sufficient to accurately define "bachelor."

We can also express our definition as follows:

If [A] someone is a bachelor, then [B] he has never married.

This is simply another way of saying that B is a necessary condition of A. In other words, you can never have an A (being a bachelor) without also having a B (never having married). Though B is a necessary condition for A, it is not sufficient for being A, as there is more to being a bachelor than never having married. For example, my six-year-old daughter has never married, and she is hardly a bachelor! But suppose we wrote the following:

Someone is a bachelor [A] if and only if
                    [B] he has never married,
                    [C] he is an adult, and
                    [D] he is male.

In this case conditions B, C, and D combined would be sufficient for being a bachelor. So conditions B, C, and D are, considered individually, necessary conditions for A (being a bachelor), and combined they are sufficient to fully explain what being a bachelor involves.

TWO THINGS TO AVOID IN DEFINITIONS

As we have seen, providing the necessary and sufficient conditions for a word, such as "bachelor," results in a good definition. Good definitions also avoid vagueness and ambiguity.

Vagueness

Definitions that are lacking in clarity may be suffering from vagueness. **Vagueness** results when the words are not precise enough to refer to any one thing in particular. So, when we hear a vague statement, we may respond with, "What exactly do you mean by that?" For example the following statement is vague:

> You are going to be here for a long time.

How long is "long"? It could range from two minutes to two days to two years. Unless we obtain more information, we have no way of determining precisely what "long" means here. Often, if we understand the context of the claim, we can figure out the particular meaning of the claim. For example, three hours is a long time at the dentist, but not for a professional football game.

Here's another example:

> You are an average American.

This may seem straightforward, but in this context "average" is vague. Average in what sense? The word could mean any of the following:

> Average looks
>
> Average income
>
> Average personality
>
> Average height or weight
>
> Average with respect to political views
>
> Average family situation (spouse and two kids)

Other vague terms include the following:

> *Big*—How big is a "big" person? Remember that *big* and *tall* have different meanings, and a person can be tall without being big, and big without being tall.
>
> *Expensive*—How expensive is an "expensive" vacation?

Be careful how you phrase important questions. THE FAR SIDE © FARWORKS, INC. Used by permission. All rights reserved.

THE FAR SIDE   By GARY LARSON

© 1984 FarWorks, Inc. All Rights Reserved

"Well, of COURSE I did it in cold blood, you idiot! I'm a reptile!"

Short—How short is a "short" woman?

Wonderful—What does it mean to have had a "wonderful" time?

Dark—What exactly does it mean to say "it is dark outside"?

Successful—What is meant by the statement "Vladimir is a successful person"?

In short, vagueness often undermines our efforts to communicate clearly, so we should make every attempt to use words in a clear and precise manner.

Ambiguity

A second thing to avoid in definitions is **ambiguity.** Words or statements are ambiguous when they have more than one meaning and the context of the statement does not make it clear which meaning is intended. A common word in the English language is *love.* As mentioned previously, however, there is no one definition of the word that is appropriate for every situation. Consider the following possibilities:

Sasha loves Alexandra. (maternal love)

Franky loves Sandi. (romantic love)

God loves me. (unconditional love)

Dante loves his car. ("material possession" love)

Sarah loves Melvina. (friendship love)

I got beat love and love. (a score in tennis)

Tyrone loves reading. ("activity" love)

As you can see, "love" has many possible meanings. So, when you use this word—or any word—it should be clear from the context how you intend for it to be interpreted.

EXERCISE 3.1

With the six requirements of a good definition in mind, define each of the following words.

1. Human

2. Dog

3. Love (romantic)

4. Honesty

5. Kindness

6. Happiness

7. Politician

8. Boat

9. God

10. Justice

THE TRUTH ABOUT DICTIONARIES

Many people falsely assume that if something is in the dictionary then it must necessarily be true or correct or accurate. Unfortunately this is not an altogether reasonable thing to assume. Dictionaries are like people: some are more trustworthy than others, and some offer much more information than others. For example, the prestigious *Oxford English Dictionary*, which spans twenty volumes and offers detailed definitions of more than 500,000 words, is an excellent one for several reasons. The product of exhaustive research, it offers a wealth of information on almost any word imaginable, including definitions, linguistic origins, and usage history. Another dictionary defines the word *libertarian* as (1) "a believer in free will as a doctrine" and (2) "an advocate of liberty." The problem is that free will and liberty are two fundamentally different things. Free will has to do with the ability to choose between options or to do as one pleases, and most philosophers believe that all humans (barring mental illness or other handicaps) possess this ability. For example, although right now I am typing words, clearly I have the ability to stop any time I choose. So free will is something virtually all humans have.

Liberty, though, is a political concept involving "the absence of legal coercion." In other words, you are at liberty to do X if there are no laws or legal restrictions preventing you from doing so. For example, suppose the government makes it a crime to call the president a bozo. This means that I am not at *liberty* to call the president a bozo but I still have the *free will* to do so. That is, I can go out in public, call the president a bozo, and perhaps get arrested for it.

All this confusion is compounded by the fact that the same word—*free* or *freedom*—is used to refer to both free will and liberty. Imagine if Patrick Henry had said, "Give me free will or give me death!" The silliness of this request highlights how different the two concepts are. Governments certainly have the ability to grant or restrict liberty, but free will is something we are born with. So, just as we should choose our words carefully when we are writing a paper, we should choose our dictionaries carefully. The *Oxford English Dictionary* is excellent; many others are not as good.

THE FUNCTIONS OF LANGUAGE

Language is a complex and multifaceted phenomenon. We cannot think clearly unless we learn to use language clearly and effectively. Language has at least seven functions:

1. **Descriptive.** This involves the statement of facts and is intended to convey information. For example, each of the following gives us information about something else:
   a. The book in front of me now is pink.
   b. I am from New Jersey.
   c. Nashville is in Tennessee.

2. **Evocative.** This involves the use of language intended to draw an emotional response. Consider the following:
   a. It doesn't get any better than this.
   b. I am poor and hungry and in need of a job.
   c. You deserve a break today.

3. **Evaluative.** This is when we make a value judgment by saying that something is good or bad. Here are some examples:
   a. Descartes was a good philosopher.
   b. She is a nice person.
   c. Hitler was evil.

4. **Expressive.** This involves language used to express emotions. Examples include the following:
   a. I hate brussels sprouts.
   b. I love you.
   c. I made it through the exam.

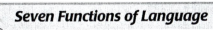

> ### *Seven Functions of Language*
>
> 1. **Descriptive.** This involves the statement of facts and is intended to convey information.
> 2. **Evocative.** This involves the use of language intended to draw an emotional response.
> 3. **Evaluative.** This is when we make value judgments.
> 4. **Expressive.** This involves language used to express emotions.
> 5. **Persuasive.** This is when we try to persuade someone to believe or do something.
> 6. **Interrogative.** This refers to a search for information.
> 7. **Recreational.** This is when we use language for the pleasure of it.

5. **Persuasive.** This is when we try to persuade a person to believe or do something. Here are a few examples:
   a. If you really love me, you won't do it.
   b. I can think of seven good reasons to vote for Senator Smith. Would you like to hear them?
   c. Don't you think you have had enough cookies already?

6. **Interrogative.** This refers to a search for information, which can involve questions or other modes of discourse. Consider these examples:
   a. What time is it?
   b. What day are you coming?
   c. I'll go along if you give me one good reason to do so.

7. **Recreational.** This is when we use language for the pleasure of it. Jokes, puns, limericks, and nursery rhymes are all examples of recreational language.[1]

EXERCISE 3.2

Each of the following real-life examples has a problem with vagueness and/or ambiguity. How might you rephrase each to make it as clear as possible?

1. "Consciousness is a being such that in its being, its being is in question insofar as this being implies a being other than itself." (Jean-Paul Sartre)

---

[1] For an excellent introduction to the various facets of language, see William Alston, *Philosophy of Language* (Englewood Cliffs, NJ: Prentice-Hall, 1964).

THE FUSCO BROTHERS   by J.C. Duffy

This is a good example of the ambiguity of language. THE FUSCO BROTHERS © 1993 Lew Little Ent. Reprinted with permission of UNIVERSAL PRESS SYNDICATE. All rights reserved.

2. "Being as such determines speaking in such a way that language is attuned to the Being of being." (Martin Heidegger)

3. "Foreclosure Listings: Entire state of New Jersey available." (Jay Leno)

4. "Three-year-old teacher needed for preschool. Experience preferred."

5. "Auto Repair Service. Free pick-up and delivery. Try us once, you'll never go anywhere again."

6. "Wanted: Man to take care of cow that does not smoke or drink."

7. "Our bikinis are exciting. They are simply the tops."

8. "Wanted: Widower with school-age children requires person to assume general housekeeping duties. Must be capable of contributing to growth of family."

9. "Used cars: Why go anywhere else to be cheated. Come here first."

10. "We do not tear your clothing with machinery. We do it carefully by hand."

11. "My friends, we can and we will never surrender to what is right." (Dan Quayle)

12. "I stand by all the misstatements I have made." (Quayle again)

13. "Semi-annual after-Christmas sale."

14. "Drought turns coyotes to watermelons." (Leno again)

15. "Mozart was a child prodigy. He practiced on a spinster in the attic."

LET ME MAKE THIS PERFECTLY CLEAR

Students frequently think their instructor is being "picky" when the instructor comments on the lack of clarity or precision in their writing. But whether we are at school or work or home, we must interact with a variety of people every day. If our communication is to be effective, we need to use words

Examples of Language Gone Astray

PHRASE	TRANSLATION
Tragic unavoidable contact with the ground	Plane crash
Ballistically induced apertures	Bullet holes
Permanently relocated	Murdered
Too short for one's weight	Fat
Optically inconvenienced	Blind
Involuntarily leisured	Out of work
Uniquely coordinated	Clumsy or klutzy
Chronologically gifted	Old
Client of the correctional system	Prisoner
Least best	Worst
Follicularly challenged	Bald
Chronically winning challenged	Long-time loser
Success challenged	Failure
Success-inconvenienced situation	Fatal accident
Revenue enhancement	Tax hike
Circumferentially maximized	Fat
Freedom fighter	Terrorist
Right-sized	Fired
Alternative moral code	Sleazy
Maritally challenged behavior	Extramarital affair
Final episode	Death

with care and precision, so that we keep both vagueness and ambiguity to a minimum.

Suppose a student made the following claim:

Everyone needs to be connected with reality.

This sounds nice, but what exactly do the words *connected* and *reality* mean here? There is not widespread consensus as to the nature of reality, and the sort of "connection" suggested could be physical or mental or spiritual. Also, what kind of "need" is meant here? There are physical needs (food and water), emotional needs (to be loved and accepted), intellectual needs (for order and coherence), and possibly even spiritual needs (to be properly related to God). So the claim is not nearly as clear or straightforward as we think.

Let's look at another example:

> Humans are always planning their own futures, and thus are basically selfish creatures.

The problem here revolves around the definition of a key term—in this case "selfish." Many students think that focusing on one's own needs is selfish, which it may or may not be. Philosophers distinguish between being selfish and being self-interested. The former means putting oneself first at the expense of others; the latter means showing concern for oneself. In this sense we could say that all selfish people are self-interested, while only some self-interested people are selfish. So a more precise way of writing this claim would be: "Humans are always planning their own futures, and thus are basically self-interested."

Consider this statement:

> Our welfare is our own business, so government should reform the welfare system.

This may seem fairly straightforward, but there is some confusion involving the word "welfare." In its first use it means "well-being," while in the second sense it refers to a government program designed to assist the needy.

Now look at this example:

> Grab for all the gusto you can get.

"Gusto" is a notoriously vague word. It is difficult to grab for something if one has no idea what it is. Given that "gusto" is not a physical object and that most of the things we grab are physical objects, then in what sense can we "grab" something nonphysical? This may sound nice, but it is not at all clear what it means!

Finally, let's look at this familiar phrase:

> "To boldly go where no man has gone before."

Many will recognize this phrase from the TV show *Star Trek*. Apart from the split infinitive, the phrase is relatively clear. Of course the word "man" here presumably is intended to refer to all of humanity (Lt. Uhura would concur). Otherwise, the phrase is clear enough.

SUMMARY

It's important to provide good definitions, but coming up with good definitions is no easy matter. There are many ways to "mess up" a definition, and as the six requirements for a good definition suggest, coming up with clear and precise ones is often a challenge. This highlights the importance of using a good dictionary. Not all dictionaries are created equal; rather, as George Orwell once wrote, some are "more equal"—that is, better—than others. The humorous examples of language gone astray remind us that word choice and word order are closely connected to the meaning of a given sentence.

EXERCISE 3.3

1. Define the following terms as precisely as possible, spelling out the necessary and sufficient conditions for each.
   a. Round (geometry)
   b. Square (geometry)
   c. Gorilla
   d. Society
   e. Culture
   f. Liberal (political)
   g. Conservative (political)
   h. Pornography
   i. Smile
   j. Depression (psychological)
   k. Truth

2. Write two sentences that are examples of each of the seven functions of language we discussed: (a) descriptive, (b) evocative, (c) evaluative, (d) expressive, (e) persuasive, (f) interrogative, and (g) recreational.

3. For each of the following, indicate whether there is a problem with vagueness or ambiguity.
   ★ a. Martina is smart.
   b. Omar is short.
   c. Cabell is rich.
   ★ d. Chan is average.
   e. John is loaded.
   f. Rosa is cool.
   ★ g. Juan loves dogs.
   h. Sasha is poor and loves sports, so she is a poor sport.
   i. That is a hot item.

EXERCISE 3.4

Many of the following are vague and/or ambiguous. Rewrite them to make them as clear as possible (some of them may be beyond salvaging). Items 23–50 are all quotes from former vice president Dan Quayle.

1. "It's isn't over until it's over." (Yogi Berra)

2. Calvin doesn't like TaNisha.

3. Did we do anything in class yesterday?

4. "Reagan OK After Brain Surgery." (newspaper headline)

5. "X-ray of Dean's Head Reveals Nothing." (newspaper headline in the 1930s, after baseball pitcher Dizzy Dean had been hit in the head with a line drive)

6. "Danger Slow Children." (roadside sign)

7. People are getting older.

8. She left school about one year into the ninth grade.

9. Ms. Smith is currently employed full time in a part-time temporary position.

10. He continues to be married to his wife.

11. "Shortly after the surgery, he turned into an emergency room."

12. Her father died from a heart attack at age twelve.

13. "Don't let worry kill you off—let the church help."

14. "The ladies of the church have cast off clothing of every kind, and they may be seen in the church basement on Friday afternoon."

15. "This being Easter Sunday, we will ask Mrs. Johnson to come forward and lay an egg at the altar."

16. "Tuesday evening there will be an ice cream social. All ladies giving milk come early."

17. Beethoven started out as a young musician.

18. "The Spring Council Retreat will be hell May 10 and 11."

19. "Proceeds will be used to cripple children."

20. "The choir invites any member of the congregation who enjoys sinning to join the choir."

21. "How Therapy Can Help Torture Victims."

22. I walk the floor over you.

23. "Welcome to President Bush, Mrs. Bush, and my fellow astronauts."

24. "Republicans understand the importance of bondage between a mother and a child."

25. "If we do not succeed, then we run the risk of failure."

26. "What a waste it is to lose one's mind. Or not to have a mind is being very wasteful. How true that is."

27. "The loss of life will be irreplaceable."

28. "It's rural America. It's where I came from. We always refer to ourselves as real America. Rural America, real America, real, real America."

29. "I was known as the chief grave robber of my state."

30. "The Holocaust was an obscene period in our nation's history. I mean in this century's history. But we all lived in this century. I didn't live in this century."

31. "Hawaii has always been a very pivotal role in the Pacific. It is in the Pacific. It is part of the United States that is an island that is right here."

32. "It isn't pollution that's harming the environment. It's the impurities in our air and water that are doing it."

33. "Let me just tell you how thrilling it really is, and how, what a challenge it is, because in 1988 the question is whether we're going forward to tomorrow or whether we're going to go past to the—to the back."

34. "I love California. I practically grew up in Phoenix."

35. "It's wonderful to be here in the great state of Chicago."

36. "Somewhere between real and real real."

37. "Speaking as a man, it's [breast cancer] not a woman's issue. Us men are tired of losing women."

38. "Most women do not want to be liberated from their essential natures as women."

39. "Verbosity leads to unclear, inarticulate things."

40. "I stand by all the misstatements I have made."

41. "[It's] time for the human race to enter the solar system."

42. "I am the future."

43. "I have made good judgments in the past. I have made good judgments in the future."

44. "The future will be a better tomorrow."

45. "How about if we say when it's wet, it's wet?" (defining *wetlands*)

46. "I am not part of the problem; I am a Republican."

47. [I support efforts] to limit the terms of members of Congress, especially members of the House and members of the Senate."

48. "I want to be Robin to Bush's Batman."

49. "I hope there's some dignity and respect for things I did not do." (defending himself against allegations of involvement with Paula Parkinson)

50. "Because. Because I say it isn't." (explaining why questions about his parents' connection to the John Birch Society aren't relevant)

GLOSSARY

essential   A characteristic such that something cannot exist without that characteristic. More formally, X is essential to Y if Y cannot exist without X.

accidental   A characteristic such that something can cease having that characteristic and still be the same something. For humans, skin color is an accidental characteristic. One is fully human regardless of one's skin color.

vagueness   When a word or phrase is unclear in the sense that there is no clear-cut boundary between what is and what is not. For example, the words *tall* and *big* are both vague, as there is no clear line between what is tall and what is not.

ambiguity   When a word or phrase has more than one meaning, and the context does not make it clear which meaning is intended. For example, the word *poor* can refer to a lack of money or to a lack of ability.

CHAPTER 4

The Basic Elements of an Argument

A knockdown argument: 'tis but a word and a blow.
   —John Dryden, "Oedipus"

Ignorance is not innocence but sin.   —Robert Browning, "The Inn Album"

Nothing in all the world is more dangerous than sincere ignorance and conscientious stupidity.   —Martin Luther King, Jr., Strength to Love

The study of arguments is at the heart of critical thinking. Just as a medical student must understand the human body before he or she can be a good doctor, so the critical thinker must know much about arguments and what they involve. But before we dive into our study of arguments, we need to address two questions: (1) Why should we spend our time learning about arguments? and (2) How can we distinguish an argument from one of the many forms of nonargument?

REASONS FOR USING ARGUMENTS

The following dialogue illustrates how learning to argue well can benefit us in making important decisions.

Elena: How many important matters are there in life?

Maria: I'm not sure. A bunch, I guess.

Elena: And in how many of these important matters does it matter what we believe?

Maria: At least some of them; maybe most of them.

Elena: So why do you think it might be important to know something about critical thinking?

Maria: What do you mean?

Elena: Well, can we think whatever we want about these important matters?

Maria: Sure we can—what's wrong with that?

Elena: What I mean is, could having poorly reasoned beliefs about an important matter have bad or undesirable consequences?

Maria: I guess so. Can you give me an example?

Elena: Sure I can. Remember when Eddie asked you to marry him last June?

Maria: Of course I do, and be careful here!

Elena: Well, how close were you to saying "yes" to him?

Maria: Pretty close; you know that.

Elena: So why didn't you say "yes"?

Maria: Well, because you and my mother talked me out of it.

Elena: That's right. Now did you agree just to make us happy or because we threatened to whack you with a baseball bat if you didn't turn him down?

Maria: No way. I turned him down because you and mom gave me good reasons for turning him down. At least three or four good reasons, if my memory is correct.

Elena: That's right.

Maria: So what's the point you're making?

Elena: My point is that we basically gave you an argument as to why you shouldn't marry Eddie. We said you shouldn't marry him because of reasons we had.

Maria: So if I had known something about how to argue well, I might not have been ready to make the decision to marry Eddie?

Elena: The disastrous decision to marry Eddie!

Maria: OK, I get the point. If you guys hadn't been around to talk me out of it, I would have done it.

Elena: With what kind of consequences?

Maria: We don't want to go there!

Elena: So if life is full of important matters that require a decision, how important might it be to be able to know how to argue well?

Maria: Pretty important—though I still think Eddie is cute!

Elena: He is cute. Just don't marry him!

As this dialogue illustrates, not being able to reason well can have negative consequences. Many of the dumbest decisions we have made in our lives were the ones that were the most poorly reasoned. Thinking critically helps us keep our bad decisions to a minimum.

Since evaluating arguments is at the heart of critical thinking, we need to know how to both identify and evaluate arguments. Learning how to evaluate arguments can help us do all of the following:

1. Better understand why others disagree with us.
2. Better understand why we believe what we believe.
3. Modify our beliefs when we find out that either our view is flawed or someone else's is more persuasive than we had previously thought.
4. Decrease our chances of making foolish decisions, as many of our worst decisions are based on faulty reasoning and poor argumentation. Decisions about major purchases, relationships, or even job offers can all be significantly aided by our having some idea of how to evaluate arguments. And we also need to know the basic reasons for forming arguments.

Persuading Others

What might the following situations all have in common?

1. Thinking you deserve a raise at work
2. Considering whether you need to party less
3. Wanting to convince your best friend that your religious view is correct
4. Convincing a potential significant other that you really are the one for him or her

So what do these four situations have in common? Among other things they all involve the importance of making a good argument.

Let's begin with your work situation. Suppose that, believing you deserve a raise, you go to the boss and say, "How about a raise?" The likely response will be, "Give me one good reason why I should give you one." Unless you can give the boss one or more good reasons, you're unlikely to get a raise. Fortunately you have done your homework and politely list *three* good reasons: (1) your department has been more productive since you were put in charge of it, as can be measured in sales figures, (2) you work very hard, and (3) you have a good attitude, which rubs off on your co-workers, making them happier and more productive. In other words you have given the boss an **argument**—a main claim, with reasons offered in support of that claim—and there's a good chance you will get some kind of raise.

Knowing about arguments greatly improves our ability to persuade others to adopt our position—not only in the workplace but in a number of other important situations as well. For example, suppose you know you've been partying too much. You also know that if you partied less you could do better at work and actually enjoy life more because you wouldn't be so tired all the time. So, in a "conversation" with yourself, you give this argument: I need to party less and get more sleep because (1) I will do better at work and (2) I will be less tired and enjoy life more. Here, again, an argument is center stage, and again it is on a matter of some importance—it's *your* life, after all! Sometimes students think of arguments and/or philosophy as focusing on questions such as "How many angels can fit on the head of a pin?" and similar matters that seem to have little bearing on their everyday life. But we would handle many real-life situations much better if we only had some idea of how to reason or argue better.

What about the situation in which you want your friend to adopt your religious view? We all have a natural desire to have our fellow humans agree with us. This is especially true if the matter is an important one and if the other person is a friend or loved one. If that person disagrees with us, we can still reason with him and see if we can persuade him to agree with us. But to do this, we must have some idea of how to argue and thus must know something about arguments themselves.

For example, consider the following claims:

1. God exists.

2. God exists because God exists.

3. God exists because today is Tuesday.

4. God exists because that's what I was raised to believe.

5. God exists because the universe exists, has not always existed, and needs a cause for its coming into existence, and God is that cause.

Here we have one nonargument (claim 1) and four arguments (claims 2–5). The approach taken in claim 1 will not convince any rational human being. Simply asserting something does not make it true. Claims 2–4 are examples of arguments, though they are poor ones in that they all offer very weak reasons for believing in God. Only the approach taken in claim 5 represents a decent argument. It offers a number of supporting reasons, or **premises**, for the main claim, and its main point, or **conclusion**, has a ring of plausibility to it. Whether this last approach is a *good* argument is another matter, but it certainly is a *genuine* argument worthy of our consideration.

Finally, with regard to our fourth common situation, it's important to remember that humans are passionate creatures. We care deeply about life and much of what it involves. We come to love many things, including other people. Suppose you are head over heels in love with someone and she loves you too. However, whereas you are sure she should marry you, she is not convinced. So, being the reasonable person she is, she throws out the following challenge: "If you can give me one or more good reasons for marrying you, then I will. Otherwise I think we will need to part as friends!"

You think about it, talk to your friends, and come up with five possible approaches:

1. You really don't love her enough to marry her.

2. She should marry you because you're so good-looking.

3. She should marry you because you have a good job and are a decent person.

4. She should marry you because you'll be crushed if she doesn't.

5. She should marry you because you love each other, have a similar outlook on life, and enjoy being together.

All five of these are arguments, but clearly some are more persuasive than others. If the three conditions mentioned in claim 5 are all true, then obviously it is the best and thus most persuasive of the five arguments. So you try this one out on her, she is impressed by the time and thought you put into it, and, more important, she is persuaded by it—so you get married.

In short, the attempts to persuade your boss that you deserve a raise, to convince yourself to party less and improve your life, to sway your friend to your view concerning God, and to get your loved one to agree to marry you are all examples of one of the central functions of arguments, namely, to persuade others of something you believe.

Making Decisions

Besides persuasion there are at least two other good reasons to know something about what arguments are and how to evaluate them. The first relates to the simple fact that we all need to make decisions in life, and some of these decisions are important. So it is crucial that we make as many wise decisions and as few foolish ones as possible.

One key decision involves what you want to do with your life. Suppose you are interested in doing all of the following:

1. Being a carpenter, because you are good at working with your hands and like building things

2. Being a salesperson, because you enjoy meeting people and work well with others

3. Being an electrician, because you are fascinated by electricity and love wiring things

4. Being a teacher, because you love being in front of the class and encouraging and challenging kids to learn

5. Being a wildlife biologist, because you are interested in science and love animals

Of course it is possible to change careers along the way, but you probably would not have time to become really good at all of these. Knowing how to argue could help you choose the one that best suits your abilities, your interests, and your current situation. Many people don't think through their career options and end up bored or unhappy with their work life. Since meaningful work is an essential part of a fulfilling life, this is a choice of no small importance. So, once again, we can see that gaining a clear understanding of arguments and good reasoning has significant practical consequences.

Explaining Things

Besides our interest in persuading others and ourselves and in making important decisions wisely, a third reason for learning how to argue well involves our natural curiosity and desire to explain things. We are naturally curious creatures. We want to know, among other things, the following:

1. Where the fire truck that just went by was going

2. Why bad things happen to decent people

3. What that couple over there is talking about

4. Why we were born with more abilities than some people and fewer than others

5. Whether we will meet the person of our dreams

6. How long our life will be

Many philosophers have wondered, for example, why something (the universe) exists as opposed to nothing. Learning how to approach and make good use of arguments helps us satisfy our curiosity. It would be a strange world indeed if humans were generally curious but lacked the ability to satisfy that same curiosity! But, for whatever reason, we are both curious creatures and thinking creatures, and we have the ability to pursue many of the issues we find particularly interesting.

Think about the following situations:

1. You are late for an important meeting, and the boss wants to know why.

2. You are not as happy as you were a few years ago.

3. You wonder why your favorite sports team rarely wins the big game.

4. You realize modern American society has many problems.

In each case you have a desire and/or a need to explain something.

In the first case your job may hinge on your having a good explanation of why you were late. When you tell the boss that there was a major accident and you got stuck in traffic, she will realize that there was nothing you could have done to make the meeting on time. The argument you give her is an explanation and justification of why you were late.

In the second case you think about your life over the past few years to see if you can figure out why you are not as happy as you once were. Here you are trying to explain why your general state of mind has changed. Obviously the more thought you give to this, the more likely you will be able both to understand the problem and to take steps to address it. The sports team situation is not a matter of cosmic importance, though many Americans take their favorite teams very seriously. Is the failure to win the big one the result of a lack of talent, poor coaching, a few bad breaks, or some combination of these?

Serious sports fans want to know why their team is not doing as well as they had hoped.

Finally, thinking about the leading social problems in this country, such as poverty, racism, crime, child and spouse abuse, alcoholism, illiteracy, drug abuse, and divorce, is no easy task. But if you want to be an informed citizen, you must have some idea of the problems the country faces. It is very difficult to have any idea as to how to fix something if you do not even know that something is broken. One of the fundamental steps in this process is to explain why each of these problems occurs to the extent that it does. Only then can we begin to propose meaningful and concrete solutions. Knowing how to argue well, then, provides us with a crucial tool in learning how to explain the world around us and to respond effectively to the challenges life presents.

Clearly it is important to learn about arguments and how to use them effectively. But there is another obstacle in our path here: it is sometimes difficult to know when an argument is being offered and when it is not. So, not only do we need to be motivated to understand and use arguments effectively, but we also need to learn how to detect them.

HOW TO DETECT AN ARGUMENT

At a costume party it is not always easy to figure out who is who. This is because people dress up as somebody else; they are wearing disguises. Thus, if you're looking for your best friend at the party, you might have trouble unless you first know what you are looking for. This is similar to the situation with arguments. We must detect or identify them before we can begin to evaluate them, so we must also learn how to detect them. So let us begin by giving a few tips for spotting arguments.

1. **Search for premise and conclusion indicator words.** Words and phrases such as *since, because, for, follows from, therefore, thus, so, it follows that,* and *accordingly* often point to the existence of a premise or conclusion. An important point here is that common indicator words do not guarantee the presence of a premise or conclusion. Consider the following examples:

1. All Americans like baseball. Mark is an American. So, Mark likes baseball.
2. April 15 is when federal income taxes are due. So, Americans take April 15 seriously.

In example 1 the word "so" is a conclusion indicator. The main claim follows it, and the other two claims are clearly intended to offer support for it. But this is not the case in example 2, because the word "so" is not a conclusion indicator. This example is an **explanation** rather than an argument, in that it attempts to explain *why* Americans take April 15 seriously. Often explanations are given by spelling out the causes of an event or the reasons it happened.

Common Premise Indicators

as shown by	for the reason that
because	given that
follows from	since
for	

Common Conclusion Indicators

accordingly	so
consequently	then
hence	therefore
in conclusion	thus
it follows that	we can conclude that

Although indicator words do not guarantee the presence of an argument, they still often signal the presence of one.

2. **Determine if the purpose of the words is to persuade someone.** The most common reason for presenting an argument is to persuade someone of something. If there is no attempt to persuade, then chances are no argument is lurking in the neighborhood. Think about the difference between these examples:

1. I was late for the appointment because my car broke down and an accident slowed down the traffic.
2. I think Hitler was the worst person in the twentieth century because he was responsible for the death of millions of people and because he promoted hate and violence.

Example 1 is an attempt to explain why the individual was late. Example 2 presents an argument—it offers a main claim and then support in the form of two other claims. It also may be understood as an attempt to persuade the reader that Hitler was in fact one of the worst people of that century. And since there is clearly an attempt to persuade, an argument is present.

3. **Make an effort to understand the context of the passage in question.** Suppose abortion is being discussed and someone says, "I disagree with you; let me tell you why." There is good reason to believe that an argument will be forthcoming. This is because if that person disagrees with you, then

> ### *Guidelines for Detecting an Argument*
>
> 1. Search for premise and conclusion indicator words.
> 2. Determine if the purpose of the words is to persuade someone.
> 3. Make an effort to understand the context of the passage in question.

he has reasons for disagreeing with you. And when he shares those reasons with you, he is trying to persuade you that his position is superior to yours. In general, if a controversial issue is being discussed and there is disagreement, there is a good chance that one or more arguments are involved. Note that it is much easier to determine context if you are there in person, as opposed to reading about some particular conversation.

Or suppose that you and a friend are trying to figure out why the economy is doing so well. You ask, "Why is it doing so well?" and she responds, "How about the following reasons?" Here she is merely trying to explain why something is true. Although she is offering reasons, she is not trying to persuade you of anything.

As with many worthwhile things in life, if you want to become good at identifying arguments, you will have to work at it. But if you keep the preceding three suggestions in mind, your ability to detect arguments will improve over time.

OTHER KINDS OF NONARGUMENTS

Familiarity with common types of nonarguments helps us learn to identify genuine arguments. We have already touched on explanations, so let's look at two more possibilities: descriptions and reports.

Descriptions

If you are telling someone about the way things are, then you are using descriptive language. Here are some examples:

Abraham Lincoln was president.

Winters are cold in Alaska.

Bach was a composer.

My older brother is forty-five years old.

Soccer is the most popular sport in the world.

Each of these five claims is a **description**, as each is offering information about someone or something. Similarly people may describe a play they went to see without giving an argument of any sort:

The play had three acts.

The leading roles were for women.

It was set in Italy in the 1500s.

It lasted over two hours.

It has been nominated for three awards.

Here they are attempting to provide you with information concerning the play. The more information they give, the clearer a picture you have.

Reports

Suppose you are watching the news and learn that country X has just attacked country Y. This may properly be called a **report**—a spoken or written account of something that has happened. A typical report will include many descriptions, and generally the more descriptive claims are included, the more useful the report will be. Reports can be long and involved and still not offer a single argument. This reminds us that a good deal of all communication, both spoken and written, does not involve arguments. Well-known reports of the following events from the twentieth century include:

The dropping of atomic bombs on the Japanese cities of Hiroshima and Nagasaki (1945)

The trans-Atlantic flight of Charles Lindbergh (1927)

The acquittal of O. J. Simpson in the murder of Nicole Simpson and Ron Goldman (1995)

The formation of the United Nations (1945)

The many AIDS-related deaths (1980s–1990s)

The assassination of President Kennedy (1963)

The development of the war in Vietnam (1960s)

The first human on the moon (1969)

Reports can include not only descriptions but also explanations. For example, a student might present a report on the fall of the Roman Empire that includes both descriptions and explanations. The descriptions might address the size, duration, and power of the empire, while the explanations might focus on the reasons for the decline and fall of the empire in the fifth century A.D.

EXERCISE 4.1

For each of the following, determine whether an argument is present.

★ 1. I am against capital punishment because it is cruel and barbaric.

2. The NFC team won the 2000 Super Bowl because it was the better team.

3. Richard was late because he overslept.

★ 4. Marsha is not committed to marriage. We know this because each of her first six marriages ended in divorce.

5. The Warren Commission reported that President Kennedy was killed by a lone assassin.

6. That belief is contrary to what we both know is true.

★ 7. Alberto couldn't possibly be a bachelor, because he has been married before.

8. The team was wearing different uniforms, because they had left theirs at the hotel.

9. Abortion clearly is morally justified. This is because the woman has a right to do as she pleases with her body, and the fetus is part of her body.

★ 10. Patricia shared with the class that the United States was a very wealthy country because it had such a high standard of living and so many high-paying jobs.

11. Maria told Sarah that Alberto was not a bachelor because he had been married before, and bachelors, by definition, cannot have been married before.

12. "Thus the value of money is *derived* from the value of the value of liberty. Therefore liberty is higher on the scale of values than money." (Phil Washburn, *Philosophical Dilemmas*).

★ 13. The plane never crashed but rather made tragic, unavoidable contact with the ground.

14. You cannot say we are all equal, because though we are equal, some of us are more equal than others.[1]

15. We know that the victim's death was not an accident—he was both hit in the head with a bat and shot twice.

★ 16. If we want to gather knowledge, we must first know what knowledge is. And if we would do that, we must then devise a reliable method for acquiring knowledge. So, if we want knowledge, we must devise a reliable method for acquiring it.[2]

17. WalMart is one of the most successful stores of its kind. We know this because of the number of new stores that have been built recently and also because of its annual earnings report.

18. Sigmund Freud argued that God did not exist and that religion was a crutch for the psychologically weak and dependent.

★ 19. Animals have as much value as human beings and thus should have all the rights humans do.

---

[1] The basic idea here comes from George Orwell's masterful *Animal Farm,* a satire on the Russian Revolution of 1917.

[2] This line of thought was developed by the great French philosopher René Descartes, who is discussed in Chapter 2.

20. Modern businesses engage in a variety of questionable practices. Sometimes these businesses cross the line. We know this because there are ethical standards and because we can document that many businesses have engaged in practices that clearly violate one or more of these standards. The Ford Motor Company's behavior in the Ford Pinto matter is just one of many such examples.[3]

CHARACTERISTICS OF ARGUMENTS

The Elements of an Argument

Before we look at actual arguments, we need to familiarize ourselves with the basic parts of an argument: premise(s) and conclusion.

We regularly engage in conversations both with others and with ourselves (when we think about what we believe on a particular matter). In your daily discussions you will often encounter some amount of disagreement—someone believes X is true while you believe it is false. The next step is to ask, "Why do you believe X to be true?" The typical response here involves an appeal to an argument of some sort. For example, the person might say, "I believe in X [the main claim, or conclusion] *because* of Y and Z [the supporting claims, or premises]." Arguments, like houses, are never any stronger than their foundations, or premises. False or unreasonable premises will destroy an argument, just as surely as a poorly laid foundation will eventually lead to the ruin of the house it supports.

People often confuse claims with arguments, as in this dialogue:

Jorge: I've got an argument for you, so tell me what you think.

Juan: Go ahead; fire away.

Jorge: Everyone should be a vegetarian.

Juan: That's a claim, but it's not an argument. For it to be an argument, you have to make a claim *and* give some support or reasons for it.

Jorge: OK. How about, everyone should be a vegetarian because my grandmother says so.

Juan: That *is* an argument. You have now made a main claim—that everyone should be a vegetarian—and offered at least one reason—that your grandmother says so—in support of it

Jorge: But is it a good argument?

Juan: Well, I'm not so sure about that. It's not clear to me why your grandmother's saying so would settle the matter, but we will save that discussion for later [for Chapter 6, actually].

Suppose someone who is talking about politics says the following:

---

[3] Ford knew that the Pinto's gas tank tended to explode when the car was rear-ended and that it would cost $11 per vehicle to fix the problem. But Ford did a cost-benefit analysis and their analysis told them the human lives lost would not be worth the cost of fixing the cars. As a result a number of people were badly burned and even killed.

Calvin and Hobbes

by Bill Watterson

Calvin's argument is based on some rather shaky premises. CALVIN AND HOBBES © Watterson. Reprinted with permission of UNIVERSAL PRESS SYNDICATE. All rights reserved.

> If Gore is committed to balancing the budget, then we should vote for him.
>
> He is committed to balancing the budget. So we should vote for him.

In this argument the first two claims support the third. They provide reasons (hopefully good ones) why voters should cast their vote for Gore. The two supporting reasons are both premises, while the main point that they support is the conclusion. In a good argument, if both (or all) of the premises are true and the conclusion follows logically from the premises, then the conclusion must also be true. For *deductive* arguments, at least. (The difference between deductive and inductive arguments will be discussed later in this chapter.) Consider another example, in which the conclusion comes first:

> Lili should buy some food, since she is out of food, and anyone who is out of food should buy some more.

In fact conclusions may be found at the beginning, in the middle, or at the end of an argument, so we need to study arguments carefully to determine what claims are being offered in support of another claim. In this example we can clearly identify three claims being made: two supporting premises and one main conclusion.

The Standard Form for an Argument

When presenting an argument it is helpful to put the argument into a standardized format. The **standard form** for an argument involves the following:

1. Listing the premises, numbering each separate premise.

2. Drawing a line below the last premise.

3. Writing the conclusion below the line. The conclusion should be preceded by three dots (∴), which are simply shorthand for the word *therefore*.

The argument about Lili buying food can be written in standard form as follows:

1. Anyone who is out of food should buy some more.

2. Lili is out of food.
    _____

∴   Lili should buy some food.

Note that when we write an argument in standard form we omit both premise and conclusion indicators, as well as the word *and* unless it is found within a premise or conclusion.

Much of what we read (or hear) does not come prepackaged in standard form. Here are some general guidelines for putting a passage into standard form:

1. Read the passage carefully. If it is long or complicated, read it twice.

2. Determine whether an argument is present. Many passages have much to say but do not contain any arguments—for example, a detailed description of the city of Rome. A few suggestions are in order here:

    a. See if any indicator words are present. Note that the presence of a word like *since* or *because* does not guarantee that an argument is in the neighborhood. Look at this example:

        Since Katya met Sergei, she has dated no one else.

        Here "since" relates to time and so is not a conclusion indicator.

    b. See if there is some main point that the writer is trying to support or justify. Whenever someone gives reasons in support of some claim, there is probably an argument to be found. So, whenever a main point (or conclusion) is either stated or implied, you should search for claims offered in support of this conclusion. Then the argument can be clearly identified and evaluated.

3. If an argument is present, begin by identifying the conclusion. This is the main point being made, and it will often be preceded by a conclusion indicator. If no such indicator is present, try to determine which claims are being offered in support of another claim. The conclusion is always a claim being supported by one or more other claims.

4. After you have identified the conclusion, try to identify the claims offered in support of it. These supporting claims are the premises.

5. Ignore any material that is not part of a premise or conclusion—for example, descriptions, editorial comments, or introductory remarks.

6. Number all the premises and draw a line under the last premise.

7. Compare your version of the argument, now in standard form, to the original to see if anything crucial has been left out of either a premise or the conclusion.

One Important Principle

Assume a virtue, if you have it not. — *William Shakespeare,* Hamlet

In everyday life people often do not write or speak as clearly as we might wish. In these cases we may not be sure how to interpret what they are saying. Suppose Lisa says something that can be interpreted in one of two ways— with the first way being reasonable enough but the second being less so. Given that life is difficult enough, why not graciously grant her the more reasonable of the two interpretations? This might be called the **principle of charity:** when more than one reading of an argument is possible, interpret the argument in the way most flattering to its presenter.[4] Making regular use of this principle can help us accomplish the following:

1. Present someone else's view fairly, thus avoiding the straw man fallacy. (See Chapter 6 for more on this fallacy.)

2. Avoid an obstacle to thinking well—the will to be right. If we fairly represent all sides of an argument, it will increase the chance of all sides receiving a fair hearing.

3. Avoid the human tendency to be lazy, another obstacle to thinking well. If we recognize that we have a duty to accurately represent others' views, as well as our own, it will lessen the chances of our arriving at the wrong conclusion.

Inductive versus Deductive Arguments

The kinds of arguments we have been examining are deductive arguments. A valid **deductive argument** occurs when the truth of the premises guarantees the truth of the conclusion. But this is not so with **inductive arguments,** in which we focus on the strength or weakness of the argument rather than on the question of validity. In a weak argument the truth of the premises does not make the conclusion probably true. By contrast, in a strong argument the truth of the premises is such that the conclusion probably is true.

Look at this argument:

Eighty percent of American men are serious sports fans. Wally is an American man. So, Wally is a serious sports fan.

---

[4] I am indebted on this point to Jerry Cederblom and David Paulsen, *Critical Reasoning,* 4th ed. (Belmont, CA: Wadsworth, 1996), p. 22.

This is not a valid argument, because even if the premises are true there is no guarantee that the conclusion is also true. But this does not mean the argument has no value. Though the truth of the premises does not guarantee the truth of the conclusion, it does provide solid support for it. Given that rational people gear their beliefs to the level of evidence provided, we could reasonably conclude that Wally is a serious sports fan.

Not only can inductive arguments be strong or weak; they can also be sound or unsound. An argument is inductively sound if (1) it is strong and (2) all its premises are true. An argument is inductively unsound when either (1) it is weak or (2) it is strong but has at least one false premise.

There are several significant differences between deductive and inductive arguments. We will focus on three of them here.[5] First, remember that a deductively sound argument cannot have a false conclusion. This is because such an argument has all true premises and is valid, with these two factors combining to guarantee the truth of the conclusion. This is not the case with inductively sound arguments. If an argument is strong (as opposed to valid) and has all true premises, it is still possible, though unlikely, that its conclusion is false. Statistically speaking, the chances of the conclusion being true are greater than 50% but less than 100%.

Suppose you have knee problems and the doctor advises surgery based on this argument:

1. If you have the surgery, there is a 95% probability your problem will be fixed.

2. You should have the surgery.

∴ There is a 95% probability your problem will be fixed.

You should not go into the surgery thinking there is a 100% guarantee that the operation will fix your problem. But you can reasonably believe that it is highly probable that the operation will succeed and so decide to go through with it. But note that you could have the surgery and still end up in the unfortunate 5% whose problem is not fixed. Indeed, in many important decisions in life, inductive soundness is the best we can hope for; the kind of certainty that deductively sound arguments offer is hard to come by.

A second significant difference between deductive and inductive arguments has to do with form. It is the form (or pattern) of an argument that determines whether it is valid. To illustrate, consider the following inductive arguments:

---

[5] This discussion is indebted to Stephen Layman, *The Power of Logic* (Mountain View, CA: Mayfield, 2000), pp. 377–385.

ARGUMENT 1   1. Most (80%) of the people from New Jersey are familiar with air pollution.

2. Joe is from New Jersey.

∴ Joe is familiar with air pollution.

ARGUMENT 2   1. If Joe is from Ocean County in New Jersey, then he probably (80%) is not familiar with air pollution.

2. Joe is from Ocean County.

∴ Joe is not familiar with air pollution.

Although both arguments seem to be inductively strong, their conclusions are contradictory; that is, they cannot both be true. Unlike their deductively valid counterparts, inductive arguments can have differing, if not contradictory, conclusions. Note that, given premise 2 in the second argument, the first argument should not be viewed as inductively strong as it omits relevant information. So, while the form of an argument can guarantee its deductive validity, the form of an inductive argument does not guarantee its strength.

There is a third significant difference between deductive and inductive arguments. Validity can profitably be compared to pregnancy in that each is an all-or-nothing proposition. But with inductive arguments, strength is not like validity, as it admits to degrees. In other words, we could have three inductively strong arguments, but one might be stronger than the other two. Consider these three possibilities:

ARGUMENT 1   1. Almost all (98%) Californians like the beach.

2. Manuel is a Californian.

∴ Manuel likes the beach.

ARGUMENT 2   1. Most (80%) Californians are laid back.

2. Linda is a Californian.

∴ Linda is laid back.

ARGUMENT 3   1. The majority of Californians (51%) like their governor.

2. Calvin is a Californian.

∴ Calvin likes the governor.

All three arguments are inductively strong, yet they are not equally strong. Argument 1 is the strongest, as the conclusion has a 98% chance of being true, while the conclusions to arguments 2 and 3 are less likely (at 80% and 51%, respectively) to be true.

EXERCISE 4.2

1. For each of the following, indicate whether the statement is true or false.
   ★ a. If an argument has a false premise, then it must be inductively unsound.
   b. If an argument is inductively sound, then it is invalid.
   c. If an argument is inductively sound, then it is strong.
   ★ d. If an argument is inductively sound, then it has one true premise.
   e. If an argument is strong, then it is valid.
   f. If an argument is inductively unsound, then it is weak.
   ★ g. If an argument has true premises and a false conclusion, then it is weak.
   h. If an argument is valid and has at least one false premise, then it is inductively unsound.
   i. If an argument is weak, then it must be invalid.
   ★ j. If an argument is weak, then it is inductively unsound.
   k. If an argument is strong and has only true premises, then it is inductively sound.
   l. If an argument is weak, then it is probable that if its premises are true its conclusion is false.
   ★ m. If an argument is strong, then it is possible that its conclusion is false even if its premises are true.
   n. If an argument is inductively sound, then it has true premises.
   o. If an argument is weak, then it is not likely that if its premises are true its conclusion is true.

2. For each of the following, indicate how strong the argument is. Which are the three strongest arguments?
   ★ a. Sixty percent of Texans own guns. Marvin is a Texan. So, Marvin owns a gun.
   b. Most human beings are inclined to be selfish. LaDonna is a human being. Therefore, LaDonna is selfish.
   c. Every man I have met is a dweeb. James is a man. So, James is a dweeb.
   ★ d. Ninety-nine percent of all who take cyanide die shortly thereafter. Goering took cyanide. Goering died shortly thereafter.
   e. Half of all Americans like the president. Cesar is an American. So, he likes the president.
   f. The majority of Americans think that God exists. Nancy is an American. So, she thinks that God exists.
   ★ g. Most college students do not work full-time. Pedro is a college student. Therefore, Pedro does not work full-time.
   h. Ninety percent of Americans have IQs of 100 or higher. Jethro is an American. So, Jethro's IQ is 100 or higher.
   i. Most rich people are not happy. Donald is rich. So, Donald is not happy.
   ★ j. Almost all humans have a need to interact with others. Alan is a human. So, Alan has a need to interact with others.

SEVEN GOOD ARGUMENT PATTERNS

Just as some arguments are more reasonable than others, so some argument **patterns,** or structures or forms, are better than others. Consider this argument:

> If John is tired, then he doesn't think well. John doesn't think well. John is tired.

There are at least two ways we can interpret this argument:

INTERPRETATION 1
1. If John is tired, then he doesn't think well.
2. John doesn't think well.

∴ John is tired.

INTERPRETATION 2
1. If John is tired, then he doesn't think well.
2. John is tired.

∴ John doesn't think well.

In looking at these two possible interpretations, how can we tell which is the more charitable of the two? The pattern in interpretation 1 can be represented as follows:

1. If A [John is tired], then B [he doesn't think well].
2. B [he doesn't think well].

∴ A [John is tired].

In this pattern the conclusion does *not* follow from the premises. In other words all the premises could be true and the conclusion still be false. After all, there could be *three* possible reasons for John's not thinking well, of which being tired is only one—and we have no way of knowing which it is. A good argument will have premises that, if true, *guarantee* the truth of the conclusion. And since this argument pattern (often called affirming the consequent) has premises that, even if true, do not guarantee the truth of the conclusion,[6] we know that it is a flawed or faulty pattern.

But what about interpretation 2? This interpretation can be represented as follows:

1. If A [John is tired], then B [he doesn't think well].
2. A [John is tired].

∴ B [he doesn't think well].

---

[6] Good argument patterns can profitably be viewed as truth-preserving or truth-guaranteeing.

In this interpretation the conclusion follows from the premises. In other words, if all the premises are true, then the conclusion *must* be true. Any argument that has this particular pattern (often called modus ponens) is preferable to any argument having the flawed pattern in interpretation 1. So, given the principle of charity, we should interpret the example in a way that puts it into a good argument pattern (modus ponens) rather than a flawed one (affirming the consequent).

Of course, modus ponens is not the only good argument pattern. In fact there are many good patterns, but fortunately we can identify seven basic ones, on which there are many variations.

PATTERN 1: Modus Ponens (the positive mode)

1.	If A, then B.	1.	If I study, then I will pass.
2.	A.	2.	I will study.
∴	B.	∴	I will pass.

PATTERN 2: Modus Tollens (the negative mode)

1.	If A, then B.	1.	If Tamika is healthy, then she's happy.
2.	Not B.	2.	Tamika is not happy.
∴	Not A.	∴	Tamika is not healthy.

PATTERN 3: Disjunctive Argument

1.	Either A or B.	1.	Either I sleep or I eat.
2.	Not A.	2.	I am not sleeping.
∴	B.	∴	I am eating.

PATTERN 4: Hypothetical Syllogism

1.	If A, then B.	1.	If I work, then I'll get paid.
2.	If B, then C.	2.	If I get paid, then I'll be happy.
∴	If A, then C.	∴	If I work, then I'll be happy.

PATTERN 5: Chain Argument

1.	A.	1.	Antoine is short.
2.	If A, then B.	2.	If Antoine is short, then Camille won't date him.
3.	If B, then C.	3.	If Camille won't date him, then Antoine will ask LaDonna out.
∴	C.	∴	Antoine will ask LaDonna out.

Seven Good Argument Patterns

PATTERN 1: Modus Ponens

1. If A, then B.
2. A.

∴ B.

PATTERN 2: Modus Tollens

1. If A, then B.
2. Not B.

∴ Not A.

PATTERN 3: Disjunctive Argument

1. Either A or B.
2. Not A.

∴ B.

PATTERN 4: Hypothetical Syllogism

1. If A, then B.
2. If B, then C.

∴ If A, then C.

PATTERN 5: Chain Argument

1. A.
2. If A, then B.
3. If B, then C.

∴ C.

PATTERN 6: Predicate Instantiation

1. All A's are B's.
2. M is an A.

∴ M is a B.

PATTERN 7: Universal Syllogism

1. All A's are B's.
2. All B's are C's.

∴ All A's are C's.

Calvin and Hobbes

by Bill Watterson

This probably is not what Gaugin had in mind. CALVIN AND HOBBES © Watterson. Reprinted with permission of UNIVERSAL PRESS SYNDICATE. All rights reserved.

PATTERN 6: Predicate Instantiation

1. All A's are B's.	1. All carpenters are good at building.
2. M is an A.	2. Kahlil is a carpenter.
∴ M is a B.	∴ Kahlil is good at building.

PATTERN 7: Universal Syllogism

1. All A's are B's.	1. All whales are mammals.
2. All B's are C's.	2. All mammals nurse their young.
∴ All A's are C's.	∴ All whales nurse their young.

Once you are familiar with these patterns, you should be able to address this question: What do all good argument patterns have in common that separates them from bad argument patterns?

MISSING PARTS OF ARGUMENTS

It would be very convenient if arguments always fit into one of the seven good patterns. But reality is often more complicated, and people are often less than precise in their writing and speaking. So in many arguments either a premise (or premises) or the conclusion is missing. These may be called implicit (unstated) as opposed to explicit (stated) premises and conclusions. When one or more parts of an argument are left unstated, we need to figure out how to best fill in or reconstruct the argument.

Implicit Conclusions

It is not uncommon for a speaker or writer to let the audience to draw the obvious but unstated conclusion. Consider this example:

If Brian is late, then Gail will be angry. Brian is very late.

Putting this into standard form, we have the following:

1. If Brian is late, then Gail will be angry.

2. Brian is late.

∴ Gail will be angry.

But how do we know exactly what is missing? This is where the seven good argument patterns come into play. The example can be symbolized as follows:

1. If A, then B.

2. A.

∴ B. (implicit)

We know that the conclusion is B because that is the only conclusion that follows from the premises given. Neither A nor Not A nor Not B will do as a conclusion because none of them follow from the premises. Remember that we are looking for a conclusion such that, if the premises are true, then the conclusion must also be true. Given this fact and the principle of charity, B is the implicit conclusion, which represents the claim "Gail will be angry."

Consider another example:

If Luke loves Laura, then he will treat her well. But he often does not treat her well.

Putting this into standard form, we have the following:

1. If Luke loves Laura, then he will treat her well.

2. He often does not treat her well.

∴ ?

But what is the missing conclusion? By symbolizing the premises and thinking back to our seven good patterns, we can determine what is missing:

1. If A, then B.

2. Not B.

∴ ?

Of the seven good patterns, this one clearly fits into modus tollens, the second one. This tells us that what is missing must be Not A, because if we entered anything else (A or B or Not B), then the conclusion would not follow from the premises and the principle of charity would be violated. So the conclusion is Not A, which stands for the claim "Luke does not love Laura." Now we can fill in the implicit conclusion:

1. If Luke loves Laura, then he will treat her well.

2. Luke often does not treat her well.

∴ Luke does not love Laura. (implicit)

Implicit Premises

It is also common for premises to be implicit. Consider this example:

Martha did not tell the truth, so she lied.

Here we have one premise ("Martha did not tell the truth") and one conclusion ("so she lied"—notice the conclusion indicator "so"). In standard form it looks like this:

1. Martha did not tell the truth.

2. ? (implicit)

∴ She lied.

Here we have two pieces of information, but they are not connected in any way. So we are looking for a missing or implicit premise that somehow connects these two pieces of information, such as "If Martha did not tell the truth, then she lied." How do we know that this is the missing premise? First, we need a premise to connect the two claims given to us; second, we need to put it into a good argument pattern. This statement succeeds on both counts. The argument can now be symbolized in this way:

1. If A, then B.   If Martha did not tell the truth,
                          then she lied. (implicit)
2. A.
                          Martha did not tell the truth.
∴ B.
                          ∴ She lied.

Consider another example:

Maria works hard, since all medical doctors work hard.

First, notice that the word "since" is present, so what follows it is a premise. Putting it into standard form, we have this:

Calvin and Hobbes   by Bill Watterson

It's easy to draw wrong conclusions from true premises.   CALVIN AND HOBBES © Watterson.
Reprinted with permission of UNIVERSAL PRESS SYNDICATE. All rights reserved.

1. All medical doctors work hard.

2. ? (implicit)
   _____

∴ Maria works hard.

Again, knowledge of the good patterns is important here. By symbolizing we can write this:

1. All A's are B's.

2. ?
   _____

∴ M is a B.

Of the seven good patterns, only predicate instantiation (pattern 6) seems appropriate here. Keeping that and the principle of charity in mind, we know that "M is an A" is missing. In words this becomes "Maria is a medical doctor." So we can now write this:

1. All A's are B's.   All medical doctors work hard.

2. M is an A. (implicit)   Maria is a medical doctor. (implicit)
   _____   _____

∴ M is a B.   ∴ Maria works hard.

As these examples show, it is important to become familiar with the seven good argument patterns if you are to have much success filling in missing premises or conclusions. That knowledge, combined with the principle of charity and lots of practice, should made this task increasingly easy as time goes by.

SUMMARY

All arguments have a main point, or conclusion, for which supporting claims, or premises, are offered. Arguments can also be written in what is commonly called standard form. Here the premises are numbered, a line is drawn under the premises, and the conclusion is preceded by the use of three dots, which is shorthand for the word *therefore*. According to the principle of charity, if more than one interpretation of someone's argument is possible, we should choose the interpretation most favorable to that person. The structure of an argument can also be called its pattern. There are seven good patterns, such that any argument that fits into one of these patterns guarantees that if the premises are true then the conclusion is as well. Finally, by standardizing arguments, we can identify implicit premises and conclusions.

EXERCISE 4.3

To complete these exercises, you should (1) be familiar with the seven good patterns of arguments, (2) know how to label (with A's and B's) the various claims, and (3) know how to put the argument into a good pattern.

1. For each of the following, identify the premises and the conclusion, as well as the argument pattern.

★ a. If Olga dates Fred, then Sally will be happy. Sally is not happy. Olga is not dating Fred.

   b. Either Sam goes to McGill or he goes to Vanderbilt. He is not going to McGill. He is going to Vanderbilt.

   c. Anyone who reads Tolstoy will be impressed. Yolanda is reading Tolstoy. Yolanda will be impressed.

★ d. If Bettina marries Boris, then Ivan will move to Berlin. Bettina will marry Boris. Ivan is moving to Berlin.

   e. All plumbers are conscientious. All conscientious people charge fairly for their work. All plumbers charge fairly for their work.

   f. If welfare is modified, then the country will improve. If the country improves, the president will get the credit. Welfare is being modified. The president will get the credit.

★ g. If affirmative action is ended, then blacks and women will suffer. If blacks and women suffer, then the country will be worse off. If affirmative action is ended, then the country will be worse off.

   h. If human nature is fundamentally selfish, then we need laws to prevent humans from harming each other. Human nature is fundamentally selfish, so we need laws to prevent humans from harming each other.[7]

   i. Either Microsoft is a monopoly or it is not. A judge rejected the idea that it is not a monopoly. Therefore, it is a monopoly.

---

[7] This point of view was developed by the British philosopher Thomas Hobbes in the 1600s and later applied in a literary context by William Golding in his *Lord of the Flies*.

★ j. If something is real, then it is knowable. If it is knowable, then it is un-changing. The physical world is constantly changing. So the physical world is ultimately unreal.[8]

   k. If the Berlin Wall comes down, then there will be many changes in eastern Europe. The Berlin Wall did come down, so there will be many changes in eastern Europe.

   l. Any philosopher appointed to a prominent university holding unpopular views will create some controversy. Peter Singer, recently appointed to a distinguished post at Princeton University, believes that human infanticide is morally acceptable in certain circumstances. Therefore, there will be some controversy.[9]

2. In each of the following, a premise or conclusion is missing. Write the argument in standard form, and then add the missing premise or conclusion.

★ a. We know Ed will get in trouble because he is not paying his taxes. (Think how we can connect the two claims here—for example, "If Ed does not pay his taxes, then . . .)

   b. If the New York Yankees are the best team in baseball, then they are better than the Atlanta Braves. If they are better than the Braves, then they are better than the Florida Marlins. So the conclusion is obvious.

   c. All Republicans favor a hands-off policy toward big business, and Jesse Helms is a Republican.

★ d. All "Cheeseheads" are Green Bay Packer fans. All Packer fans live in Wisconsin.

   e. I think. So I must exist.

   f. Linda is a human being, so Linda must be inclined to be selfish.

★ g. Either we vote for Senator Fussmire or the country will go down the tubes. And we certainly do not want the country to go down the tubes.

   h. If a fetus is a person, then it has the right to life. If it has the right to life, then it cannot be justifiably killed. And since a fetus is a person, the conclusion is clear.

   i. If a fetus is a person, then it should be self-conscious. So we know that a fetus is not a person.

★ j. All Americans like apple pie. So all Americans like at least one kind of fruit.

   k. All North Dakotans know what cold weather feels like, and Lena is a North Dakotan.

   l. If God (as traditionally understood) existed, then there would be no evil. But there is lots of evil.

★ m. All we do crumbles to the ground. Yesterday I did lots of things.

3. Reality, like life, now gets more complicated. The following arguments don't exactly fit into any of the seven good patterns. Rather, they can be seen as variations on the good patterns. Identify the premises and conclusions, and then try to determine the pattern.

---

[8] This rather abstract argument is sometimes attributed to the great Greek philosopher Plato. The argument is simply a slightly more involved example of modus tollens.

[9] Singer is a modern philosopher whose views are seen as potentially dangerous by disabled rights groups and various other groups. His ethical orientation is one version of utilitarianism, which is discussed in Chapter 8.

★ a. All Republicans believe in a strong national defense. Some people from Maine are Republicans. So some people from Maine believe in a strong national defense.

b. I will read either Dr. Seuss or Santayana. If I don't read Santayana, then I will not be happy. I will be happy. I will read Santayana.

c. All North Dakotans like cold weather. Hans does not like cold weather, so Hans is not a North Dakotan.

4. For the following arguments provide the missing part (premise or conclusion), and indicate what the pattern is.

★ a.　1.　All bachelors are unmarried males.
　　　2.　Ed is a bachelor.

　　　———————————

　　　∴　?

b.　1.　If you are rich, then I am single.
　　2.　?

　　———————————

　　∴　You are not rich.

c.　1.　All teachers work hard.
　　2.　?

　　———————————

　　∴　All teachers pay taxes.

★ d.　1.　?
　　　2.　I will go south.

　　　———————————

　　　∴　I will need a new car.

e.　1.　If you like to watch *The Simpsons,* then you are well adjusted.
　　2.　You like to watch *The Simpsons.*

　　———————————

　　∴　?

f.　1.　All Chicago Cubs fans know about the pain of losing.
　　2.　All who know about the pain of losing appreciate victory when it comes along.

　　———————————

　　∴　?

★ g.　1.　If God exists, then evil does not exist.
　　　2.　?

　　　———————————

　　　∴　God does not exist.

h.　1.　Today is either Tuesday or Wednesday.
　　2.　?

　　———————————

　　∴　Today is Tuesday.

i.　1.　All Merkins are unwazuvenated.
　　2.　All who are unwazuvenated are unrepentant.[10]

　　———————————

　　∴　?

---

[10] Don't be confused by the fact that there is no such thing as a "Merkin" or being "unwazuvenated." You should still be able to figure out what is missing. As will become clearer in Chapter 5, the conclusion can follow from the premises even if one or more of the premises is false or downright ridiculous.

★ j. 1. If you are a Manchester United fan, then you like to go to pubs.

2. If you like to go to pubs, then you like to drink beer.

3. ?

_____

∴ You like to drink beer.

5. Each of the following doesn't neatly fit into any pattern. Provide the implicit claim and indicate the pattern.

★ a. 1. Either I will go to school or I will stay home.

2. If I go to school, then I will see Sue.

3. ?

_____

∴ I will stay home.

b. 1. ?

2. Some New Jerseyans are New York Giants fans.

_____

∴ Some New Jerseyans threw snowballs.

c. 1. If Alice winks at Charlie, then Charlie will be thrilled and George will be peeved.

2. ?

_____

∴ Alice did not wink at Charlie.

GLOSSARY

argument   A statement containing a main point (claim) and one or more reasons in support of it.

premise   A claim offered in support of a conclusion.

conclusion   The main point of an argument.

indicator   A word that often signals the presence of either a premise or a conclusion.

explanation   A type of nonargument that spells out why something happens.

description   A type of nonargument that gives information about someone or something.

report   A type of nonargument that gives an account of what happened.

standard form   A widely accepted way of writing arguments.

principle of charity   The principle that, if one or more interpretations of an argument are possible, we should choose the interpretation most favorable to its advocate.

deductive argument   An argument in which the premises are intended to guarantee the truth of the conclusion. Here, if the premises are true, then it is impossible for the conclusion to be false.

inductive argument   An argument in which the premises are intended to make the conclusion probable or likely but not guaranteed. Here, though it is unlikely, it is possible for the premises to be true and the conclusion to be false.

pattern   The structure or form of an argument.

CHAPTER 5

Distinguishing Good Arguments from Bad Ones

Seventy minutes had passed before Mr. Lloyd George arrived at his proper theme. He spoke for a hundred and seventeen minutes, in which period he was detected only once in the use of an argument.
  —Arnold Bennett, "After the March Offensive"

VALIDITY

All deductive arguments can be judged either valid or invalid. But what does it mean for an argument to be valid? An argument is **valid** if the conclusion logically follows from the premises. This is another way of saying that if the premises are true then the conclusion is also true. Put yet another way, an argument is valid if and only if it is impossible for all the premises to be true and the conclusion to be false. For any given argument we need to ask whether there are any possible circumstances in which all the premises could be true but the conclusion be false. If the answer is no, then the argument is valid.

Note that the concept of validity is an *internal* one in that it has to do with how all the parts of an argument relate to each other, with how well the parts "fit" together. Validity thus reflects how different claims are related to one another. A valid argument involves a "good fit," while an invalid argument involves a "poor fit." The seven good patterns, presented in Chapter 4, are all valid argument patterns.

To understand the idea of validity, think about working a jigsaw puzzle. If the pieces fit together well, then it is valid; if there is a poor fit, it is invalid. But even if the pieces fit together well, it does not mean that the overall picture is a "true" one. For examples, we can imagine a cow flying though we know that cows do not have the ability to do any such thing. A puzzle could "be valid"—that is, all its pieces fit together well—even though the picture it shows does not correspond with reality as we know it. Similarly an argument can be valid even if its premises and conclusion are false or even downright ludicrous.

To illustrate validity, consider this example:

1.   If the minimum wage is raised, then the Democrats will be happy.

2.   The minimum wage will be raised.

∴   The Democrats will be happy.

Here the conclusion follows from the premises. In other words, if the premises are true, then the conclusion must also be true with 100% certainty. So it is a valid argument. This should not surprise us, as this is an example of good argument modus ponens (pattern 1), discussed in the previous chapter.

Now consider a second example:

1.   If the minimum wage gets raised, then the Democrats will be happy.

2.   The Democrats are happy.

∴   The minimum wage got raised.

Here the conclusion does not follow from the premises. All the premises may be true but the conclusion still be false—the essence of an invalid argument. Suppose there are *seven* things that would make the Democrats happy, only one of which is an increase in the minimum wage. Therefore, if someone tells us that the Democrats are happy (premise 2), there is no guarantee that the cause involves the minimum wage. It could be any one of the other six things. It is important to note here that, although the truth of the conclusion *could* follow from the truth of the premises, there is no guarantee of its doing so, and validity always involves a 100% certainty of the conclusion following. In short, if there is no guarantee, then there is no validity.

Note that validity deals only with the pattern, structure, or form of an argument; it has nothing to do with its content. For example, all of the houses in a particular subdivision may have the same form, or pattern—the same square footage, the same floor plan, and so forth. But individual families will fill up these houses with different things (the content). Or suppose a family makes 72 Christmas cookies using the same cookie cutter: 24 chocolate chip, 24 sugar, and 24 gingerbread. Each of these three kinds of cookies will have the same shape (form) but their individual content will differ.

SOUNDNESS

In addition to validity, we need to consider the **soundness** of arguments. An argument is sound if and only if:

1. It is valid.
2. All its premises are reasonable, or rationally acceptable.[1]

Note that soundness involves both form and content. If either one (or both) of these two conditions is violated, then the argument is unsound. Validity and soundness are somewhat like pregnancy in that they are "all-or-nothing" concepts. That is, just as there is no such thing as being "somewhat pregnant," the idea of an argument being semivalid or partially sound is a silly one.

Keeping the concepts of validity and soundness in mind, we come up with four combinations:

1. A valid and sound argument   Best possibility
2. A valid but unsound argument   ↓
3. An invalid but sound argument   ↓
4. An invalid and unsound argument   Worst possibility

Combos 1, 2, and 4 are all genuine possibilities, while combo 3 is not, because the concept of soundness includes the idea of validity within it. In other words, if an argument is sound, then, by definition, it is also valid.

Let's look at an example of each of the three remaining possibilities, beginning with the first one.

A VALID AND SOUND ARGUMENT

1. All whales are mammals.

2. All mammals nurse their young.

∴ All whales nurse their young.

This is a valid argument in which the conclusion follows from the premises, as there is no way for all the premises to be true and the conclusion to be false. But it is also a sound argument, because it is valid and both of its premises are true.

Now let's look at our second possibility.

A VALID BUT UNSOUND ARGUMENT

1. All who vote Republican are also conservative.

2. Bob votes Republican.

∴ Bob is a conservative.

---

[1] By "rationally acceptable" we mean there is more evidence in favor of the claim being true than false. More will be said about rational acceptability in Chapter 7. For further study on this matter, see Louis Pojman, *What Can We Know?* (Belmont, CA: Wadsworth, 1995).

Validity and Soundness

STATUS OF THE ARGUMENT	ARE ALL THE PREMISES TRUE?	DOES THE CONCLUSION FOLLOW?
Invalid	Not relevant	No
Valid	Not relevant	Yes
Sound	Yes	Yes

This example fits one of the seven good argument patterns (pattern 6, predicate instantiation) and is thus a valid argument. There is no way for both premises to be true and the conclusion to be false. But it is not a sound argument, because premise 1 is false. That is, it is not necessarily the case that all people who vote Republican are conservatives. It *might* be true that most who vote this way are conservatives, but the claim here involves the much stronger word "all." Someone certainly could vote Republican and be, say, a liberal or a Socialist. Since one can vote Republican and not be a conservative, there is sufficient reason to reject this premise. Remember that universal claims ("All X are Y") are considered false if there are one or more exceptions to the claim. And since it is clearly possible, even if not likely, for someone to vote Republican and not be a conservative, the premise should be regarded as false.

What about our final possibility?

AN INVALID AND UNSOUND ARGUMENT

1. If Jenna is in Massachusetts, then she is in the United States.

2. She is in the United States.

∴ She is in Massachusetts.

Here the conclusion does not follow from the premises, making it an invalid argument. Though it is possible to be both in the United States and in Massachusetts at any given moment, most of the people in the United States in fact are not in Massachusetts. The issue is whether the two premises guarantee the conclusion—that Jenna is in Massachusetts—and clearly they do not. And because this is an invalid argument, it is also, by definition, unsound.

EXERCISE 5.1

For each of the following, indicate whether it is (1) valid and sound, (2) valid but unsound, or (3) invalid and unsound.

★ 1. 1. All lions are mammals.
       2. In the local zoo there is a lion. (Assume this is true.)
       _____
       ∴ In the local zoo there is a mammal.

   2. 1. If Tyrone is rich, then Tyrone is happy.
       2. Tyrone is rich. (Assume this is true.)
       _____
       ∴ Tyrone is happy.

   3. 1. If Bonnie is a physician's assistant, then she will enjoy her job.
       2. Bonnie enjoys her job.
       _____
       ∴ Bonnie is a physician's assistant.

★ 4. 1. Deon is either a Democrat or a Republican.
       2. Deon is not a Republican.
       _____
       ∴ Deon is a Democrat.

   5. 1. If someone is healthy, then that person is happy.
       2. That person is healthy.
       _____
       ∴ That person is happy.

   6. 1. If Diego is sick, then he will not go to work.
       2. If Diego does not go to work, he will miss the office party.
       3. Diego will miss the office party.
       _____
       ∴ Diego is sick.

★ 7. 1. All mammals are dogs.
       2. All dogs are Socialists.
       _____
       ∴ All mammals are Socialists.

   8. 1. If the fetus is not a person, then it does not have the right to life.
       2. If the fetus does not have the right to life, then it is morally acceptable to abort it under some circumstances.
       _____
       ∴ If the fetus is not a person, then it is morally acceptable to abort it under some circumstances.

   9. 1. All triangles are three-sided figures.
       2. Mahmood did not draw a three-sided figure.
       _____
       ∴ Mahmood did not draw a triangle.

★ 10. 1.   If Santa Claus exists, then I am the president of IBM.

2.   I am not the president of IBM.

∴   Santa Claus does not exist.

SYMBOLIZING CLAIMS

The grammatical structure of a claim often gives us insight into its logical structure. Learning how to symbolize claims, using letters to stand for each claim, helps us analyze claims. We will focus on four kinds of claims:

1. **Negations**—"not" claims

2. **Conjunctions**—"and" claims, with two claims typically joined by *and*

3. **Disjunctions**—"or" claims, with two claims typically joined by *or*

4. **Conditionals**—"if . . . then" claims

With negations, we use the symbol "~" when symbolizing claims. Consider the following examples of negation:

CLAIM	NEGATION
It is raining.	It is not raining.
Today is Sunday.	Today is not Sunday.
Pele is the best soccer player ever.	Pele is not the best soccer player ever.

Any simple (one-part) claim can be represented by a letter of our choosing. So, instead of saying "It is raining," we can substitute a capital R (for "rain") as a symbol for that claim. And since the symbol for negation is ~, we can write the negation of R as ~R, which is simply shorthand for "It is not raining." Similarly we can use a capital S to stand for "Today is Sunday" and ~S to represent the claim "Today is not Sunday."

Just as we can use symbols to represent claims and their negations, we can also use symbols for conjunctions, disjunctions, and conditional claims. Consider the following conjunctions:

1. San Jose is in California, and Irvine is in California.

2. Woodrow Wilson was president, and so was Abraham Lincoln.

3. Watching too much TV is a problem, and so is child abuse.

Note that all of these claims have two parts (claims), linked by a conjunction ("and"), that together form one longer (compound) claim. Again, choosing letters to represent each single claim, we use the symbol "&" to represent "and." Suppose we decide to have S (for "San Jose") represent the claim "San

---

Examples of Negation

CLAIM	NEGATION OF THE CLAIM
It is raining.	It is not raining.
Today is Sunday.	Today is not Sunday.
Michael Jordan is the greatest basketball player ever.	Michael Jordan is not the greatest basketball player ever.
Madrid is in Spain.	Madrid is not in Spain.
The ball is green.	The ball is not green.
Lincoln is considered a great president.	Lincoln is not considered a great president.
I like apples.	I do not like apples.
Women get paid less than men for comparable work.	Women do not get paid less than men for comparable work.
Murder is morally wrong.	Murder is not morally wrong.
All politicians can be trusted.	Not all politicians can be trusted.

Jose is in California" and I (for "Irvine") represent "Irvine is in California."
We now can write

$$S \,\&\, I$$

to represent the claim. Notice how easy this is to do, and also how much less writing it involves. Likewise we can symbolize claim 2 as

$$W \,\&\, L$$

and claim 3 as

$$T \,\&\, C$$

Now consider the following disjunctions:

1. Either Phan wins the lottery or he will need to get a better job.
2. Either you love me or you don't.
3. Either Theresa will go to work or Yolanda will.

For claim 1 we can represent "Phan wins the lottery" as P and "he will need to get a better job" as J (for "job"). The symbol for the word *or* is "∨," so we can now symbolize this claim as

$$P \vee J$$

In similar fashion we can represent the other two disjunctions as follows:

$$L \vee \sim L$$

$$T \vee Y$$

Finally, consider these conditional claims:

1. If it rains, then we will play inside today.
2. If Eduardo wins the lottery, then he will retire pronto.
3. If the economy continues to do well, many people will benefit.

For claim 1 we can symbolize "If it rains" as R and use I (for "inside") to stand for "then we will play inside today." The symbol for a conditional claim, representing the structure of "if . . . then" claims, is an arrow (→). So we can now write

$$R \rightarrow I$$

to symbolize this claim. Similarly we can represent the other two conditional claims as follows:

$$E \rightarrow R$$

$$E \rightarrow B$$

EXERCISE 5.2

Each of the following is either a conditional, a conjunction, a disjunction, or a negation. Translate them into symbols according to the rules just discussed. Note that items 13–24 are not straightforward.

★ 1. If humans have souls, then they are not animals. (Here, if we use H to stand for humans and A to stand for animals, then we can symbolize this as $H \rightarrow \sim A$.)

2. If racism continues, then American society will suffer.

3. Either Roberto is wise or he is foolish.

★ 4. Eleanor will go to the party, and so will Jack.

5. Latrell will not go to the grocery today.

6. If Katrina gets an A in her last class, then she will get a scholarship for college.

★ 7. Las Vegas is in Nevada, and many people visit it.

8. Either Polly will play tennis or Emmett will.

9. God does not exist.

★ 10. Either same-sex marriages will be legally recognized or homophobia will continue.

11. Kevin can dribble well and dunk a basketball.

12. Nancy wants to be a doctor and a mother.

★ 13. Terrell is in Michigan only if he is in Detroit.

14. It is not true that both Miranda and Althea will go to the party.

15. The Anteaters would have won if Billy had not dropped the ball.

★ 16. Fred was a gifted dancer though he was also very hard on himself.

17. You can say that to him but you might regret it later.

18. Either Marcel or Hans or Claude will get the job.

★ 19. Bozo is tall, red-haired, and a clown.

20. Unless you shape up you're going to get in big trouble.

21. If this figure is a square, then it has four sides and four right angles.

★ 22. If Jackson Lake is not in Colorado, then it must be in either Wyoming or Utah.

23. The theory failed to get much support from the experts in the field.

24. Mercy killing is justified only if the patient is dying, is in significant pain, and gives permission.

A PRELIMINARY WORD ABOUT TRUTH TABLES AND VENN DIAGRAMS

With regard to truth tables and/or Venn diagrams, you may wonder, "Why do we need to learn these things?" Rest assured that truth tables and Venn diagrams are not included in the text merely to make your life difficult. For several reasons it's important to become familiar with these two methods for evaluating arguments.

The primary reason has to do with critical thinking itself. The major goal of this book is to improve your ability to think clearly and precisely, and the use of truth tables and Venn diagrams will help you achieve this goal. An argument along these lines might run as follows:

1. If one wants to better oneself, then one should learn how to think critically.

2. If one wants to learn how to think critically, then one needs to know how to argue well.

3. If one needs to know how to argue well, then one needs to know all about validity and soundness.

4. If one needs to know all about validity and soundness, then one needs to know about the various techniques for testing the validity of arguments.

5. Truth tables and Venn diagrams are two such techniques.

6. One should want to better oneself.

∴   One should learn about truth tables and Venn diagrams.

Many of you will recognize this as merely an extended chain argument (good argument pattern 5).

A second reason for learning about truth tables and Venn diagrams has to do with language and our grasp of it. As discussed in Chapter 3, arguing well requires careful and precise use of language. Truth tables actually offer very precise definitions of some of the key words in the English language: *and, or, not,* and *if . . . then*. You must have a firm grasp of the meaning of these seemingly simple words if you are to fully understand truth tables. Also, it never hurts to solidify an already decent understanding of something of importance, and learning to use language properly is definitely important. And both truth tables and Venn diagrams actually are enjoyable and relatively easy to work with!

TRUTH TABLES

Claims of the sort we have been examining are either simple or compound. A claim is simple if it has only one part and so makes only one claim. Here is an example:

It is raining.

By contrast, a compound claim has two or more parts. Here are some examples:

Marty will go to work and so will Joe. (conjunction)

Either Marty will go to work or Joe will go to work. (disjunction)

Note that a conjunction is considered true only if both of its parts—called **conjuncts**—are true; a disjunction is true whenever one or more of its parts—called **disjuncts**—are true. So a conjunction is a stronger claim than a disjunction, as it is claiming that both of its conjuncts are true, while a disjunction can be true when only one disjunct is true.

A conditional claim is also made up of two simple claims, phrased in the "if . . . then" form. Look at this example:

If Marty goes to work, then Joe will go to work.

Examples of Conjunctions

SIMPLE CLAIMS	CONJUNCTION
1. It is raining. 2. Today is Sunday.	It is raining, *and* today is Sunday.
1. It is sunny outside. 2. Olaf is happy.	It is sunny outside, *and* Olaf is happy.
1. Lincoln was from Kentucky. 2. Lincoln was president.	Lincoln was from Kentucky, *and* Lincoln was president.
1. Dmitra is a politician. 2. Politicians cannot be trusted.	Dmitra is a politician, *and* politicians cannot be trusted.
1. I like apples. 2. Fruit is good to eat.	I like apples, *and* fruit is good to eat.

Here the claim introduced by the word "if" is called the **antecedent** (meaning "to come before"), and the claim introduced by the word "then" is called the **consequent** (meaning "to come after"). Conditionals should not be understood as making the claim that both the antecedent and the consequent are true. The two parts do not have that kind of relationship. Rather, the truth of the consequent *depends upon* the truth of the antecedent. In other words, if A (short for "antecedent") is true, then we can expect C (for "consequent") to be true. So, if A is true and C follows (is also true), then it is a *true* conditional claim; if A is true and C is false, then it is a *false* conditional.

One last kind of claim we are interested in is that of negation. Here's an example:

1. Marty goes to work. (claim)
2. It is false that Marty will go to work. (negation)

We now have in place the building blocks to introduce the idea of truth tables. **Truth tables** record all the possible truth values of the claims in an argument and enable us to do two very important things:

1. Determine whether a number of argument patterns are valid.
2. Come to a clearer understanding of some fundamental words in the English language.

Let us begin by letting P stand for any simple claim. For any claim P there are two and only two possibilities—either it is true (T) or it is false (F). This can be represented as follows:

Examples of Disjunctions

SIMPLE CLAIMS	DISJUNCTION
1. It is raining.	
2. Today is Sunday.	It is raining, *or* today is Sunday.
1. It is sunny outside.	
2. Olaf is happy.	It is sunny outside, *or* Olaf is happy.
1. Lincoln was from Kentucky.	
2. Lincoln was president.	Lincoln was from Kentucky, *or* Lincoln was president.
1. Dmitra is a politician.	
2. Politicians cannot be trusted.	Dmitra is a politician, *or* politicians cannot be trusted.
1. I like apples.	
2. Fruit is good to eat.	I like apples, *or* fruit is good to eat.

$$\frac{P}{\begin{array}{c} T \\ F \end{array}}$$

This graphic displays the possible truth values of any simple claim. Truth tables are helpful not only for determining the validity of arguments but also for giving us a better understanding of some crucial words in arguments and critical thinking. Recall that the crucial words have accompanying symbols:

WORD	SYMBOL	CLAIM
Not	~	Negation
And	&	Conjunction
Or	∨	Disjunction
If . . . then	→	Conditional

The truth table for negation is written as follows:

$$\begin{array}{c|c} P & \sim P \\ \hline T & F \\ F & T \end{array}$$

The left-hand column lists both possible truth values for P (its being true and its being false), while the right-hand column presents the truth values for ~P

Examples of Conditionals

SIMPLE CLAIMS	CONDITIONAL
1. It is raining.	*If* it is raining, *then* we will not play baseball today.
2. We will not play baseball today.	
1. It is sunny outside.	*If* it is sunny outside, *then* Olaf is happy.
2. Olaf is happy.	
1. Lincoln freed the slaves.	*If* Lincoln freed the slaves, *then* Lincoln was a good president.
2. Lincoln was a good president.	
1. Dmitra is a politician.	*If* Dmitra is a politician, *then* she cannot be trusted.
2. She cannot be trusted.	
1. I like apples.	*If* I like apples, *then* I eat one every day.
2. I eat one every day.	

based on the truth values for P. So far this is fairly straightforward: whenever P is true, then its negation is false, and vice versa. But suppose we are considering two claims, P and Q, where Q stands for another simple claim. Since we have two claims and both P and Q can be either true or false, these factors combine to give us four (two claims times two possibilities) overall possibilities. The resulting truth table is written as follows:

P	*Q*	
T	T	(P is true and Q is true.)
T	F	(P is true and Q is false.)
F	T	(P is false and Q is true.)
F	F	(P is false and Q is false.)

This table shows us that there are four possibilities, with each row representing one possibility.

In addition to negation ("not") and disjunction ("or"), truth tables can be used to investigate conjunction ("and"). Recall that the claim P and Q can be written as "P & Q." The truth table for a conjunction looks like this:

P	*Q*	*P & Q*
T	T	T
T	F	F
F	T	F
F	F	F

Suppose the claim P & Q stands for this situation:

Heather will go to work and Maurice will go to work.

This conjunction is true only if the following occurs:

Heather goes to work and Maurice goes to work. (row 1 in the truth table)

It is false given any of the other three possibilities:

1. Heather goes to work and Maurice does not. (row 2)

2. Heather does not go to work and Maurice goes to work. (row 3)

3. Heather does not go to work and Maurice does not go to work. (row 4)

Note that a conjunction can have many more than two parts, and for it to be true as a whole, every single part must be true.

P and Q can be combined in a number of ways. For example, for the (inclusive) disjunction P ∨ Q ("Either P is true or Q is true, or both"),[2] the truth table can be written in this way:

P	*Q*	*P* ∨ *Q*
T	T	T
T	F	T
F	T	T
F	F	F

Note that the disjunction is false *only* in those cases in which all (two or more) of its disjuncts are false. The last row in the table shows this possibility, while the other three rows are all regarded as true in that one or more of the disjuncts are true. Suppose P ∨ Q represents this claim:

Either Heather will go to work or Maurice will.

This disjunction is true if any of the following occurs:

1. Heather goes to work and Maurice does too. (row 1 in the truth table)

2. Heather goes to work and Maurice does not. (row 2)

3. Heather does not go to work and Maurice goes to work. (row 3)

It is false only if this occurs:

Heather does not go to work and neither does Maurice. (row 4)

_____

[2] Disjunctions can be either inclusive (when both disjuncts can be true) or exclusive (when one and only one disjunct is true). In this text we will focus on only inclusive disjunctions.

A fourth kind of claim to consider is the conditional ("if . . . then"). Conditionals are not as easy to grasp as conjunctions, disjunctions, and negations, because they have two parts rather than one, and many students fail to remember just what a conditional is (and is not). Consider this example:

If Elena wins the lottery, then she will take us out to dinner.

We need to begin by asking ourselves under what conditions this claim would be false. It would be false only if the antecedent (the "if" part) were true and the consequent (the "then" part) were false. Under all other circumstances we would regard the conditional as true, even though it might seem contrary to what many people would think. This claim can also be phrased as follows:

It will not be the case that Elena wins the lottery and does not take us out to dinner.

The truth table for a conditional looks like this:

P	*Q*	*P → Q*	
T	T	T	*(Elena wins the lottery and takes us out to dinner.)*
T	F	F	*(Elena wins the lottery and does not take us out to dinner.)*
F	T	T	*(Elena does not win the lottery and takes us out to dinner.)*
F	F	T	*(Elena does not win the lottery and does not take us out to dinner.)*

The first two rows of the truth table are fairly straightforward. In the first row, P is true (Elena wins the lottery) and Q is true (she takes us out to dinner). This is exactly as promised, so we regard this value as true. And in the second row, P is true (Elena wins the lottery) and Q is false (she does not take us out to dinner). This clearly makes her initial claim ("If P, then Q") untrue, so we regard this value as false.

But what about rows 3 and 4? Why do we write "T" and "T" when the antecedent is false in both cases? Remember that conditional claims are not blanket (sometimes called "categorical") claims like this one:

Elena will take us out to dinner no matter what.

Rather, they are conditional—"*If* Elena wins the lottery, then she will take us out to dinner." Elena is not lying if she does not win the lottery and takes us out to dinner anyway. Nor is she lying if she does not win the lottery and does not take us out to dinner. The word "if" can roughly be understood to mean "on the condition that" or "whenever." So, in the event that she does not win the lottery (rows 3 and 4), then she is under no obligation to take us out to dinner. She could do so out of the goodness of her heart, but it would be

Kinds of Truth Tables

NEGATION			CONJUNCTION				DISJUNCTION				CONDITIONAL		
A	~*A*		*A*	*B*	*A* & *B*		*A*	*B*	*A* ∨ *B*		*A*	*B*	*A* → *B*
T	F		T	T	T		T	T	T		T	T	T
F	T		T	F	F		T	F	T		T	F	F
			F	T	F		F	T	T		F	T	T
			F	F	F		F	F	F		F	F	T

something above and beyond what she has promised to do. Thus, whenever the antecedent is false, we regard the value of P → Q as true, regardless of whether the consequent is true or false.

The following diagram illustrates the logic of a conditional claim:

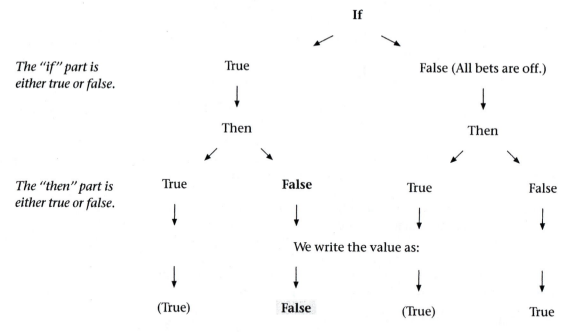

This diagram merely represents graphically what the truth table tells us in another manner. The expression "All bets are off" is simply another way of stating that a person who makes a conditional promise is obligated to fulfill that promise *if and only if* the antecedent of the conditional is true. Otherwise, as just discussed, the promise maker is under no obligation to make the consequent come true.

So truth tables help us determine the validity of many different kinds of arguments. Let's look at some examples, beginning with this one:

1.   P → Q   (If P, then Q.)

2.   ~Q   (Not Q.)

∴   ~P   (Not P.)

The truth table for this claim looks like this:

P	*Q*	*P → Q*	*~Q*	*∴ ~P*	
T	T	T	F	F	
T	F	F	T	F	
F	T	T	F	T	
F	F	T	T	T	*(key row)*

Remember that a valid argument is one in which the truth of the premises guarantees the truth of the conclusion. There is only one row (row 4) in which all the premises are true. So we check to see if the conclusion is also true—and it is. This tells us that, whenever all the premises are true, the conclusion is also true. And that is what validity is all about. The other three rows in this table are not relevant, given that validity is only concerned with whether the conclusion must follow from all true premises.

Our second example has a different outcome than the first:

1.   P → Q

2.   Q

∴   P

The truth table for this claim looks like this:

P	*Q*	*P → Q*	*Q*	*∴ P*	
T	T	T	T	T	*(relevant row)*
T	F	F	F	T	
F	T	T	T	F	*(key row)*
F	F	T	F	F	

In this truth table two rows (rows 1 and 3) have all true premises. Remember that a valid argument is one in which, if all the premises are true, then the conclusion is also true. Row 1 has all true premises and a true conclusion; so far, so good. But row 3 has all true premises and a false conclusion. Thus this is an invalid argument pattern, as there is no guarantee that all true premises will be followed by a true conclusion. It is important to note here that, even if a truth table had thirty rows with all true premises and true conclusions and only one row with all true premises and a false conclusion, that would be sufficient to make it an invalid pattern (something like "one bad apple spoils the whole bunch").

Our third example gets a little more complicated:

1. P & Q

2. Q → R

3. P
_____

∴   R

Note that the truth table for this example has eight rows, because there are three premises (variables) and two possibilities (T or F) for each ($2 \times 2 \times 2 = 8$):

P	*Q*	*R*	*P & Q*	*Q → R*	*P*	*∴ R*	
T	T	T	T	T	T	T	*(key row)*
T	T	F	T	F	T	F	
T	F	T	F	T	T	T	
T	F	F	F	T	T	F	
F	T	T	F	T	F	T	
F	T	F	F	F	F	F	
F	F	T	F	T	F	T	
F	F	F	F	T	F	F	

Here row 1 is the only one in which all the premises are true. And since the conclusion is also true in row 1, we know that this is a valid argument pattern, as it is not possible for all the premises to be true and the conclusion false.

The fourth example looks like this:

1. P → Q

2. P & (Q ∨ R)

3. ~Q
_____

∴   R

The truth table for this example will again contain eight rows, as there are three premises and two possibilities (T or F) for each:

Guidelines for Using Truth Tables

1. Fill in the columns for all negative variables—for example, ~A and ~B.

2. Fill in the columns for all simple claims—for example, A or ~B.

3. Fill in the truth value for all remaining variables (all compound claims).

4. Remember the rules for the different operations:

   a. "And" statements are false if any one part of the conjunction is false. They are true if and only if all the parts are true.

   b. "Or" statements are false if and only if all the parts are false. They are true if any one part is true.

   c. "If . . . then" statements are false if and only if the antecedent ("if") part is true and the consequent ("then") part is false. They are considered true under all other circumstances.

5. Work from within the parentheses out—just as in math.

6. Apply the rule of the particular operation (&, ∨, →, or ~) to that column.

7. Find all the rows with all true premises, and mark them with an asterisk (*).

   a. Remember that a valid argument is one in which, whenever all the premises are true, the conclusion is also true.

8. Determine if all these relevant rows have true conclusions.

9. If yes, then write "valid by row(s) ——————."

10. If no, then write "invalid by row(s) ——————."

P	Q	R	P → Q	P & (Q ∨ R)	~Q	∴ R	
T	T	T	T	T	T	T	(relevant row)
T	T	F	T	T	T	F	(key row)
T	F	T	F	T	F	T	
T	F	F	F	F	F	F	
F	T	T	T	F	T	T	
F	T	F	T	F	T	F	
F	F	T	T	F	F	T	
F	F	F	T	F	F	F	

Here the first two rows are of interest to us, for they represent all the situations in which all the premises are true. Row 1 has all true premises and a true conclusion, but row 2 has all true premises and a false conclusion. So row 2

The big questions in life are not easily answered. Frank and Ernest reprinted by permission of Newspaper Enterprise Association, Inc.

tells us that it is possible for all the premises to be true and the conclusion false. Since this is the very essence of invalidity, we now know that this is an invalid argument pattern.

To illustrate, let's apply the guidelines in the box on page 99 to the following pattern:

A	*B*	*C*	*A* → (*B* ∨ *C*)	~*A* & ~*C*	*B* ∨ *C*	~*A*	∴ *A* & *B*
T	T	T					
T	T	F					
T	F	T					
T	F	F					
F	T	T					
F	T	F					
F	F	T					
F	F	F					

Step 1 tells us to fill in the columns for all negative variables. There is one negative variable, ~A, the fourth premise. So our table looks like this:

A	*B*	*C*	*A* → (*B* ∨ *C*)	~*A* & ~*C*	*B* ∨ *C*	~*A*	∴ *A* & *B*
T	T	T				F	
T	T	F				F	
T	F	T				F	
T	F	F				F	
F	T	T				T	
F	T	F				T	
F	F	T				T	
F	F	F				T	

Note that the column for ~A is simply the negation (or opposite) of the A column on the far left. So far, so good.

Step 2 tells us to fill in the column for all single variables. But there aren't any more single variables, so we move on to step 3 and fill in all the remaining columns, beginning with the columns for the simpler claims and finishing with the more complicated ones. This means we want to work on the conclusion next. Here we remember that "and" claims (conjunctions) are true only if all of their parts are true. This means that A & B is true only when both A and B are true. Since A and B are both true only in rows 1 and 2, we can fill the column in as follows:

A	B	C	A → (B ∨ C)	~A & ~C	B ∨ C	~A	∴ A & B
T	T	T				F	T
T	T	F				F	T
T	F	T				F	F
T	F	F				F	F
F	T	T				T	F
F	T	F				T	F
F	F	T				T	F
F	F	F				T	F

The simplest of the three remaining claims is the third premise, B ∨ C. We remember that "or" claims (disjunctions) are true whenever at least one part (disjunct) is true. Looking at the values for B and C, we see that either B or C (or both) is true in rows 1–3 and 5–7. The result now looks like this:

A	B	C	A → (B ∨ C)	~A & ~C	B ∨ C	~A	∴ A & B
T	T	T			T	F	T
T	T	F			T	F	T
T	F	T			T	F	F
T	F	F			F	F	F
F	T	T			T	T	F
F	T	F			T	T	F
F	F	T			T	T	F
F	F	F			F	T	F

Three columns down and two to go—we are making good progress! Next let's tackle the second premise, ~A & ~C. Given that this is an "and" statement (conjunction), we know that it is true only if all of its parts are true. We know that, since A is true for rows 1–4, ~A, being the negation of A, must be false for rows 1–4. And since A is false for rows 5–8, ~A must be true for those rows. We reason similarly about the ~C part of this claim. That is, for any row in which C is false, ~C must be true. So, whenever A is false and C is false, then ~A & ~C will be true. We see that A is false and C is false only in rows 6 and 8. Our updated table looks like this:

A	B	C	A → (B ∨ C)	~A & ~C	B ∨ C	~A	∴ A & B
T	T	T		F	T	F	T
T	T	F		F	T	F	T
T	F	T		F	T	F	F
T	F	F		F	F	F	F
F	T	T		F	T	T	F
F	T	F		T	T	T	F
F	F	T		F	T	T	F
F	F	F		T	F	T	F

Only one more premise to go! The first premise is a little more complicated than the others in that it involves *two* operations. Working within the parenthesis first, on the B ∨ C part, we remember that "or" statements are true whenever at least one part is true. Note that we enter the value for B ∨ C in smaller letters, as we are not yet assigning the final truth value for the entire premise but only determining the truth value for a part of the premise. Our latest update gives us the following:

A	B	C	A → (B ∨ C)	~A & ~C	B ∨ C	~A	∴ A & B
T	T	T	T	F	T	F	T
T	T	F	T	F	T	F	T
T	F	T	T	F	T	F	F
T	F	F	F	F	F	F	F
F	T	T	T	F	T	T	F
F	T	F	T	T	T	T	F
F	F	T	T	F	T	T	F
F	F	F	F	T	F	T	F

Now we turn our attention to the other side of the premise, the A part. Here we simply copy the A column from the far left column, again using smaller letters to indicate that this is not the final truth value for the entire premise. Filling in this column, we now have the following:

A	B	C	A → (B ∨ C)		~A & ~C	B ∨ C	~A	∴ A & B
T	T	T	T	T	F	T	F	T
T	T	F	T	T	F	T	F	T
T	F	T	T	T	F	T	F	F
T	F	F	T	F	F	F	F	F
F	T	T	F	T	F	T	T	F
F	T	F	F	T	T	T	T	F
F	F	T	F	T	F	T	T	F
F	F	F	F	F	T	F	T	F

We're getting close. All we have to do now is apply the rules for conditional claims to the truth values for both A and B ∨ C. Remembering that conditionals can seem a little odd, we know that a conditional claim is seen as false if and only if the "if" part (antecedent) is true and the "then" part (consequent) is false. Looking at the latest version, we see that this is the case only in row 4, for there and only there is the "if" part true and the "then" part false. Our latest version looks like this:

A	*B*	*C*	*A* → (*B* ∨ *C*)			~*A* & ~*C*	*B* ∨ *C*	~*A*	∴ *A* & *B*
T	T	T	T T	T		F	T	F	T
T	T	F	T T	T		F	T	F	T
T	F	T	T T	T		F	T	F	F
T	F	F	T F	F		F	F	F	F
F	T	T	F T	T		F	T	T	F
F	T	F	F T	T		T	T	T	F
F	F	T	F T	T		F	T	T	F
F	F	F	F T	F		T	F	T	F

Now that we have filled in the entire truth table, we still need to interpret it. Remember that a valid argument pattern is one in which the truth of the premises guarantees the truth of the conclusion. In other words, whenever all the premises are true, then the conclusion is also true. So we look at the truth table to see which rows have all true premises. We discover that only row 6 fits the bill here; all other rows have at least one false premise, and so we are not concerned with them. (Remember, testing for validity focuses on the cases in which all the premises are true.) We now look at the conclusion for row 6 and see that it is false. This means that it is possible, given this pattern, to have all true premises and a false conclusion—the very essence of an invalid argument! So we mark the argument as "invalid by row 6," as there is no guarantee that all true premises will produce a true conclusion. The final result looks like this:

A	*B*	*C*	*A* → (*B* ∨ *C*)			~*A* & ~*C*	*B* ∨ *C*	~*A*	∴ *A* & *B*	
T	T	T	T T	T		F	T	F	T	
T	T	F	T T	T		F	T	F	T	
T	F	T	T T	T		F	T	F	F	
T	F	F	T F	F		F	F	F	F	
F	T	T	F T	T		F	T	T	F	
F	T	F	F T	T		T	T	T	F	*Invalid by row 6*
F	F	T	F T	T		F	T	T	F	
F	F	F	F T	F		T	F	T	F	

As arguments become more complicated, truth tables become more and more helpful in determining the validity of the patterns. It is not always easy simply to look at an argument and know whether it is valid or invalid. Another helpful tool for determining the validity of an argument pattern is the Venn diagram.

EXERCISE 5.3

Write the truth table for each of the following. Be sure to indicate, using an asterisk, all relevant rows, and note whether the pattern is valid.

★ 1.

P	Q	$P \rightarrow Q$	~Q	$\therefore$ ~P
T	T			
T	F			
F	T			
F	F			

2.

P	Q	$P \vee Q$	~Q	$\therefore P$
T	T			
T	F			
F	T			
F	F			

3.

P	Q	R	$P \& (Q \vee R)$	$P \& {\sim}R$	$\therefore Q$
T	T	T			
T	T	F			
T	F	T			
T	F	F			
F	T	T			
F	T	F			
F	F	T			
F	F	F			

★ 4.

P	Q	R	$P \rightarrow Q$	$P \vee R$	$\therefore P \& R$
T	T	T			
T	T	F			
T	F	T			
T	F	F			
F	T	T			
F	T	F			
F	F	T			
F	F	F			

★ 5.

P	Q	$P \vee (P \& {\sim}Q)$	${\sim}P \vee Q$	$\therefore$ ~Q
T	T			
T	F			
F	T			
F	F			

6. | **P** | **Q** | **R** | **P & (~Q ∨ R)** | **P ∨ Q** | **∴ ~R** |
|---|---|---|---|---|---|
| T | T | T | | | |
| T | T | F | | | |
| T | F | T | | | |
| T | F | F | | | |
| F | T | T | | | |
| F | T | F | | | |
| F | F | T | | | |
| F | F | F | | | |

7. | **P** | **Q** | **R** | **P → (Q ∨ R)** | **~(P & ~Q)** | **~P** | **∴ R** |
|---|---|---|---|---|---|---|
| T | T | T | | | | |
| T | T | F | | | | |
| T | F | T | | | | |
| T | F | F | | | | |
| F | T | T | | | | |
| F | T | F | | | | |
| F | F | T | | | | |
| F | F | F | | | | |

8. | **P** | **Q** | **R** | **~(P ∨ Q) → (R & P)** | **(P & ~Q) ∨ ~R** | **∴ P ∨ R** |
|---|---|---|---|---|---|
| T | T | T | | | |
| T | T | F | | | |
| T | F | T | | | |
| T | F | F | | | |
| F | T | T | | | |
| F | T | F | | | |
| F | F | T | | | |
| F | F | F | | | |

9. | **P** | **Q** | **P → (P ∨ Q)** | **~Q → ~(P & Q)** | **∴ P ∨ Q** |
|---|---|---|---|---|
| T | T | | | |
| T | F | | | |
| F | T | | | |
| F | F | | | |

★ 10. | **P** | **Q** | **R** | **P ∨ Q ∨ R** | **R → (P & Q)** | **~P** | **∴ Q ∨ R** |
|---|---|---|---|---|---|---|
| T | T | T | | | | |
| T | T | F | | | | |
| T | F | T | | | | |
| T | F | F | | | | |
| F | T | T | | | | |
| F | T | F | | | | |
| F | F | T | | | | |
| F | F | F | | | | |

TRUTH TABLES: THE SHORT METHOD

Some truth tables, especially those with sixteen or more rows, can be tedious to work on. Fortunately there is a shorter method, one that can save valuable time. If we can construct one row of a truth table and show the argument to be invalid (by finding a row with all true premises and a false conclusion), we have saved ourselves much work. Remember that an invalid argument has a truth table with at least one row in which all the premises are true and the conclusion is false.

To illustrate, consider the following example:

1. $A \vee (B \,\&\, C)$

2. $C \rightarrow D$

3. $A \rightarrow E$

∴ $D \rightarrow E$

If this argument is invalid, then we know that it is possible for all the premises to be true but the conclusion still to be false. Looking at the conclusion, we know that, being a conditional, it is false only if the antecedent (D) is true and the consequent (E) is false. So for our one row, D will be true and E will be false.

So far we have assigned the following truth values:

A	B	C	D	E
			T	F

E is also found in premise 3. We know that the third premise must be true here (remember our assumption of invalidity here and what that involves), so if E is false, then A cannot be true, for that would make this premise false. So we assign a truth value of false to A. We now have this:

A	B	C	D	E
F			T	F

Premise 2 is also a conditional. We already know that D is true, so we can assign a truth value of either T or F to C, as the conditional would be true in either case. But a close look at premise 1 shows that we must assign a truth value of T to C. Since we already know that A is false, premise 1 can be true only if both B and C are true. So we assign T to C. We now have the following:

A	B	C	D	E
F		T	T	F

Only the first premise remains. Given that A is false and that this is a disjunction, we know that the second disjunct, B & C, must be true for the entire disjunction to be true. Since B & C is a conjunction, all of its conjuncts must be true for it to be true. So B and C must be true. The result is as follows:

A	*B*	*C*	*D*	*E*
F	T	T	T	F

The complete row of the truth table looks like this:

A	*B*	*C*	*D*	*E*	*A* ∨ *(B & C)*	*C* → *D*	*A* → *E*	∴ *D* → *E*
F	T	T	T	F	T	T	T	F

Rather than writing out all thirty-two rows of this truth table, we have shown with only one row that it is possible for all the premises to be true and the conclusion false. Thus we know that this argument is invalid. Note that the conclusion's being false required us to assign D and E particular truth values. But sometimes neither the conclusion nor any of the premises force us to do this. In such cases we must use a trial-and-error method. Begin with an assignment that makes the conclusion false (or some premise true), and see how well it works. If it does not work, try another assignment. If all such assignments fail, then the argument is valid. It may take three or four such attempts for a particular argument, but it's still much faster than filling in all thirty-two rows of the truth table!

EXERCISE 5.4

For each of the following, use the short truth table method to test for validity.

★ 1. 1. A ∨ B
    2. B
    ―――――
    ∴ A

2. 1. A → B
    2. B → C
    3. C
    ―――――
    ∴ A

3. 1. A ∨ (B → C)
    2. B & ~C
    ―――――
    ∴ ~A

★ 4. 1.   A ∨ ~B
   2.   C → B
   _____
   ∴   A → ~C

5. 1.   ~(A & B)
   2.   ~A → C
   3.   ~B → D
   _____
   ∴   C & D

6. 1.   A ∨ (B & C)
   2.   ~A
   _____
   ∴   (A & B) ∨ (A & C)

★ 7. 1.   (A & B) → C
   2.   ~C
   _____
   ∴   ~A

8. 1.   (A & B) → C
   2.   D & (C → E)
   3.   D → B
   _____
   ∴   A & E

9. 1.   A → (B → C)
   _____
   ∴   A → (B & C)

★ 10. 1.   A ∨ (B & C)
   2.   ~B ∨ D
   3.   B → (A ∨ D)
   _____
   ∴   B & D

11. 1.   A → ~(B & C)
   2.   A & C
   _____
   ∴   ~B

12. 1.   A ∨ B ∨ C
   2.   ~C & D
   3.   D → (B ∨ ~A)
   _____
   ∴   B ∨ ~C

★ 13. 1. $(A \mathbin{\&} B) \to (C \vee D \vee {\sim}E)$

   2. $B \mathbin{\&} (A \vee D)$

   3. ${\sim}C \mathbin{\&} B$

   ───────────────

   ∴ $B \mathbin{\&} C$

14. 1. $A \to B$

   2. $(B \mathbin{\&} C) \to D$

   3. $D \to E$

   ───────────────

   ∴ $(A \vee C) \to E$

VENN DIAGRAMS

One shortcoming of truth tables is that they can't be used to determine the validity of arguments with claims using the words *all, some,* and *no*. But **Venn diagrams**[3] can. Let's begin by considering a large rectangular box, which represents everything that exists in the universe:

Instead of focusing on the entire universe (a difficult task), let's instead focus our attention on this claim:

   All cats are mammals.

Here we can represent "cats" as C and "mammals" as M. Then we can draw two circles, with the first circle representing where the cats live and the second one where the mammals live, and label them with C and M. The result would look like this:

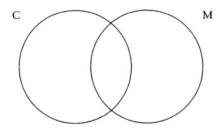

───────────────

[3] Named after the British philosopher John Venn (1834–1923), who developed this method.

Note that the living areas for cats and for mammals overlap, so the two circles overlap as well. We can also, for simplicity's sake, number the three areas represented in this diagram. As "cats" is our subject, we can count on finding any cat in area 2. Additionally we can see that area 1, representing all cats that are not mammals, is empty. In other words, there are no cats that are not mammals. A convenient way of representing this is to shade it in (this tells us that no cats live here). We now have this diagram:

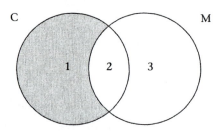

This method of drawing overlapping circles, with one circle for each claim variable, enables us to determine the validity of a variety of arguments that truth tables are of no help with. Venn diagrams help us with three basic kinds of claims:

KIND OF CLAIM	EXAMPLE
"All" claims	All cats are mammals.
"Some" claims	Some Republicans are conservatives.
	Some Republicans are not conservatives.
"No" claims	No fish are mammals.

Here are the Venn diagrams for each of these claims:

All cats are mammals.

Some Republicans are conservatives.

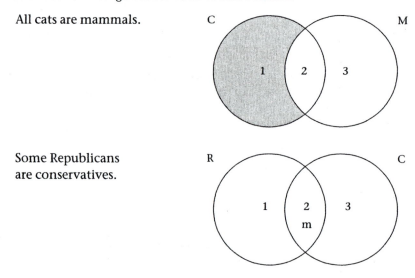

Some Republicans
are not conservatives.

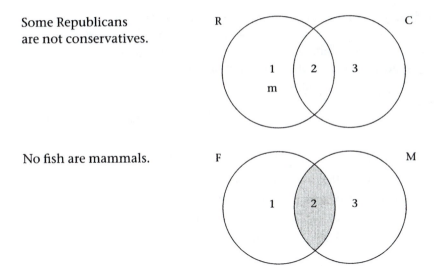

No fish are mammals.

Venn diagrams give us a method for determining the validity of a fairly wide variety of arguments. Let's begin by considering this example:

1. All dogs are four-legged.

2. Fido is a dog.

∴   Fido is four-legged.

Here we draw two overlapping circles, one for the class of dogs (D) and the other for the class of four-legged creatures (F). We then write the letter *m* (which refers to a specific or named example of) to represent the idea that there is at least one creature (Fido) that is a dog. Our latest diagram looks like this:

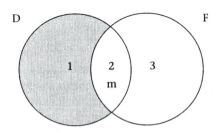

For premise 1 we shade in area 1, to illustrate the claim "All dogs are four-legged." For premise 2 we write an m (which means "is a specific named example of") in area 2, as this is the only part of the first (dogs) circle available to us. If the argument is valid, then the conclusion should be accurately represented by what we have drawn. The conclusion "Fido is four-legged" is accurately represented by the diagram, as the m (representing Fido) is in area

2, which is also a part of the second circle, representing four-legged creatures. So for any m in area 2, it must be a member of the first circle (dogs) and the second circle (four-legged creatures). Because the diagram accurately depicts the conclusion, this argument pattern is valid.

Notice that we diagram only the premises. The diagram itself is our assumption that the premises are true, so diagramming the conclusion would undermine this assumption. Remember also that all Venn diagrams share three characteristics:

1. Shading, which indicates the area is empty
2. Using an m, which means the area is occupied
3. Blank spaces, which mean that we do not know whether the area is occupied on the basis of the information provided

Venn diagrams can also illustrate invalid patterns. Consider a second example:

1. All dogs are mammals.

2. Fido is a mammal.
   _____

∴ Fido is a dog.

The first premise can be drawn as follows:

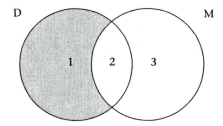

The second premise is a bit more involved. Using m to represent Fido, the second premise tells us to place m in the second circle (representing mammals). But there are two areas available (2 and 3) in this circle. So where do we put m? We know that m is in the circle, but we do not know where. So we write "m?" meaning that m could be here but might not be, in both area 2 and area 3. Combining the first two premises, we now have this diagram:

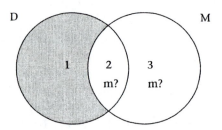

The conclusion is "Fido is a dog." Looking at the diagram, we ask if that situation is accurately represented. In other words, does the diagram guarantee that if the premises are true then the conclusion is also true? It does not seem to. The m could be either in area 2 or in area 3. But for the argument pattern to be valid, there must be a guarantee that m (Fido) is in the first circle. So, if there is a guarantee that m is in area 2, then the argument is valid. But as there is no such guarantee (it's a "maybe yes, maybe no" sort of thing), the argument pattern is invalid.

Here is a third example:

1.   No dogs are human.

2.   All humans are rational.
   _____

∴.   No dogs are rational.

Premise 1 is illustrated as follows:

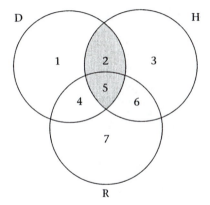

In this case we draw three circles, one for each of the three things represented (dogs, humans, being rational). We illustrate the second premise by shading in areas 2 and 3, so that we now have this diagram:

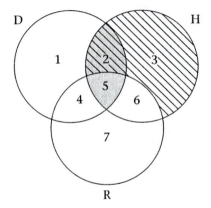

We shade area 2 a second time to show that both premise 1 and premise 2 apply to it. Our conclusion is "No dogs are rational." If the argument is valid, then the area common to these two classes (areas 4 and 5) should be shaded. Since area 5 is shaded but area 4 is not, the argument pattern is invalid, as there is no guarantee that if the premises are both true then the conclusion will also be true.

Our final example is a little more involved:

1.   All A's are B's.

2.   All C's are B's.

3.   m is not a B.
   _____

∴   m is not an A and m is not a C.

Premises 1 and 2 are represented in the following manner:

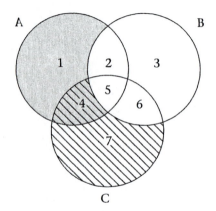

Premise 3 requires that we place m outside of area B. But all of areas A and C are shaded and thus are not available. So we put an m outside of all three circles, as shown here:

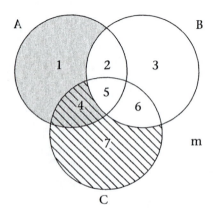

Looking at the conclusion, "m is not an A and m is not a C," we can see that it is accurately represented by the diagram. Since it is true that if all the premises are true then so is the conclusion, we know that this is another example of a valid argument pattern.

THE SQUARE OF OPPOSITION

The Venn diagrams we have been working with involve four kinds of claims:

1. "All" claims ("All A are B")
2. "No" claims ("No A are B")
3. "Some" claims ("Some A are B")
4. Negative "some" claims ("Some A are not B")

Aristotle, who lived in the fourth century B.C., developed a system for analyzing these claims. He also chose the first four vowels in the alphabet to stand for the claims,[4] labeling them as follows:

A   Universal affirmative ("all") claims

E   Universal negative ("no") claims

I   Particular affirmative ("some") claims

O   Particular negative ("some") claims

These four kinds of claims have different logical relationships. First, corresponding **A** and **O** statements are **contradictories** in that they cannot both be true and they cannot both be false. In other words, if one is true then the other must be false, and vice versa. For example, the **A** claim "All dogs are mammals" is contradicted by the **O** claim "Some dogs are not mammals." Given that these two claims are contradictory, we know that one and only one of them can be true.

Similarly, corresponding **E** and **I** statements are contradictories. For example, "No dogs are mammals" contradicts "Some dogs are mammals." Therefore, given that no dogs are mammals, we can logically conclude that it is false that some dogs are not mammals. And if it is true that some dogs are mammals, then we know it is false that no dogs are mammals.

A second logical relationship that exists between these kinds of claims involves **contraries**. Two claims are contrary if they cannot both be true but can both be false. For example, corresponding **A** and **E** claims are contraries. The claims "All dogs are mammals" and "No dogs are mammals" cannot both be true, though they could both be false. For instance, if it were true that "Some dogs are mammals," then both "All dogs are mammals" and "No dogs

---

[4]By convention these letters are set in boldface type.

are mammals" would be false. And if either the **A** claim or the **E** claim is true, then the other must be false.

A third logical relationship exists between corresponding **I** and **O** claims, namely, that of **subcontraries.** Two claims are subcontrary if they can both be true but cannot both be false. So the claims "Some dogs are mammals" and "Some dogs are not mammals" can both be true (if some dogs are mammals and some dogs are not), but clearly they cannot both be false.

These three kinds of logical relationships can be captured in a single diagram called the square of opposition, as shown here.

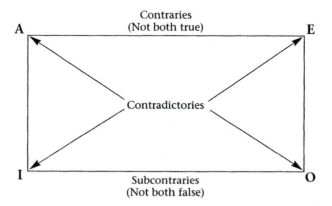

The relationships between these four kinds of claims (**A, E, I,** and **O**) also include three other possibilities. The first one is **conversion.** The converse of a claim is obtained by switching its subject (what the claim is about) and its predicate (the information about the subject) and terms. For example, "All mammals are dogs" is the converse of "All dogs are mammals."

All of the following are examples of converse statements:

	STATEMENT	CONVERSE
A	All dogs are mammals.	All mammals are dogs.
E	No cats are dogs.	No dogs are cats.
I	Some Republicans are conservatives.	Some conservatives are Republicans.
O	Some Republicans are not conservatives.	Some conservatives are not Republicans.

Conversion is valid for **E** and **I** statements. In other words, **E** and **I** claims and their converses are equivalent—they mean the same thing. By contrast, conversion generally is not valid for **A** and **O** statements. For example, the following are both valid arguments:

1. No dogs are cats. So, no cats are dogs.

2. Some plants are trees. So, some trees are plants.

But the following examples show that conversion is not valid for **A** and **O** statements:

1. All cats are animals. So, all animals are cats.

2. Some plants are not trees. So, some trees are not plants.

A second kind of relationship is that of **obversion,** such that every class (group) of things has a complement. For example, for the class of tigers, the complement would be nontigers. To find the obverse of a claim, we must do two things:

1. Change it from affirmative to negative, or vice versa.

2. Replace the predicate term with its complementary term.

Here are a few examples:

	STATEMENT	OBVERSE
A	All humans are mammals.	No humans are nonmammals.
E	No fish are humans.	All fish are nonhumans.
I	Some humans are females.	Some humans are not nonfemales.
O	Some athletes are wealthy.	Some athletes are not nonwealthy.

Claims of all four types are equivalent to their obverses.

Besides conversion and obversion, a third possibility is **contraposition.** To find the contrapositive of a claim, we do two things:

1. Switch the subject and predicate terms, just as we did with conversion.

2. Replace both terms with their complementary terms.

The result looks like this:

	STATEMENT	CONTRAPOSITIVE
A	All dogs are mammals.	All nonmammals are nondogs.
E	No monkees are rats.	No nonrats are nonmonkees.
I	Some plants are weeds.	Some nonweeds are nonplants.
O	Some plants are not weeds.	Some nonweeds are not nonplants.

Contraposition is valid for **A** and **O** statements, but generally not for **E** and **I** statements. For instance, consider the following valid arguments:

1. All dogs are mammals. So, all nonmammals are nondogs.

2. Some trees are maples. So, some nonmaples are nontrees.

But the following **E** claim is not valid:

No fish are humans. So, no nonhumans are nonfish.

EXERCISE 5.5

1. For each of the following, identify whether it is a contradictory, contrary, or subcontrary.
   ★ a. All politicians are honest. Some politicians are not honest.
   b. All men are direction askers. No men are direction askers.
   c. All Texans are tall. Some Texans are not tall.
   ★ d. Some people are creative. Some people are not creative.
   e. No frogs are happy. Some frogs are happy.
   f. Some cows are not mooers. All cows are mooers.
   ★ g. No girls are boys. Some girls are boys.
   h. All dancers are talented. No dancers are talented.
   i. Some giraffes are not tall. Some giraffes are tall.
   ★ j. All priests are godly. Some priests are not godly.

2. For each of the following, form the converse, obverse, and contrapositive.
   ★ a. All politicians are wealthy.
   b. Some cowboys are horse riders.
   c. No heros are cowards.
   ★ d. Some historians are theists.
   e. All felines are finicky.
   f. No dogs are reptiles.
   ★ g. No snakes are vegetarians.
   h. Some ministers are virtuous.
   i. All lawyers are contentious.
   ★ j. Some wars are not justified.
   k. Some dogs are noncats.
   l. Some women are not married.
   m. All choices are free.
   n. All soccer fans are enthusiastic.
   o. No pirates are law abiders.

MORE ABOUT SOUNDNESS: CHALLENGING PREMISES

Counterexamples to Universal Generalizations

Venn diagrams and truth tables are helpful for determining the validity of arguments, but what about determining the soundness of arguments? This is not quite as straightforward. Suppose we know that an argument is valid. How do we go about determining if it is sound? Remember that a sound argument is a valid argument, with all its premises being rationally acceptable. So, if we know that an argument is valid, the only unresolved issue is whether all the premises are rationally acceptable.

Let's begin with this example:

1. All men are lazy.

2. Robert is a man.

∴   Robert is lazy.

This is clearly a valid argument, as it fits one of the basic patterns. So, to decide whether it is sound, we need to determine if *both* premises are rationally acceptable. We can readily accept the second premise as true (assuming no unusual circumstances here). But what about the first premise? Is it really true that *all* men—past, present, and future—are lazy? This is doubtful, to put it mildly. If we can cite just one exception, or **counterexample**, then the premise is false, making the argument itself unsound. So one method of challenging a premise is to think of possible counterexamples. Given how strong "all" claims are (they allow for no exceptions whatever), it often is not too difficult to think of one or more counterexamples, thus making the claim false and the argument unsound.

Consider another example:

1. All cats can meow.

2. Whiskers is a cat.

∴ Whiskers can meow.

Suppose we grant that the second premise is rationally acceptable and that the argument is valid. The argument's soundness hinges on whether the first premise is true. Is it true that all cats can meow? Probably not, for it's likely that, due to injury or disease, at least one cat is now unable to meow. It would still be a cat, just a nonmeowing sort of cat.

Counterexamples such as this can be real ("I know of such-and-such a cat who can't meow") or imagined ("It is perfectly sensible to imagine a creature that was a cat but that couldn't meow"). Remember that counterexamples are responses to **universal generalizations** ("All X are Y"). For example, if someone claimed that all professional basketball players in the past ten years were less than 7 feet 5 inches tall, you could respond with "What about Manute Bol and Gheorghe Muresan?" both of whom were over that height. Citing either one of these players would be sufficient to make the universal claim false. If the person then said, "Most NBA players in the past ten years were less than 7 feet 5 inches tall," then they would have conceded that the universal claim was false and retreated to a much safer "most" claim.

Exceptions to Conditional Claims

A second method of casting doubt on premises involves citing exceptions to conditional ("if . . . then") claims. Consider the following dialogue:

Donna: Do you think it is true that if you are rich then you are happy?

Roberto: I'm not so sure. That would mean that anyone who is rich is also happy, and that seems doubtful, to say the least! For example, I know of two people who are rich and yet very unhappy. And even if I did not know of two real-life exceptions, it is not at all clear how being rich would somehow guarantee being happy.

Donna: I think you're probably right. So if we can show that the consequent, happiness, does not necessarily follow from the antecedent, being rich, then we have cast enough doubt on the premise to make the claim false.

Roberto: That's right, and remember that we don't have to show that the consequent does not follow from the antecedent, but only that there is no guarantee that it follows.

Casting doubt on a premise does not prove it is false, but it does require that the person making the claim give us good reasons why we should accept the claim as true. Universal claims ("All P's are Q's") and conditional claims ("If . . . then") are both regarded as false if there is even one counterexample or exception.

Unacceptable Consequences

A third method for challenging premises involves identifying unacceptable consequences. Suppose that someone who does not care for the sport of boxing makes the following claim:

All violent sports should be banned.

We might ask what the consequences of this claim might be. For starters, everyone might agree that boxing, bullfighting, and dogfights should all be banned. So far, so good. But football and hockey are, by most definitions, violent sports, so they would have to be banned as well. And if we did not find this consequence acceptable and could rationally support our belief, we would have sufficient reason to reject the claim. In short, we are justified in rejecting any claim that has clearly unacceptable consequences.

References to Common Knowledge

Common knowledge refers to what virtually everyone knows. For example, it is common knowledge that all of the following are true:

1. Columbus sailed west in 1492.
2. The Holocaust happened.
3. Cancer kills many people.
4. Women have not always had the right to vote in the United States.
5. The New Orleans Saints have never won a Super Bowl.

For whatever reason, some have questioned whether the Holocaust really occurred. But there is an incredible amount of evidence supporting the claim that it happened and no good reason for thinking that it did not. This is a classic example of a reasonable belief: much evidence in its favor and no evidence to the contrary.

Contradictions by Proper Authorities

Proper authority refers to when a duly qualified expert speaks to his or her field of expertise. Of course, this does not guarantee that the authority is correct, but it merits our taking the claim seriously and places the burden of proof on those who would disagree. A proper authority must have expertise in the area in question, as well as genuine credentials, such as education and/or experience.

Consider the following possibilities:

1. Bill James predicts the Tigers will not win the World Series this year.

2. Robert Redford eats octopus for his health and thinks you should too.

3. Ted Kennedy thinks the current welfare system needs overhauling.

With respect to claim 1, Bill James is widely acknowledged as an expert when it comes to major league baseball. This hardly guarantees that he will be correct, but it places the burden of proof on anyone who might disagree with him. With regard to claim 2, Robert Redford is a fine actor and director, but it's unlikely that he is a proper authority in the area of health and nutrition. Finally, with regard to claim 3, Ted Kennedy certainly knows more about the current welfare system than the average American, though it is not clear that he would qualify as a proper authority in this area. We might grant that he is well informed and be open to the possibility that he is indeed a genuine authority.

Poorly Supported Testimony

Another shortcoming of some premises involves testimony that is poorly supported. Consider the following four claims:

1. I ate lunch today.

2. Tasaki is the world's best tennis player.

3. Joe Bob ate lunch with Elvis and space aliens today.

4. Marisa experienced God today.

The first one is so ordinary that the mere claim is sufficient evidence for believing its truth. With regard to claim 2, people might rightly demand significant supporting evidence—a Wimbledon championship, a number one ranking, or the like—before they take the claim seriously. Claims out of the ordinary, such as this one, clearly require more evidence than the common sort given in claim 1. And the third claim practically defies belief. Given that there is excellent evidence that Elvis died and a serious lack of evidence that space aliens exist, the extraordinary nature of the claim means that a massive amount of supporting evidence is needed. So unless some special evidence is forthcoming (undoctored video footage would be nice), Joe Bob's claim clearly is lacking in sufficient support. Finally claim 4 is a rather complicated one involving several interwoven issues. The first concerns whether it is reasonable to believe that God exists. The second issue concerns claims about religious experience. There may be no doubt that Marisa had an experience and that she *believes* this experience was of God. But how might we distinguish between a genuine experience of God and an imaginary one?

Calvin and Hobbes

by Bill Watterson

Most worthwhile things in life involve hard work. CALVIN AND HOBBES © Watterson. Reprinted with permission of UNIVERSAL PRESS SYNDICATE. All rights reserved.

SUMMARY

A valid argument is an argument in which, if all the premises are true, then the conclusion must also be true. That is, the conclusion follows from the premises. In an invalid argument the truth of the premises does not guarantee the truth of the conclusion. An argument is sound if it is valid and has rationally acceptable premises. An argument is unsound if either it is invalid or one or more of its premises are false. The concepts of validity and soundness apply only to arguments while premises and conclusions should be characterized as either true or false. Truth tables and Venn diagrams are useful tools for determining the validity of certain argument patterns. Methods of challenging premises include finding counterexamples, questioning the "if . . . then" connection in a conditional claim, showing that the consequences of taking a premise seriously are unappealing or undesirable, and identifying claims that are contrary to common knowledge, contrary to proper authority, or poorly supported by testimony.

EXERCISE 5.6

1. Complete these truth tables.

★ a.

A	B	$A \rightarrow B$	A	$\therefore B$
T	T			
T	F			
F	T			
F	F			

b.
A	*B*	*A* → *B*	~*B*	∴ ~*A*
T	T			
T	F			
F	T			
F	F			

c.
A	*B*	*A* → *B*	*B*	∴ *A*
T	T			
T	F			
F	T			
F	F			

★ d.
A	*B*	*A* ∨ *B*	~*A*	∴ *B*
T	T			
T	F			
F	T			
F	F			

e.
A	*B*	*C*	*A*	*A* → *B*	*B* → *C*	∴ *C*
T	T	T				
T	T	F				
T	F	T				
T	F	F				
F	T	T				
F	T	F				
F	F	T				
F	F	F				

f.
A	*B*	*C*	*A* → *B*	~(*C* & *B*)	*C*	∴ ~*A*
T	T	T				
T	T	F				
T	F	T				
T	F	F				
F	T	T				
F	T	F				
F	F	T				
F	F	F				

★ g.
A	*B*	*C*	*A* ∨ *B*	*A* → ~*C*	*C*	∴ *B*
T	T	T				
T	T	F				
T	F	T				
T	F	F				
F	T	T				
F	T	F				
F	F	T				
F	F	F				

h.

A	B	C	$(A \mathbin{\&} B) \lor C$	$\sim A$	$\therefore C$
T	T	T			
T	T	F			
T	F	T			
T	F	F			
F	T	T			
F	T	F			
F	F	T			
F	F	F			

i.

A	B	C	$(A \mathbin{\&} B) \lor C$	$\sim(A \lor B)$	$\therefore C$
T	T	T			
T	T	F			
T	F	T			
T	F	F			
F	T	T			
F	T	F			
F	F	T			
F	F	F			

★ j.

A	B	C	$A \lor (\sim B \mathbin{\&} C)$	$B \to \sim A$	$\therefore \sim B$
T	T	T			
T	T	F			
T	F	T			
T	F	F			
F	T	T			
F	T	F			
F	F	T			
F	F	F			

k.

A	B	C	$A \lor (B \lor C)$	$(\sim A \mathbin{\&} \sim B)$	$\therefore C$
T	T	T			
T	T	F			
T	F	T			
T	F	F			
F	T	T			
F	T	F			
F	F	T			
F	F	F			

l.

A	B	C	$A \lor (B \to \sim C)$	$B \to \sim C$	$\therefore \sim A$
T	T	T			
T	T	F			
T	F	T			
T	F	F			
F	T	T			
F	T	F			
F	F	T			
F	F	F			

★m.

A	B	C	A → B	B → C	C	∴ A
T	T	T				
T	T	F				
T	F	T				
T	F	F				
F	T	T				
F	T	F				
F	F	T				
F	F	F				

n.

A	B	~A → B	A	∴ B
T	T			
T	F			
F	T			
F	F			

o.

A	B	A ∨ ~B	B	∴ ~A
T	T			
T	F			
F	T			
F	F			

★p.

A	B	C	A → (B ∨ C)	A & ~C	~B & C	∴ B
T	T	T				
T	T	F				
T	F	T				
T	F	F				
F	T	T				
F	T	F				
F	F	T				
F	F	F				

q.

A	B	C	D	(A & B) → (~C & D)	~B → (C ∨ D)	A → (B & ~D)	∴ ~(A & C)
T	T	T	T				
T	T	T	F				
T	T	F	T				
T	T	F	F				
T	F	T	T				
T	F	T	F				
T	F	F	T				
T	F	F	F				
F	T	T	T				
F	T	T	F				
F	T	F	T				
F	T	F	F				
F	F	T	T				
F	F	T	F				
F	F	F	T				
F	F	F	F				

r.	*A*	*B*	*C*	*D*	*(A & B) ∨ (C ∨ D)*	*A → (C ∨ D)*	*B ∨ D*	∴ *~A*
	T	T	T	T				
	T	T	T	F				
	T	T	F	T				
	T	T	F	F				
	T	F	T	T				
	T	F	T	F				
	T	F	F	T				
	T	F	F	F				
	F	T	T	T				
	F	T	T	F				
	F	T	F	T				
	F	T	F	F				
	F	F	T	T				
	F	F	T	F				
	F	F	F	T				
	F	F	F	F				

★ s.

	A	*B*	*C*	*D*	*(A → B) → (C ∨ D)*	*A & ~(C & ~D)*	*B → C*	∴ *B ∨ D*
	T	T	T	T				
	T	T	T	F				
	T	T	F	T				
	T	T	F	F				
	T	F	T	T				
	T	F	T	F				
	T	F	F	T				
	T	F	F	F				
	F	T	T	T				
	F	T	T	F				
	F	T	F	T				
	F	T	F	F				
	F	F	T	T				
	F	F	T	F				
	F	F	F	T				
	F	F	F	F				

2. Create truth tables for determining whether the following argument patterns are valid.

★ a. 1. Either A or B.

2. If B, then C.

∴ If not A, then C.

b. 1. If A, then not B.

2. Not B.

∴ Not A.

c. 1. If not A, then B.
   2. If C, then not B.

   ∴ If not A, then C.

★ d. 1. If A, then not B.
     2. Either not B or C.
     3. A.

     ∴ C.

e. 1. If A and B, then C.
   2. A and C.

   ∴ Not B.

f. 1. If A, then B or not C.
   2. A and not B.
   3. A or not C.

   ∴ Not B.

★ g. 1. If A and B, then C.
     2. Not C.

     ∴ Not A and B.

h. 1. A or B or C.
   2. A and not B.
   3. Not C.

   ∴ A.

3. Construct Venn diagrams to test the validity of the following arguments.

★ a. 1. All Republicans are conservatives.
     2. No conservatives are liberals.

     ∴ No Republicans are liberals.

b. 1. All whales are mammals.
   2. All humans are mammals.

   ∴ No whales are humans.

c. 1. All teachers are conscientious.
 2. Ed is not a teacher.

 ∴ Ed is not conscientious.

★ d. 1. All dogs have tails.
 2. No tail owners are humans.
 3. Edna has a tail.

 ∴ Edna is a dog.

e. 1. No dogs are cats.
 2. All cats have whiskers.

 ∴ No dogs have whiskers.

f. 1. No plumbers are poor.
 2. All poor people are short.
 3. Fran is short.

 ∴ Fran is not a plumber.

★ g. 1. All koalas are cute.
 2. Some animals are koalas.

 ∴ Some animals are cute.

h. 1. No politicians are honest.
 2. Some men are politicians.

 ∴ Some men are not honest.

i. 1. All New Jerseyans have an accent.
 2. All women have an accent.

 ∴ All New Jerseyans are women.

★ j. 1. All lions are carnivorous.
 2. Some lions are big.

 ∴ Some carnivores are big.

k. 1. Some Californians are surfers.
 2. Some surfers have a tan.

 ∴ Some Californians have a tan.

l. 1. No men ask for directions.
    2. Some men get lost.
    _____
    ∴   No direction-askers get lost.

★ m. 1. All Italians love wine.
    2. Some wine lovers are men.
    _____
    ∴   Some men are Italian.

n. 1. No tigers are persons.
    2. All humans are persons.
    _____
    ∴   No tigers are humans.

o. 1. Some girls have curls.
    2. All cute kids are girls.
    _____
    ∴   Some cute kids have curls.

★ p. 1. All tables are made of wood.
    2. All chairs are made of wood.
    _____
    ∴   No tables are chairs.

q. 1. All dragons snort fire.
    2. All fire snorters are big.
    _____
    ∴   All dragons are big.

r. 1. All rodents are small.
    2. No rats are small.
    _____
    ∴   No rats are rodents.

★ s. 1. All Democrats are liberals.
    2. All liberals spend money.
    _____
    ∴   No Democrats spend money.

t. 1. All book lovers love reading.
    2. No reading lovers are aliens.
    _____
    ∴   No aliens are book lovers.

u. 1.   Some rectangles are squares.
   2.   Some figures are squares.

   ∴   Some figures are rectangles.

★ v. 1.   All men go bald.
   2.   No men are rich.

   ∴   All bald men are rich.

w. 1.   All omelets have eggs in them.
   2.   No omelets have ham in them.

   ∴   No things with egg in them also have ham.

x. 1.   All birds can fly.
   2.   Some ostriches are birds.

   ∴   No ostriches can fly.

★ y. 1.   All humans die.
   2.   Some dogs are not human.

   ∴   Some dogs do not die.

4. Construct Venn diagrams to test the validity of the following arguments.

★ a. 1.   No mice eat cake.
   2.   No cake eaters are dogs.

   ∴   No mice are dogs.

b. 1.   No Republicans are mean.
   2.   Some women are not Republicans.

   ∴   Some women are not mean.

c. 1.   No pigs can fly.
   2.   Some birds can fly.

   ∴   Some pigs are birds.

★ d. 1.   All cows chew their cud.
   2.   Some cud chewers are not rodents.

   ∴   Some cows are not rodents.

e. 1.   All southerners like grits.

  2.   Some people are not southerners.

  ∴   Some people do not like grits.

f. 1.   All camels are ornery.

  2.   Some furry creatures are not camels.

  ∴   Some ornery creatures are not furry.

★ g. 1.   Some card games are fun.

  2.   Some fun games are not complicated.

  ∴   Some card games are not complicated.

h. 1.   All soccer fans know of Pele.

  2.   Some men do not know of Pele.

  ∴   Some men are not soccer fans.

5. Determine the truth value of the following statements. Assume in each case that A is true, B is false, C is true, and D is false.

★ a.   A & D
  b.   A ∨ B ∨ C
  c.   ~(C → D)
★ d.   B → D
  e.   (A ∨ C) → (B & D)
  f.   C ∨ D
★ g.   ~A & ~C
  h.   (A & D) → C
  i.   B → (A → ~C)
★ j.   A ∨ ~B ∨ ~D
  k.   ~(C → B)
  l.   B & C & ~D
★ m.   ~(A ∨ ~B) → (C & ~D)
  n.   D → C
  o.   (A & C) ∨ (B ∨ D)
★ p.   ~(A → B) → (~A → ~B)
  q.   (D & B) ∨ (A ∨ C)
  r.   A → (B → C) → (D ∨ ~C)
★ s.   (B ∨ D) → ~C
  t.   ~(A ∨ B ∨ C)
  u.   ~(B & D)
★ v.   (A & B & C) → ~(B ∨ D)
  w.   D → ~A
  x.   D → (~A ∨ ~C)
★ y.   ~A & ~B & C
  z.   ~(C ∨ D) → (A & B & ~D)

6. Determine whether each of the following is an acceptable premise. If the premise is not acceptable, indicate why not.

★ a. Kansas City is in Texas.
  b. All dogs have four legs.
  c. My proposal is to eliminate all federal and state taxes.
★ d. If Dennis is rich, then he is happy.
  e. If humans lie, then they feel guilty.
  f. Gravity does not exist.
★ g. God exists.
  h. Humans are generally selfish.
  i. The Holocaust did not occur.
★ j. Women are treated the same as men in the United States today.
  k. All men are more intelligent than all women.
  l. Chess is more difficult than checkers.
★ m. Racism no longer exists in the United States.
  n. Life is worth living.
  o. If you work hard, then you will be rewarded.
★ p. The wealthy should be taxed at a higher rate than the poor.
  q. Hitler was a decent man.
  r. There is no evil (undeserved pain or suffering) in the world.
★ s. Boston is west of Cleveland.
  t. Humans have a need to be accepted.
  u. If couples work at it, then their relationship will last a long time.

GLOSSARY

validity A characteristic of any argument that has a conclusion that logically follows from the premises.

soundness A characteristic of any argument that is valid and that has all true (rationally acceptable) premises. All sound arguments are, by definition, valid, but not vice versa.

negation The opposite of a claim. The negation of P is ~P.

conjunction Two or more claims joined by the connective *and*. All parts of a conjunction must be true if the whole claim is to be considered true.

disjunction Two or more claims joined by the connective *or*. For a disjunction to be true, only one disjunct must be true.

conditional An "if . . . then" claim. It is considered false only if the antecedent is true and the consequent is false; it is considered true under all other circumstances.

conjunct One part of a compound "and" claim.

disjunct One part of a compound "or" claim.

antecedent The "if" part of a conditional claim.

consequent The "then" part of a conditional claim.

truth table A method of determining the validity of certain types of arguments by recording all possible truth values in table form.

Venn diagram   A method of drawing interlocking circles that demonstrates the validity or invalidity of certain argument patterns.

contradictories   Two claims that cannot both be true and cannot both be false.

contraries   Two claims that can both be false but cannot both be true.

subcontraries   Two claims that can both be true but cannot both be false.

conversion   The process of switching the subject and predicate terms in a claim.

obversion   The process of changing a claim from the affirmative to the negative, or vice versa, and then replacing the predicate term with its complementary term.

contraposition   The process of switching the subject and predicate terms in a claim and then replacing both terms with their complementary terms.

counterexample   An exception to the contrary.

universal generalization   Any claim of the sort "All A's are B's," or that all members of one group have one characteristic in common.

CHAPTER 6

Fallacies

With how much ease believe we what we wish.
—*John Dryden, "Oedipus"*

Irrationally held truths may be more harmful than reasoned errors.
—*T. H. Huxley,* The Coming of Age of the Origin of Species

A **fallacy** is a flawed or defective argument that may still be persuasive and even convincing. Without knowledge of the many fallacies of reasoning in their various guises, all of us are susceptible to them. Having false or unreasonable beliefs can cause problems both in our personal lives and at school or work, so it is important to know how to detect and avoid fallacious reasoning.

To illustrate, suppose Eduardo is very sick, and his doctor tells him he needs an operation. But Eduardo hears that vitamin Q will cure his condition, and there's even a money-back guarantee if the vitamin does not succeed as advertised. Eduardo reasons that the spokesperson promoting vitamin Q seems sincere and is even a doctor of some sort and that vitamins are good for us, so he decides to go the vitamin route instead of getting the more traditional operation. Unfortunately, after taking all of the (very expensive) vitamins as prescribed, not only is he not better, but his very life is in jeopardy.

As you can see, it's easy to make dangerous decisions about health, relationships, jobs, money, and many other matters simply because we fail to reason properly about the particular situation. By avoiding reasoning fallaciously, we can make good decisions on a daily basis. Fallacious reasoning can be viewed as a form of manipulation (intentional or otherwise) and as something that undermines our autonomy and control of our own lives. Fallacies can be conveniently grouped according to the kind of reasoning they promote. Depending on how precisely they are defined, among other things, there are at least 150 fallacies; here we will focus on some of the most common ones. The first two fallacies we discuss—affirming the consequent and denying the antecedent—are considered formal in that they both involve an argument pattern that is invalid. The remaining fallacies are generally considered informal in that the problem does not necessarily involve the form or structure of the argument pattern.

FORMAL FALLACIES

Fallacy 1: Affirming the Consequent

This is a common way of arguing for many people. Affirming the consequent involves this pattern:

1. If A, then B.
2. B.
   _____
∴   A.

We know from truth tables and from specific examples that this is an invalid argument pattern. That is, an argument could have this pattern and have all true premises, and yet its conclusion could be false. The truth of the premises does not *guarantee* the truth of the conclusion, so it is an invalid pattern.

Consider the following example:

1. If you are in Paoli, then you are in Pennsylvania.
2. You are in Pennsylvania.
   _____
∴   You are in Paoli.

If this were a valid pattern, then the truth of the premises would guarantee the truth of the conclusion. So does being in Pennsylvania guarantee that one is in Paoli? Clearly not—one could be in, say, Pittsburgh or Scranton or Lancaster. Not only are most people in Pennsylvania presently not in Paoli, but, more important, there is no guarantee that being in Pennsylvania involves being in Paoli. So any argument that fits this pattern is an invalid one and should be rejected.

This pattern may be profitably contrasted with the pattern called modus ponens (Chapter 4):

1. If you are in Paoli, then you are in Pennsylvania.
2. You are in Paoli.
   _____
∴   You are in Pennsylvania.

Here the truth of the premises guarantees the truth of the conclusion, telling us that it is a valid argument pattern. There is no way one can be in Paoli and not be in Pennsylvania; the pattern of affirming the consequent provides no such guarantee.

Fallacy 2: Denying the Antecedent

Like affirming the consequent, **denying the antecedent** is a common, though fallacious, way of arguing. Its pattern looks like this:

> 1. If A, then B.
> 2. Not A.
> _____
> ∴   Not B.

Consider the following example:

> 1. If you are in Boston, then you are in Massachusetts.
> 2. You are not in Boston.
> _____
> ∴   You are not in Massachusetts.

Clearly one could be somewhere other than Boston—say, Gloucester or Lynn—and still be in Massachusetts. Even if both of these premises are true, the truth does not guarantee the truth of the conclusion. Therefore the argument pattern is invalid. It may be true that many people who are not in Boston are also not in Massachusetts, but the lack of a guarantee is the key issue here.

Consider one more example:

> 1. If George sends Buffy flowers, then he loves her.
> 2. George does not send Buffy flowers.
> _____
> ∴   George does not love Buffy.

Their budding romance may soon be over due to some poor reasoning on Buffy's part. Buffy might come up with other reasons to suggest that George does not truly love her, but reasoning in this manner provides no good grounds for this conclusion.

This flawed pattern can be contrasted with the pattern known as modus tollens (Chapter 4):

> 1. If you are in Boston, then you are in Massachusetts.
> 2. You are not in Massachusetts.
> _____
> ∴   You are not in Boston.

Two Formal Fallacies

FALLACY	PATTERN	EXAMPLE
Denying the antecedent	1. If A, then B. 2. Not A. ——————— ∴ Not B.	1. If I'm in Albany, then I'm in New York. 2. I am not in Albany. ——————— ∴ I am not in New York.
Affirming the consequent	1. If A, then B. 2. B. ——————— ∴ A.	1. If I'm in Albany, then I'm in New York. 2. I am in New York. ——————— ∴ I am in Albany.

This is a valid pattern, as the truth of the premises guarantees the truth of the conclusion. After all, anyone who is not in Massachusetts must also not be in Boston.

INFORMAL FALLACIES OF RELEVANCE

Any premise is either relevant or irrelevant to the conclusion of the argument; the difficulty lies in deciding. The matter is further complicated by the fact that we generally assume that what a person says is relevant to the main point being made. Suppose you and a friend are discussing whether capital punishment is morally justified, and your friend makes two main claims in support of the view that capital punishment is not morally justified:

1. Friday comes after Thursday.
2. Every human being has a right to life that cannot be taken away or forfeited under any circumstances.

The first claim obviously is not relevant, as the relation of days of the week has no bearing on capital punishment. But the second claim certainly is relevant. If there is an absolute right to life, one that can never be lost or taken away, then it is not clear how capital punishment could be morally justified.

Fallacy 3: Appeal to Pity

The **appeal to pity** shifts the focus away from the reasons offered in support of a claim to the possible negative consequences that may befall the claimant if his or her position is not adopted. Consider the following:

Come on, ump, we're down 28 to 1. How can you call that a strike?

The person is trying to get the umpire to feel sorry for his team and thus call a pitch a ball, rather than arguing that there are good reasons for calling it a ball, such as that it was clearly outside the strike zone. The fact that his team is getting clobbered is irrelevant when it comes to calling balls and strikes. The relevant matter here is the location of the pitch, and not the emotional state of the losing team.

Now look at this example:

> My ego will be badly bruised if I don't get this job, so please offer it to me.

Nothing is said here about why the employer should hire this particular person; it's merely an observation that her feelings will be hurt if she is not hired. A fragile ego may be a valid reason to seek counseling of some sort, but it hardly counts as a qualification for most jobs!

However, a possible exception should be noted here. Suppose that two equally qualified people apply for a job. Also suppose that one of them is from a wealthy family, while the other is from a poor family. Finally, suppose that, following a review of their resumes and the interviews, they are in a dead heat. Would it be (morally) appropriate for the employer to hire the person with the less fortunate background? Those with politically conservative leanings might be inclined to flip a coin to decide the matter. Those with more liberal leanings might be more inclined to see the poorer background of the one candidate as relevant and be more likely to hire this individual. An underlying issue here involves affirmative action, on which there is an extensive literature and on which there is much disagreement among scholars.[1]

But now suppose a homeless man applies for a job and, when asked what his qualifications are, responds by noting that he is homeless. This is an appeal to pity, as his homelessness is irrelevant to the issue of job qualifications. If the man actually has decent qualifications, the fact that he is homeless might be enough for you to offer him the job. But his homelessness still has no bearing on the issue of his job qualifications.

Fallacy 4: Appeal to Authority

Many people are experts in one or two areas, but most of us have relatively little knowledge in most fields. If you are writing a physics paper and cite Albert Einstein, this is clearly appropriate, as Einstein is an acknowledged expert in the field of physics. But when you appeal to people outside their area(s) of expertise, the resulting claim is irrelevant. That is, you have made a fallacious appeal to authority.

---

[1] One good starting point in investigating this issue would be Albert Mosely and Nicholas Capaldi, *Affirmative Action* (Lanham, MD: Rowman & Littlefield, 1996). For a good introduction to liberalism and conservatism, see John Gray, *Liberalism* (Minneapolis: University of Minnesota Press, 1986), and Robert Nisbet, *Conservatism* (Minneapolis: University of Minnesota Press, 1994).

Consider the following examples:

1. I'm not a doctor, but I play one on TV. Take Sneezol, and you'll feel great.
2. Brett Favre says BenGay is great. You should use it too.
3. Goldie Hawn says doing research on animals is usually unjustified.
4. Jimmy Carter claims that Georgia peanuts are the best.

In claims like the first one, once we hear "I'm not a doctor . . . ," we should ask ourselves why we should take this person seriously. Actors and actresses, as a rule, know no more about medicine than anyone else. With regard to the second claim, Brett Favre may be a gifted football player, but he is hardly an expert on muscle ointments and the like. As a professional athlete he might well know *more* than the average person about such things, but that is still a long way from being an authority. So, unless we have actual evidence that Favre is an authority, it still is a fallacious appeal to authority. Similarly Goldie Hawn may know something about animals and research using them, but she is not trained in ethics or related disciplines. Finally, because Jimmy Carter was a big-time Georgia peanut farmer before he became president, he might well be an authority of sorts on peanuts.

Note that even experts can be wrong. Consider these examples:

1. Thomas Aquinas says that God exists.
2. Rudolf Bultmann says that the New Testament is highly unreliable historically and otherwise.
3. Jean-Paul Sartre says that life is devoid of meaning.

All three of these claims concern complex and controversial issues. As such, even the experts often will disagree among themselves in these areas. So, while it is generally better to cite an expert than a novice about a particular issue, this hardly settles the issue. Aquinas, Bultmann, and Sartre were brilliant scholars in the fields of religion, the New Testament, and philosophy, respectively, but many other experts in those areas would disagree with them. The bottom line is whether the individual cited can provide good reasons for a given claim.

Fallacy 5: Appeal to Popular Opinion

Suppose everyone in the United States believes that God exists. Does this mean that God does in fact exist? No. It should not count as evidence either for or against the existence of God. To claim that something is true simply because everyone believes it is to commit the fallacy of **appeal to popular opinion**. It might be sociologically interesting to ask why so many people believe in God, but this widespread belief is irrelevant to a rational discussion of the issue. A thousand years ago practically everyone believed that the earth was flat and that the earth was at the center of the solar system. We now know they were wrong on both counts. And two hundred years ago it was widely believed that bleeding the sick would get rid of the "bad blood" and thus speed their recovery. We now know that giving two or three pints of blood when you are very sick may actually worsen your condition. There is some evidence that, for example, George Washington's death may have been hastened by bleeding on top of a case of pneumonia.

The fact that many people believe or do not believe X thus hardly counts as evidence for or against X. Whether it is reasonable to believe X must be settled on other grounds. The key question is, *Why* does everyone believe X? and not, *How many* people believe X? If they believe X for good reasons, then those reasons count as evidence for X. And a single person believing X for good reasons is far more relevant than twenty people believing X for a host of bad reasons. In a sense, then, quality is more important than quantity.

One other point is in order here. Psychologists tell us that as humans we have a natural desire, often a strong one, to be accepted and to fit in. All things being equal, most of us would rather fit in with the group than be the "odd one out." This in itself is not a bad thing. But we need to be aware of this desire and to recognize how it often makes us more inclined to believe something just because everyone else believes it.

Fallacy 6: Abusive ad Hominem

The phrase *ad hominem* is from the Latin and means "against the man." The abusive ad hominem fallacy is committed whenever someone attacks the person making a claim instead of the claim itself. Instead of saying, "I think X is mistaken for the following three reasons," the attacker questions or ridicules the claimant's personality, intelligence, background, or the like. Even if there are good reasons for disliking someone, it does not follow that what that person says is erroneous. Similarly someone may be morally virtuous, but it does not follow that what that person says is correct. So we need to distinguish between *who* says something and *what* that person says.

Let's look at some examples. Consider this argument:

> You should vote against Jesse Helms's proposal because Helms is a reactionary.

Note that the claimant gives no relevant reasons for rejecting Helms's proposal. Rather, the claimant simply labels Helms as a "reactionary." Even if this is true, it is irrelevant to a consideration of the merits of Helms's position.

Here's another example:

> Jack rejected Linda's motion because, he said, she's a radical feminist.

Again, whether Linda is a radical feminist simply is not relevant to the issue at hand. The main issue is whether her motion has merit. Here we should focus on the various strengths and weaknesses of the proposed motion, and not on Linda's alleged political or social views.

Calvin and Hobbes
by Bill Watterson

In the sense that Calvin is really slamming Moe, this is an example of an abusive ad hominem.   CALVIN AND HOBBES © Watterson. Reprinted with permission of UNIVERSAL PRESS SYNDICATE. All rights reserved.

Let's look at one more example:

I voted against him because he's an idiot.

Once more we have strong words directed at a person rather than the view he or she has set forth. Here, as with the other examples, the attack on the person ultimately is irrelevant. The key issue is whether the claim deserves our rational support.

Fallacy 7: "You, Too" ad Hominem

Abusive ad hominems are not the only kind of ad hominem. Almost all of us have encountered the **"you, too" ad hominem** fallacy at some point in our lives. Here person A claims that person B is guilty of X, and B responds by claiming that A is even worse with respect to X. However, whether B is actually guilty of X is completely ignored.

Consider this example:

You call me a Commie? Well, your momma dated Karl Marx, and her maiden name is Stalin!

The issue here is whether either person is a Communist. Insulting the other person does nothing to show that the respondent is not a Communist. It may be true that the accuser is a Communist, but the respondent still has not replied to the specific charge, namely, being a Communist.

Look at this claim:

You think I'm overweight?! Well, at least I don't have to weigh myself on a trucker's scale and I don't have my own zip code!

Notice that the respondent never addresses the claim that he is overweight. He simply accuses the claimant of being worse than he is with respect to body weight. Again, the "you, too," ad hominem, like the abusive ad hominem, focuses on matters not relevant to the claim at hand.

Note that the "you, too" ad hominem does not always involve prejudicial language. Suppose that a mother who took drugs in her "hippie days" in the 1960s gives her daughter three reasons not to use drugs. The daughter responds in this way:

> If they were good enough for you, then they are good enough for me.

The daughter's response contains no prejudicial language, but it also ignores the reasons offered by the mother. Whether the mother ever used drugs simply is irrelevant to whether there are good reasons for not using drugs.

EXERCISE 6.1

For each of the following, identify the fallacy. Indicate how it is committed.

★ 1. If Sarah bakes bread for Don, then she loves him. She does not bake bread for him. She does not love him.

2. Paul Newman uses GE light bulbs, so you should too.

3. Hey, ref, we're losing 45 to 6. How about a couple of calls going our way?

★ 4. You call me bad?! Well, Attila the Hun, Hitler, and Stalin were all saints compared to you.

5. If you don't marry me, you'll be full of regret. You are full of regret, as you did not marry me.

6. "No one I know goes in and throws money around." (Rush Limbaugh, *The Way Things Ought to Be*)

★ 7. Everyone is doing it.

8. These boys are the products of a difficult environment and starved for attention. Can you honestly say you would have done any differently under these circumstances?

9. "He may be a son of a bitch, but he's our son of a bitch." (attributed to Franklin Roosevelt, commenting on Anastasio Somoza, the dictator of Nicaragua, in 1938)

★ 10. Senator Smith is slimy, sleazy, and utterly lacking in moral decency.

11. You're an East Coast, liberal, quiche-eating snob.

12. Michael Jordan wears Hanes underwear, and you should too.

★ 13. "Every American knows that the legal system is broken, and now is the time to fix it." (Dan Quayle)

14. "Whoever designed the streets must have been drunk. . . . I think it was those Irish guys." (Minnesota governor Jesse Ventura)

15. If the president does a good job, then the economy does well. The economy is doing well, so the president must be doing a good job.

★ 16. Mary Lou Retton eats Wheaties; you should too.

17. "Governor Dukakis is a card-carrying member of the ACLU." (George Bush on Michael Dukakis during the 1988 presidential campaign)

18. "When a British legislator asked him about religious liberties in the Soviet Union, [Mikhail] Gorbachev [leader of the Soviet Union at the time] replied, 'You persecute entire communities . . .'" (*Time*)

★ 19. Do you really need to buy that $45,000 sport utility vehicle. Consider all the people starving to death in the world, and how many you could save if you gave even a quarter of that money to hunger relief organizations?

20. It's a new policy for a kinder and gentler police force. And since it was proposed by Mayor Giuliani in New York, we know it must be a bad policy![2]

Fallacy 8: Appeal to Force

Suppose Juan agrees with Marie only because she threatens to hurt him if he doesn't ("Adopt my proposal or I'll flatten you"). Here we have a classic example of the fallacy of **appeal to force.** The threatened harm need not be physical. It can be economic ("I'll fire you if you do that"), social ("Agree with me or I won't go out with you anymore"), or political ("If you don't support my view, then I won't vote to reelect you"). In each case the claimant gives no reasons to support the claim but merely threatens some harm.

Consider this example of an appeal to economic force:

> If Congresswoman Jones insists on pursuing her vendetta against me, then we can arrange for the IRS to closely scrutinize her tax returns for the past seven years.

Notice how this appeal shifts the focus away from reasons offered in support of a view, where it should be, to threats of some sort of harm if that view is not agreed with or endorsed. Finally, suppose that someone whom you know to be violent says, "Agree with me or I'll slug you." This might be a good reason for *doing* as he says, but it will never be a good reason for *believing* as he does.

Fallacy 9: Two Wrongs Make a Right

Suppose Bobby has just hit his sister Sally. A classic response to the question "Why did you hit your sister?" is "She hit me first," which supposedly justifies the retaliation. But even if Sally unfairly and wrongly hit Bobby, is Bobby justified in striking her in response? The widely accepted answer is no. Given that Bobby has free will and is accountable for his behavior, he has the ability

---

[2] This is a variation on one of the main fallacies.

not to retaliate. And since, according to almost any viable standard of ethics, it is morally wrong to retaliate in such a situation unless one's life or well-being is at risk, Bobby should refrain from hitting her.

Even the Stoics of ancient Greece and Rome, who believed that we control little in life and stressed accepting what we cannot control, believed that we have control over how we respond to situations. Understandably Bobby might be angry and want to retaliate (also a choice, as the Stoics would argue), but one sign of moral maturity is the ability to control one's emotions and to do what one knows to be right in a given situation. Given that we can control our emotions, including anger, then Bobby's anger is a form of response that he chose and for which he is responsible. The bottom line here is that, even if someone has wronged you, that fact is irrelevant with regard to whether you should also wrong that person.

Some of the relatives of victims in the tragic Oklahoma City Federal Building bombing wanted the death penalty for the two convicted bombers on the grounds that "one bad turn deserves another." This is a classic example of the fallacious reasoning underlying the claim that "two wrongs make a right."

Fallacy 10: Appeal to Ignorance

Suppose we do not have enough evidence to believe that claim X is true. Does it therefore follow that we are justified in believing ~X (that is, "not X") to be true? The answer is a resounding no. A lack of evidence for X does not count as evidence in favor of believing ~X to be the case. Ultimately our ignorance is irrelevant to the issue of truth.

To illustrate, let's focus on a familiar and complex issue, namely, whether God exists. Suppose we have a debate involving three people:

The theist, who believes she is justified in believing X (where X = God exists)

The atheist, who believes he is justified in believing ~X

The agnostic, who believes she is justified in believing neither X nor ~X

During the course of the debate, the three agree that the theist is not justified in believing X. What follows from this? Assuming that these three positions are logically exhaustive for the purposes of this discussion, we are left with two options: agnosticism and atheism. But the failure of the theist to show that her belief in X is justified hardly counts as evidence for either of the other two positions. The absence of a positive does not necessarily equal the presence of a negative. If the theist is truly not justified in believing X, it follows that one of the other two must be the more reasonable alternative. But we have no good reason to prefer one to the other. So someone who claimed, "I know of no good reason to be a theist, so I'm an atheist," would be guilty of a fallacious appeal to ignorance.

Also relevant here is the issue of the burden of proof, which relates to the responsibility to come up with a good argument in a debate. In criminal law, for example, the prosecution has a clear burden to prove its case beyond a reasonable doubt. Similarly claims that are out of the ordinary have the burden of proof.

Suppose someone claims to have spoken with space aliens. This claimant obviously has a heavy burden of proof to show the reasonableness of the claim. Given that we cannot prove either that there are aliens or that there are no aliens, where do we go from here? Because the existence of space aliens is not common knowledge, the burden of proof is on our claimant. And if he or she does not have good evidence, such as an undoctored videotape, then the most reasonable conclusion is this:

> There is no good evidence for the existence of aliens; therefore, I am justified in believing that there are not any.

This belief is based on the (lack of) evidence, and it is also subject to modification if some evidence becomes available.

One final point is in order here. Even if the three debaters agree that the theist is not justified in believing X, it does not necessarily follow that belief in X is unjustified. For example, suppose that there actually is one good reason for believing X, but none of three debaters is aware of it. If the theist had put forth arguments P and Q in favor of X, and then they all agreed that P and Q were flawed, what conclusions should we draw? It might surprise you to learn that the reasonable conclusion is that P and Q do not justify X, and not the much stronger claim that X is not (or cannot be) justified. This would involve being aware of all the decent arguments for X and then successfully challenging or rebutting each and every one of them—no small feat! So, if you ever hear someone say, "You can't *prove* that there are no aliens, so I'm justified in believing in them," you will recognize this as an appeal to ignorance.

Fallacy 11: False Confidence

People are often willing to accept a claim if the person making the claim does so with confidence and sincerity. Just as we are less inclined to believe the claims of individuals who seem unsure of themselves, so we are inclined to believe those who claim something boldly and confidently and with sincerity. Again, we must learn to distinguish between the claim being made and the person making the claim. The fact is, confident and sincere people are not always correct in what they say, while people who are unsure of themselves and rather tentative in their claims are not necessarily mistaken. A lack of self-confidence on the part of a claimant has no logical relation to the issue of whether his or her claim is justifiable. Self-confidence is relevant to psychological well-being, but not to the reasonableness of claims.

The habit of not distinguishing between people and their claims is one of the factors that contributes to the success of many religious cults. The leaders of cults tend to be highly confident, charismatic, sincere-sounding figures. But does it therefore follow that their claims are more likely to be true than someone else's? Not in the least! Or consider Linus, the younger brother of Lucy in the "Peanuts" comic strip. He is a bright and wise young boy who nevertheless is convinced that on Halloween the Great Pumpkin will come to the pumpkin patch he is in because it is the most sincere of all pumpkin patches! Even if there were a Great Pumpkin, it is not at all clear why it would choose to appear in pumpkin patches solely on the basis of their "sincerity"— a characteristic seldom associated with pumpkin patches.

Recall the series of commercials put out by Holiday Inn in which a man who has had a restful night's stay at a Holiday Inn confidently gives advice to a woman confronted by a large bear and offers expert-sounding medical advice to an injured cyclist. The woman and the cyclist clearly seem to trust the person giving the advice, probably because he seems so self-confident and because the advice has a ring of expertise to it. In short, even though self-confidence is a good thing, it is no substitute for genuine evidence or reasons in support of a claim.

INFORMAL FALLACIES OF LANGUAGE

Fallacy 12: Prejudicial Language

Language is **prejudicial** (or loaded) when the words tend to stimulate certain positive or negative feelings in us. Suppose someone is below the average weight for his or her height, age, and sex. How should we refer to this individual? Here are some options:

1. *Thin*—a word that is descriptive without having particularly positive overtones
2. *Emaciated*—a word that clearly has negative overtones and so is an example of negative prejudicial language
3. *Svelte*—an example of positive prejudicial language
4. *Slender*—another example of positive prejudicial language
5. *Anorexic*—a classic example of negative prejudicial language

As one scholar has argued, "Language can become a substitute for rational argument and can work to disguise the fact that important and contested claims have not been supported by reason or evidence."[3] The philosopher Bertrand Russell focused on this feature of language when he wrote the following:

I am firm.

You are stubborn.

He is a pigheaded fool.

---

[3] Trudy Govier, *A Practical Study of Argument* (Belmont, CA: Wadsworth, 1992), p. 106.

Notice that while the word "firm" has positive overtones, "stubborn" is either neutral or negative in tone, and "pigheaded" is most certainly negative.

Now consider these examples:

Don's view is *simplistic* and *naive,* while Mary's is *sophisticated* and *progressive.*

Reagan's policies were *regressive* and *primitive.*

Clinton was a *bleeding-heart liberal.*

The italicized words are good examples of prejudicial language. Some of the words have negative connotations—such as "simplistic" and "regressive"—while others are positive—such as "sophisticated" and "progressive." Using loaded or prejudicial language is not necessarily to be avoided, but we should be aware of when it is used and how it functions.

Another kind of prejudicial language involves euphemisms, which are nice-sounding words or phrases used to express a not-so-pleasant reality. "Executive facilities" (for restrooms) and "maritally challenged" (referring to a recently divorced person) are classic examples of euphemistic language. It has even been said that zombies are the "living impaired"! In the following piece columnist Bob Herbert writes about the many euphemisms that have been coined for losing one's job.

Separation Anxiety

Bob Herbert

The euphemism of choice for the corporate chopping block is downsizing, 1
but variations abound. John Thomas, a 59-year-old AT&T employee, was told on Tuesday that his job was "not going forward." One thinks of a car with transmissions trouble, or the New York Jets offense, not the demise of a lengthy career.

Other workers are discontinued, involuntarily severed, surplussed. There are men and women at AT&T who actually talk about living in a "surplus universe."

There are special leaves, separations, rebalances, bumpings and, one of my favorites, cascade bumpings. A cascade bumping actually sounds like a joyful experience.

In the old days some snarling ogre would call you into the office and say, "Jack, you're fired." It would be better if they still did it that way because that might make the downsized, discontinued, surplussed or severed employee mad as hell. And if enough employees got mad they might get together and decide to do something about the ever-increasing waves of corporate greed and irresponsibility that have capsized their lives and will soon overwhelm many more.

Instead, with the niceties scrupulously observed, and with employment 5
alternatives in extremely short supply, the fired workers remain fearful, frustrated, confused, intimidated and far too docile. . . . The staggering job losses,
even at companies that are thriving, are rationalized as necessary sacrifices to
the great gods of international competition. Little is said about the corrosive
effect of rampant corporate greed, and even less about peculiar notions like
corporate responsibility and accountability—not just to stockholders, but to
employees and their families, to the local community, to the social and economic well-being of the country as a whole.

New York Times, January 19, 1996

The tendency toward euphemistic language has changed us from a nation of fat, bald, ignorant people to one of the "anorexically challenged," the
"follicularly challenged," and the "knowledge challenged." Though they may
be funny, euphemisms do not always accurately depict reality and so are examples of prejudicial language.

It is possible, however, to have a valid and sound argument that makes
use of prejudicial language. Look at this example:

1.   All nerds are mainstream challenged.

2.   Ned is a nerd.
     _____

∴   Ned is mainstream challenged.

Note that this is a valid argument, as the conclusion follows from the premises. But it is also a sound argument, as premise 1 reflects the basic definition
of a "nerd" while premise 2 is assumed to be true. So, although inclusion of
prejudicial language may influence how we evaluate an argument, for better
or for worse, it still leaves open the possibility that the argument is both valid
and sound.

Fallacy 13: Equivocation

The fallacy of **equivocation** occurs when a word or group of words changes
meaning from one premise to another in an argument. Given how many
words have two or more possible meanings, it should come as no surprise that
people sometimes use the same word in two or more senses. Consider the
following:

1.   If you break the law, then you should go to jail.

2.   Anyone committing adultery violates God's law.
     _____

∴   Anyone committing adultery should go to jail.

Calvin and Hobbes

by Bill Watterson

This is a wonderful example of the ambiguity of many claims in particular and of language in general. CALVIN AND HOBBES © Watterson. Reprinted with permission of UNIVERSAL PRESS SYNDICATE. All rights reserved.

The problem here is that the word "law" is used in two different senses in this argument. In premise 1 it refers to a legal statute, while in premise 2 it refers to a moral code. The shift in meaning from the first premise to the second makes the argument invalid. If "law" has a legal meaning in both premises, then premise 2 is false, as God is not the author of legal statutes. If "law" has a moral sense in both premises, then premise 1 is unreasonable, as most of us would not want to jail everyone who committed a moral wrong. So either the argument is invalid due to the shift in meaning or one of the premises is false.

EXERCISE 6.2

For each of the following, identify the fallacy and indicate how it is committed.

★ 1. Jethro heard Bubba say, "Gimme a break," so he kicked him hard and broke his leg.

2. If you don't adopt my proposal, you might not get reelected.

3. He disagrees with me, but he's an idiot.

★ 4. You don't know that I'm mistaken, so I am justified in believing in it.

5. Senator Smith seems so nice and sincere. She must be telling the truth about her personal finances.

6. The government doesn't use my money in a wise fashion, so I'm not going to disclose all my income on my federal tax form.

★ 7. Nobody knows that Janet and Leon's marriage will not last, so I believe it will.

8. "Martin Luther King's epitaph, in my opinion, can be written here in Birmingham." (Robert Shelton, quoted in Juan Williams, *Eyes on the Prize*)

9. Mary is a poor person and she often loses at sports, so she is a poor loser.

★ 10. She hit me first!

11. Do you still hold to the naive belief that God exists?

12. "[Dr. Jack] Kevorkian is the John Brown of the right-to-die movement, wild-eyed and nutty." (Arthur Caplan, quoted in John Leo, "Dancing with Dr. Death," *U.S. News & World Report*)

★ 13. "Do you know why God created woman? Because sheep can't type." (Texas state senator Kenneth Armbrister)

14. "I would warn Orlando that you're right in the way of some serious hurricanes, and I don't think I'd be waving those [gay pride] flags in God's face if I were you." (Pat Robertson)

15. "I call on Mississippi to keep the faith and courage. We will never surrender." (Ross Barnett, governor of Mississippi, quoted in Juan Williams, *Eyes on the Prize*)[4]

★ 16. Whose moronic proposal is this?

17. I heard her say, "All humans are moral creatures," so it must be true that all humans are good creatures.[5]

18. We don't know much about space aliens, so I'm justified in believing whatever I want about them.

INFORMAL FALLACIES OF MISREPRESENTATION

Fallacy 14: Straw Man

With the straw man fallacy someone makes an opponent's position appear weaker than it really is by either distorting, oversimplifying, or caricaturing it, so that we would reasonably be inclined to reject that position. Consider the following example:

Everyone who is against capital punishment sees it as barbaric.

This statement is simply false. Certainly many people oppose the death penalty because they view it as barbaric. But other reasons for opposing the death penalty include these:

1. Innocent people have been executed.

2. Mandatory life in prison is a fair and just sentence for "capital" crimes.

---

[4] The context is very important here. Governor Barnett was speaking on radio while a riot was taking place at the University of Mississippi. Barnett and others were resisting efforts to register James Meredith, a black man, at the college. The speech was in reaction to and defiance of federal efforts to peacefully enroll Meredith at the school.

[5] Hint: The word "moral" has more than one meaning.

3. The state should not kill its citizens, regardless of what they have done.

Keeping the principle of charity in mind (see Chapter 4), we should make every effort to clearly and fairly represent the position of someone with whom we disagree. And keeping the Golden Rule (we should treat others as we ourselves would wish to be treated) in mind, we should take great care to accurately portray the views of others. To do otherwise simply shows a lack of respect for other people.

Fallacy 15: Slippery Slope

We tend to view certain things in a negative light because they seem, perhaps inevitably, to lead to other things that may be even worse. For example, not only may alcoholic beverages, cocaine, and gambling be bad in and of themselves, but they also share a tendency to be addictive for many humans. So, although occasional light gambling may not be seen as harmful as such, some people become compulsive gamblers—often to their own and their family's ruination. Slippery slope refers to a situation in which event A leads to event B and eventually to event F, which is clearly bad and thus undesirable. Therefore, if you want to avoid F, you should also avoid doing A. As with dilemmas, only some slopes are genuinely slippery (A may well lead to B, and so on); other slopes are not (A does not generally lead to B, and so on).

Let's consider the following example:

If you touch that drink, you will want another and another, until finally you become an alcoholic.

Generally alcohol consumption is not a slippery slope. Many people can and do drink alcoholic beverages in moderation and never become problem drinkers. Someone may have a family history of alcoholism, and for that individual one drink may lead to further problems. But note that the problem ultimately is only with certain people, because alcohol does not usually drive us to become addicted to it.

A slippery slope argument is fallacious only when the connection between the first event (A) and the final event (F) is either nonexistent or weak—or perhaps the link is moderately strong but not strong enough to constitute a genuine slippery slope. The slippery slope fallacy might be more accurately labeled the "unslippery slope," because the fallacy is committed only when the slope is *not* slippery (when A does not necessarily lead to F). By "weak" we mean here that, more often than not, A does not lead to B, and so on. But if there is a causal guarantee or a high probability that A will lead to B, and so on, then the use of a slippery slope argument is a legitimate and acceptable form of arguing.

Although the alcohol claim is an example of a fallacious, or nongenuine, slippery slope, for some individuals, such as those already diagnosed as alcoholics, alcohol is a legitimate problem. This suggests that whether a slippery slope argument is genuine or fallacious is, to some extent, person-relative. That is, it depends to some degree on which group of people we have in mind. If we are referring to all humans, then it clearly is not a genuine slippery slope. But if we have all the members of Alcoholics Anonymous in mind, then there may well be a causal connection between the first drink (A) and the later stage of drunkenness (F).

Fallacy 16: Complex Question

A complex question is really two questions rolled into one. The questioner first assumes the answer to an unasked question and then asks a second question based on this "answer." Here are some examples:

> Have you given up your evil ways?
>
> Are you as dumb as you look?
>
> Have you stopped beating your wife?
>
> Does Barry Manilow know you raid his wardrobe?

Note that in each case there are really two questions masquerading as the one that is asked. Even worse, the questions are constructed such that, no matter how you answer them, you admit to some undesirable thing of which you may not be guilty. In the first example these are the two questions:

> Have your ways *ever* been evil? (unstated)
>
> Are your ways *still* evil?

We can imagine someone answering yes to the first but no to the second. Similarly the second example is really two questions appearing as one:

> Do you look dumb? (unstated)
>
> Are you as dumb as you look?

Here, again, one could be guilty of the former but not the latter—and, of course, one might be guilty of neither. So the proper response to a complex question is to break it down into its component questions and then answer them one at a time.

Fallacy 17: False Dilemma

Sometimes life presents us with genuine dilemmas in which both (or all) possible courses of action have negative consequences. As the old saying goes, we are caught "between a rock and a hard place." For example, if someone robs you at gunpoint and says, "Your money or your life," it is reasonable to think that these are the only options available.

How, then, does a false dilemma differ from a genuine one? A **false dilemma** results when only two possible courses of action are presented even though other options are available. Consider the following slogan, which Vietnam War protesters frequently heard in the 1960s and 1970s.

America: love it or leave it!

This would be a genuine dilemma if the two options presented were the only two possibilities:

1. Loving America (and presumably staying)
2. Disliking America and leaving

But clearly these are not the only two alternatives. Here are some other possibilities:

3. Disliking America and wanting to stay (with the hope of improving it, perhaps)
4. Loving America but wanting to leave anyway
5. Being indifferent toward America and wanting to leave
6. Being indifferent toward America and wanting to stay

Given options 3–6, this is a false dilemma.

Now consider another example:

Marry me today or the wedding is off.

Here we have two options:

1. Marriage today
2. No wedding

But surely these are not the only two potential courses of action. What about the following options, to list but a few?

3. Marriage tomorrow
4. Marriage next year
5. Marriage at some undetermined time

Given that we easily came up with three additional possibilities, this is another false dilemma.

Let's look at one more example:

Dad, would you rather:

1. Increase my allowance,
2. Give me the money I need to buy the car, or
3. Give me a no-interest loan?

Once again we have a false dilemma, as there are many more options available, including these:

4. What if you don't buy the car at all?
5. What if Dad lends you the money at low interest?

So a dilemma is a false one whenever it unreasonably restricts the options available. But how do we tell the difference between a genuine dilemma and a false dilemma? There is no easy answer to this question. Certainly having some familiarity with the issue being considered helps. Also, the knowledge and wisdom we gain as we grow older can give us insight into whether a given dilemma is indeed a false one.

EXERCISE 6.3

For each of the following, identify the fallacy, and indicate how it is committed.

★ 1. Please don't eat that donut. It will lead to a second and a third, and then you'll eventually eat the whole bag, gain weight, develop heart disease, and die prematurely.

2. It's my way or no way!

3. The only reason you are pro capital punishment is that it's cheaper than life in prison.

★ 4. Are you as silly as you look?

5. Everyone either loved or hated President Clinton.

6. "Progress is not striving for economic justice or fairness, but economic growth." (Rush Limbaugh, *35 Undeniable Truths*)

★ 7. "Does Barry Manilow know you raid his wardrobe?" (student to the assistant principal in the movie *The Breakfast Club*)

8. "They were throwing Frisbees, flying kites, and listening to Tom Cruise talk about how we have to recycle *everything* and stop corporations from polluting." (Rush Limbaugh, *The Way Things Ought to Be*)

9. You're either for us or against us.

★ 10. I am either the best or the worst tennis player.

11. If you turn on that television, you will watch that show. If you watch that show, you will want to watch it every day. Then you will no longer do your homework, you'll flunk out of school, and you'll end up on welfare. So don't touch that dial!

12. People who reject capital punishment do so only because they believe one or two innocent people have died over the years.

★ 13. "So damned if you do [have an abortion], damned if you don't. I hope you make a choice you feel comfortable with. I only wish that you had some real options to choose from." (Kristin Luker, *Harper's*)

14. One adult to another: "Do you still call your mommy every day?"

15. Cigarette smoking leads to marijuana, which leads to cocaine use, which leads to a lifelong addiction.

★ 16. Are you as big a dweeb as ever?

17. "The Democrats still blame society, not criminals, for crime." (Phil Gramm)

18. "These environmental extremists put birds and rats and insects ahead of families, workers, and jobs." (Pat Buchanan, "The Election Is About Who We Are")

INFORMAL FALLACIES OF POOR REASONING

Fallacy 18: Begging the Question

This fallacy is not always easy to detect. Essentially, when the conclusion of an argument is merely the premise(s) restated, the arguer is **begging the question.** Thus most cases of begging the question involve different ways of saying the same thing. Look at this claim:

> I know he's telling the truth because he is not lying.

This is an example of begging the question because to not be lying is not evidence for telling the truth; rather, it is *the same thing* as telling the truth. The claimant has merely stated the same thing in two different ways, one positive and one negative, without giving us any *reasons* to believe the main claim is true.

Consider another example:

> I know that Jabba is grossly overweight because he is obese.

Here "grossly overweight" and "obese" mean the same thing. So the fact that someone is obese does not count as evidence for the belief that he is grossly overweight. This amounts to arguing along the lines of "he is obese because he is obese," which is not an argument at all but merely a restatement of the same information. In other words, it is an example of circular reasoning.

To illustrate, look at this argument:

1. If Maria is reliable, this is because she is always on time.

2. If she is always on time, it is because she works at it.

∴ If she works at it, it is because she is reliable.

This argument can be symbolized as follows:

1. If A, then B.

2. If B, then C.

∴ If C, then A.

This is reasoning in circles (notice that it loops back on itself) and so is an invalid pattern.

Fallacy 19: Common Cause

Suppose that in the real world two events have an established pattern of happening one after the other. So, if event B always follows event A, is this sufficient reason for believing that A *causes* B? The answer is no. This is because A and B can be either *accidentally* related or related in that they are both products of the same **common cause**, but neither is the cause of the other.

Consider the following examples:

1. If the NFC team wins the Super Bowl, then the stock market will have a growth year.
2. If the barometer falls dramatically, then a storm will follow.
3. Whenever Shanelle wears her lucky socks, her basketball team wins.
4. Chan's fatigue is the cause of his depression.

The first example is simply an accidental relationship. It may be true that when the NFC team wins the Super Bowl the stock market usually has a good year, but no one really believes that the two are causally related. Example 2 is a bit more complicated. It is true that falling barometers and storms often happen one after the other and that the relationship is not an accidental one. The falling barometer and the storm do have a causal connection; it's just not the kind in which one causes the other. That is, they are both produced (caused) by the same thing (a common cause), namely, a low-pressure system.

Example 3 involves simple superstition. The fact that the team always wins when Shanelle wears her "lucky" socks is hardly evidence for the causal powers of the socks. Rather, it is evidence of her team's talent or work ethic, or both. Finally, in example 4, other causes of Chan's depression might include the recent death of a loved one and the stress of a new job.

To summarize, there are (at least) four kinds of relationships two consecutive events, A and B, can have:

1. A is the cause of B.
2. A and B have a common cause. (example 2)
3. A and B are causally unrelated (examples 1 and 3)
4. A is one of the causes of B. (example 4)

All this tells us that the common cause fallacy is not the only fallacy relating to the idea of cause and effect, though it is one of the more common ones. There are many possible relationships between two events, which suggests that reality is often a bit more complicated than we might think.

Fallacy 20: Hasty Generalization

We are all guilty, at one time or another, of basing a conclusion on rather limited information. Look at the following:

1. Edgar dumped Darla, so Darla concluded that all men are jerks.

2. Sully had a few beers too many. Everyone knows that the Irish are all heavy drinkers.

3. Donna sees Senators Olson and Paslawski as morally decadent and concludes that most members of Congress are similarly flawed.

With respect to the first example, even if it is true that Edgar is a jerk, it hardly follows that *all* men are like Edgar in this regard. To move from one example to a claim about billions of men is a classic example of a **hasty generalization.** Note that, while Darla's hurt feelings may well be understandable, it hardly follows that her belief is a reasonable one. Along similar lines, even if Sully is "sobriety challenged," it hardly follows that all Irish people are heavy drinkers. Recall that if there is one genuine counterexample, then the claim is false. And since we probably all know at least one Irish person who is not a heavy drinker, then the claim is false.

Example 3 is a bit different. Here the move is made from two examples to the claim that most members of Congress are decadent. Since "most" means more than half (to state it conservatively), and there are 535 members of Congress, is Donna justified in basing a claim about at least 268 people on the basis of observations concerning 2 people? The answer is a resounding no. Though Donna has not made the illogical jump from one case to an "all are guilty of . . ." claim, she has made the move from two cases to a very strong claim, and her reasoning is not much better.

The lesson to be learned here is that sweeping statements and broad generalizations are no stronger than the evidence on which they are based. And if the evidence is very limited, as it often is, then the concluding generalization is not a justified one. Evidence may exist to support the generalization, but until that evidence is forthcoming, the conclusion remains unjustified.

TWO FINAL FALLACIES

Fallacy 21: Misleading Statistics

When I was a boy I heard an advertiser proudly claim that its brand of television had more than twice the sales of its leading competitor. I asked my father, "They must be number one, huh, Dad?" He responded, "Not necessarily." And he was right. Suppose the market shares for television manufacturers were as follows:

Brand A	31%
Brand B	29%
Brand C	18%
Brand D	97%
Brand E	04%
All others	10%

Suppose further that the claim on television was made by Brand C. Is it true that their sales were more than double those of their nearest competitor? The answer is yes. This is because 18% is more than double the 8% of their nearest competitor, brand D. What was misleading was that the commercial clearly implied that brand C was the top seller when in fact it was comfortably in third place! This is a classic example of using statistics in a misleading manner.

Suppose we polled the American public to see what they thought of the most recent federal budget and obtained these results:

Strongly agree	18%
Significantly agree	24%
Moderately agree/disagree	23%
Significantly disagree	23%
Strongly disagree	12%

Suppose further that an advertisement then claimed that 58% of all Americans do not strongly agree with the budget. Technically this is correct (combining categories 3–5), but it is misleading. It is true that members of the group in category 3 do not significantly or completely agree with the budget, but they would be better described as "fence-sitters" or "in the middle" than as being against the budget. Advertisers know that if they make this sort of claim, many people will think that 58% *strongly disagree* with the budget. But we know that the absence of something positive ("strongly agree") is not equivalent to the presence of a negative ("strongly disagree"). This is because there is a fairly large group (category 3) that is neither positive nor negative but somewhere in the middle. People often wrongly assume that if you are not for something, then you are against it. As this example shows, this is not always the case.

Abortion is one of the most controversial issues in the United States today, with both pro-abortion and anti-abortion advocates claiming to be in the majority.[6] Consider the following imaginary statistics concerning the question "Under what conditions should a woman be legally allowed to have an abortion?"

If the mother's life is in danger	92%
In cases of rape and incest	83%
In cases of fetal birth defects	65%
For financial reasons	36%
On demand	25%

What could the two groups, if they were so inclined, do with these statistics? For starters, an anti-abortion advocate could claim that 75% of Americans are

---

[6] Note that the labels "pro-choice" and "pro-life" contain "loaded," or prejudicial, language. In light of this, I prefer the more descriptive labels "pro-abortion" and "anti-abortion."

against abortion on demand. A pro-abortion advocate could counter with the claim that 65% support a right to abortion when one of three conditions is met. Each side would be appealing to the same set of statistics (which is often not the case in the real world) yet making fundamentally different claims.

Consider two more examples:

1. Boys are better than girls at math.

2. Asian-Americans do better than Caucasians on standardized tests.

In the first case some studies indicate that boys *do* better than girls in math, but this is different from claiming that they *are* better than girls at math. But the studies also suggest that the difference is a small one, perhaps explainable by the different ways boys and girls are socialized in the United States today. Similarly, if Moe consistently beats Larry by a point or two in basketball, Moe may be the better player, but not by much—a fact that is certainly relevant.

In the second case studies suggest that Asian-Americans do better than virtually any other group on standardized tests. What conclusions should we draw from this? Does this mean that Asian-Americans are inherently brighter? Not necessarily. Does it mean that they have a better work ethic with respect to education than most other groups? Perhaps. So the fact that they do better may be interesting, but it doesn't necessarily tell us anything about their natural intelligence or work ethic compared to other groups.

To properly understand statistics, we need to consider many other factors, including the following:

1. **Was it a representative sample of the desired population?** If we wanted to know about the car-buying habits of Americans in general, we would not poll only people living in the greater Detroit area, as their loyalty to the three main American manufacturers would skew the results.

2. **Was it a biased sample?** If we wanted to investigate the buying habits of the poor, we would have to be careful in conducting a phone survey. This is because the sample would be biased toward phone owners, who are less likely to be poor than those who do not own a phone.

3. **How large was the sample?** For a sample to represent the whole population adequately, it must contain enough respondents to accurately represent the diversity of the overall population.

4. **Who conducted the research?** If a poll on smoking cigarettes was conducted by the tobacco companies, they clearly would have a vested (economic) interest in the results. This does not mean that whatever they reported would be wrong, but we would want to be very careful in evaluating claims under conditions such as these.

5. **What sorts of questions were asked?** If Americans were asked whether they are more properly described as being morally good or morally bad, the overwhelming majority would choose the former.

Examples of Misleading Statistics

The graphs below deal with student scores on the Scholastic Aptitude Test (SAT) over a twenty-nine-year period. Even though the two graphs present the same data, the graph on the top looks different from the one on the bottom. Notice how the graph on the top expands the scale to show a definite downward trend, while the graph on the bottom compresses the scale to minimize any change over time. Someone looking at the first graph might well say, "Scores are down," while someone looking at the second one would respond, "The scores are fairly constant over time." The point is that even statistical graphs can be "manipulated" to show preferred results.

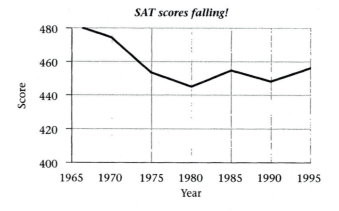

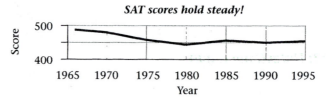

A second example involves a magazine called *Literary Digest*. In a survey of American voters in the 1930s, the magazine concluded that the Republican candidate would easily defeat the Democratic incumbent, Franklin Roosevelt. As it turned out, however, Roosevelt won in a landslide! How could the magazine have gotten it so wrong? The simple answer is that their research sample was not representative of the American population. The magazine selected respondents from telephone directories and motor vehicle registrations. The problem was that the majority of people who owned cars and phones were Republicans, and thus very few traditional Democrats were included in the survey. Shortly after their prediction proved to be way off the mark, *Literary Digest* went out of business.

But such a question is simplistic. Not everyone is morally comparable to Mother Teresa or to Adolf Hitler. Rather, most of us reside in
the expansive moral terrain falling between the two extremes. Morality is a matter of degrees, and questions involving morality must
recognize this fact, or the resulting study will be of little value.

6. **How honest were the survey participants?** Even if many questions
   were asked and answered, it does not necessarily follow that the answers were entirely truthful. Research suggests that humans are
   more likely to answer truthfully some kinds of questions than others. This fact must be taken into account when evaluating the merits
   of the particular study.

7. **How were the questions phrased?** For example, it would clearly be
   an example of loaded or prejudicial language if in an abortion survey participants were asked, "Are you in favor of murdering innocent babies in the womb?" Even the most passionate of pro-abortion
   advocates would have a hard time answering this question in the
   affirmative.

One final point is in order here. Some statistics are not misleading as such
but simply do not provide enough information for us to make an informed
decision. Such statistics might be called incomplete or out of context. If someone claims, "No other product is more widely recommended than ours," that
is an incomplete claim. It could mean that the product is the number one
seller in its field, or it could mean there is a six-way tie for first and the product has only 11% of the market! Since we have no way of knowing, unless
more information is forthcoming we should view such claims as statistically
incomplete.

Fallacy 22: Untestable Claim

Suppose you overhear one person say to another, "I hear you are mentally
ill." The other person emphatically denies the claim. The accuser follows up
with "Then you must be worse off than I ever expected! We all know that
many mentally troubled people go for help but that the worst cases involve
those who will not even admit there is a problem. They are both troubled and
deluded, and so are you." What can the accused possibly say in his defense?
There are two main possibilities:

1. Yes, I am mentally troubled, but I'm working on it.

2. No, I'm not mentally troubled, and please buzz off.

If he chooses option 1, then he is admitting to a problem of some sort. But if
he chooses option 2, then the accuser will retort that he is worse off than she
ever imagined! So the accused seems to be admitting to problems irrespective
of the option he chooses. It is a classic lose-lose situation. The problem with

Calvin and Hobbes

by Bill Watterson

Here is a classic example of an untestable claim. CALVIN AND HOBBES © Watterson. Reprinted with permission of UNIVERSAL PRESS SYNDICATE. All rights reserved.

the original claim is that there are no grounds for calling it into question. It is somewhat like saying, "Heads, I win; tails, you lose." The accused should respond, "Is there any *possible* evidence I could appeal to that would convince you of the unreasonableness of your claim?" If the answer is no, then the original claim is an *untestable* one and should not be taken seriously.

As a general rule all meaningful claims are testable claims. In other words, there is some method of determining (or testing) whether the particular claim is a reasonable one. If no such method exists, then the claim may rightly be categorized as untestable and so not worthy of further consideration.

EXERCISE 6.4

For each of the following, identify the fallacy, and indicate how it is committed.

★ 1. I met a Scotsman I didn't like. You can't trust any of them.

2. His sneezing always precedes his headaches, so we know that his sneezing causes his headaches.

3. The world is currently five minutes old. All apparent memories, fossils, historical documents, and the like were all planted by God when the universe was created five minutes ago.

★ 4. A study shows that 70% of Americans do not support Senator Wilson's plan.

5. He clearly believes in himself, and I think we should believe in him too.

6. Only 5% of our customers are significantly unhappy with our service.

★ 7. It's true because it's true.

8. Edwin dumped me, but I shouldn't be surprised, as all men are morons.

9. She has only two hits in her last ten at bats. She's definitely in a slump.

★ 10. All of that belongs to me because you're simply not entitled to it.

11. You just say you agree with me. You really and truly disagree with everything I have ever said, though you often claim to agree with me.

12. "Everything you read, when he [Adolf Hitler] came in he was good. They built tremendous highways and got all the factories going." (Marge Schott, quoted in the *Louisville Courier-Journal*)

★ 13. No product is more highly recommended than ours.

14. I've met four Irishmen in my life, and it's obvious none of them can be trusted.

15. "NOW (National Organization for Women) represents maybe 1 or 2 percent of the population." (Rush Limbaugh, *The Way Things Ought to Be*)

★ 16. Cocaine use generally follows marijuana use, so it is reasonable to conclude that marijuana use is a cause of cocaine use.

17. Clinton and Carter were both lousy presidents, and none of the Democratic presidents were any good.

18. Your brain is currently being controlled by tiny, undetectable Martian-implanted devices. That's why you're so wacky!

THE ROLE OF EMOTIONS

Emotions play an important role in arguments. If humans were unemotional creatures like Mr. Spock on *Star Trek,* then arguments would be easier to evaluate and life would be significantly less interesting. We already know that appeals to pity generally make an argument fallacious. But it is not at all clear that all appeals to emotion are illegitimate in the contexts of argument and discussion.

To illustrate, think about this example:

A mother tells her daughter that her dropping out of school is wrong and that it will hurt her (the mother) and others greatly.

Is this explicit appeal to emotions ("If you do it, I'll be hurt") illegitimate? It does not seem so. The emotional effects of our decisions on those close to us is relevant to the decision-making process. If the mother insisted that this was the only relevant factor, then the weight attached to it would be exaggerated, and it would be a fallacious appeal to emotion. But if the emotional effects are presented as only one relevant factor—along with, say, the best interests of the daughter and of society—then such an approach is clearly appropriate, and no fallacy is being committed.

Note that whether or not the mother will be upset does not, by itself, tell us whether the daughter's action is wrong. The mother has made two different, though related, claims:

FRANK & ERNEST® by Bob Thaves

Some questions do not easily fit in a true-false format. Frank & Ernest reprinted by permission of Newspaper Enterprise Association, Inc.

1. It is wrong to drop out of school.
2. Her dropping out will upset her mother and others.

The mother's appeal to emotions is clearly relevant to claim 2, but it is doubtful that it is relevant to claim 1. Apparently some appeals to emotion are legitimate, while others are not.

Consider one more example:

Defense attorney: "Ladies and gentlemen of the jury, Mr. Jones is charged with first-degree murder. But look at him! He was abused as a child, never had a father, was drawn into crime by older siblings, and one day decided he had had enough. Can you honestly find him guilty when he has endured such suffering and mental anguish?"

Here we have a straightforward appeal to an emotion, namely, pity. Are such emotions relevant to the issue of Jones's guilt? It would seem not. The fact that we might be inclined to feel sorry for Jones and his horrible upbringing does not change the fact that he is probably guilty. But if the issue is how severe his sentence should be, emotional appeals clearly are relevant. If there are extenuating circumstances and the offender shows genuine remorse (another emotion), he or she is likely to receive a lighter sentence.

It is not always evident when an appeal to emotion is legitimate and when it is not. Understanding the context of the appeal to emotion is crucial in helping us determine whether it was a fallacious appeal or one that was relevant and legitimate.

SUMMARY

Fallacies, or flawed or defective arguments, can be both formal and informal. Some fallacies are easily identified, while others tend to resist easy detection. Familiarity with the various fallacies helps us realize how often in everyday life fallacious reasoning takes place. Most of the fallacies shift attention away from what we are most interested in: whether a particular claim is supported by good enough reason(s) for us to believe it. People often use fallacious reasoning unknowingly, but sometimes people intentionally use these deceptive forms of reasoning. People also often include appeals to emotion in their arguments—again, sometimes inappropriately.

EXERCISE 6.5

For each of the following, identify the fallacy committed, and indicate how the fallacy is committed.

★ 1. Either I win the lottery or I will be flat broke.

   2. If Edna ditches Lou, then Betty will be ecstatic. And since Betty is ecstatic, Edna must have ditched Lou.

   3. If you eat that Oreo, the next thing you know you will want to eat another and another and another. You will gain weight, develop heart disease, and die prematurely. So don't eat that Oreo!

★ 4. If Karisa loves Ed, then Ed will be happy. Karisa does not love Ed, so he is very unhappy.

   5. Those who disagree with my views on welfare must believe that we should never help anyone in need for any reason.

   6. If you don't cooperate, I may have to call Cousin Vito in the city.

★ 7. Are you still as sorry a creature as you always have been?

   8. I've met two Brazilians in my life, and it is obvious that none of them can be trusted.

   9. Do you still hold to the Neolithic view that all humans are primitive and clueless?

★ 10. Ronald Reagan was a fan of the Baby Ruth candy bar, and you should be too.

   11. You call me stupid? At least my IQ is in double digits.

   12. Everyone believes that Elvis is still alive, so you should too.

★ 13. He's losing badly, so he should be allowed to take five turns in a row.

   14. Nobody can prove God's nonexistence, so Ralph is justified in believing that God does exist.

   15. One bad action deserves another.

★ 16. But he was so sincere and full of statistics. How could he be wrong?

   17. Elliot gets fined whenever he speeds, so we know he is a fine man.

   18. If you don't give my business special consideration, the boys and I will remember you at election time.

★ 19. If you don't get an A on the physics exam, you might as well not try at all.

20. Myron always loses love and love (6-0 and 6-0) whenever he plays tennis. He is the most loving man I know.

EXERCISE 6.6

For each of the following, identify the fallacy committed. A few may have more than one fallacy.

★ 1. "Kevorkian had very good luck with *60 Minutes,* too, framing the issue on his terms as a stark choice between a lethal injection or pointless suffering." (John Leo, *U.S. News & World Report*)

2. My dog ate my paper, my car broke down, and my grandma just died.

3. "PETA's (People for the Ethical Treatment of Animals) real mission is destroying capitalism." (Rush Limbaugh, *The Way Things Ought to Be*)

★ 4. "This is the last straw, I know that my opponent was committed to the State Department policy of appeasement toward Communism in the Far East, but I never dreamed she would stick to it even after we were attacked." (Stephen Ambrose, *Nixon: The Education of a Politician 1913–1962*)

5. "I once asked a long-haired maggot-infested FM-type environmentalist wacko who he thought was threatening the owl." (Rush Limbaugh, *The Way Things Ought to Be*)

6. "Well, let me tell you what they [the Democrats] did." (George Bush) This was in response to questions concerning his knowledge of some morally questionable campaign tactics used by the Republican party in the 1988 presidential election.

★ 7. "But I need a C or better to stay in the teacher education program, so you've got to change my grade from a D to a C."

8. She didn't help me with my homework, so I won't help her with hers.

9. People who support abortion do so only because it's cheaper to abort than to have the baby and raise it.

★ 10. "There is a distinct American culture—rugged individualism and self-reliance—which made America great." (Rush Limbaugh, *35 Undeniable Truths*)

11. "Sexual harassment . . . it's everyone's responsibility." (ad)

12. "This is undoubtedly a weakness. It [the opposition of the intellectuals and liberals] lays us open to the charge of being 'hicks' and 'rubes' and 'drivers of second-hand Fords.' We admit this." (Hiram Wesley Evans, "The Klan's Fight for Americanism," in *The Twenties*)

★ 13. "Some people are clearly born into more favorable circumstances than others; therefore, not everyone is equal." (Letter to the editor) (The attack here is on

Jefferson's famous words "We hold these truths to be self-evident that all men [people] are created equal.")

14. "Do they really need to shred our Constitution to persuade them to trade with us?" (Pat Buchanan)

15. "If there were a photo op involved, Giuliani would be handing these two quality-of-life vigilantes the key to the city. Instead, police arrested them." (Karen Houppert, "Jailhouse Shock," in *The Village Voice*)

★ 16. "Is not woman destined to conduct the rising generation of both sexes, at least through all the primary stages of education? Has not the Author of nature preadapted her, by constitution, and faculty, and temperament for this noble work?" (Horace Mann, "Eighth Annual Report of the Secretary of the Board of Education," in *The Way We Lived*)

17. "How could he have lied?" (This was a common reaction to President Clinton's sincere and public denial of having had "sexual relations" with Monica Lewinsky.)

EXERCISE 6.7

For each of the following, identify the fallacy or fallacies committed.

★ 1. "The natural and proper timidity and delicacy which belongs to the female sex evidently unfits it for many of the occupations of civil life." (The Supreme Court in *Bradwell v. Illinois*, 1872)

2. "Of all car owners, 68% favor the Republican candidate, so he should win in a landslide." (*Literary Digest*, 1936)

3. "Because I'm here." (The response of a somewhat inebriated friend of mine to the question "Why aren't you with your girlfriend?")

★ 4. "How the hell did they [Asians, Koreans, Vietnamese, Indians, Russians, and Hispanics] get in this country?" (John Rocker)

5. "That's why it is the most dangerous word in America. Once you start accepting it, you will tolerate anything—drugs, gangs, poor schools, teen pregnancy." (Carl Chancellor, "Toleration of the N Word Is Plain Ignorance")

6. "How do I know this? Because I do." (Rush Limbaugh, *The Way Things Ought to Be*)

★ 7. Since propane prices always rise with the advent of colder temperatures, the lower temperatures must be the cause of the increased propane prices.

8. "Why do actors engage in propaganda for the environmentalist wackos?" (Rush Limbaugh, *The Way Things Ought to Be*)

9. "Faith may be defined briefly as an illogical belief in the occurrence of the improbable." (H. L. Mencken)

★ 10. "You are a godless atheist." (letter to Ellen Goodman, cited in her "Schools Can Teach About Religion Role in Society")

11. All men are jerks.

12. "It's that she [Madonna] has reached that pitch of egomania at which celebrity supposes itself oracular." (Joseph Sobran, "Madonna Is a Vapid Pop Figure," in *Culture Wars*)

★ 13. If you're liberal then you will vote for her. And since you voted for her, you must be a liberal.

14. I know she is unemployed because she is not presently working.

15. If God exists, then the Cubs will win the World Series in the next hundred years. The Cubs will win the World Series in the next hundred years, so God must exist.

★ 16. If you pass that law, then surely another will follow. Eventually the government will regulate whom we can talk to and what we can do even in the privacy of our own homes.

17. He cut me off, so I gave him a piece of my mind.

18. "[John] Rocker is a muscle-twitching, wide-eyed specimen who happens to fling a baseball at high speed." (George Vecsey, "Ted Should Just Fire the Bigot")

EXERCISE 6.8

For each of the following, identify the fallacy.

★ 1. No one sells more cars than McCarthy Ford.

2. "So long as a regime, however repressive, allied itself with the United States' interests in the Cold War, Secretary of Stage Haig would embrace it—as so many of his predecessors had done." (Ken Silvers, "Still in Control," in *Mother Jones*)

3. If you regulate Uzis and AK-47s, then the next thing you know they'll want to regulate handguns and hunting rifles. Eventually, even kitchen knives and what we do in the privacy of our own homes will be regulated.

★ 4. "Only fruits wear earrings." (Marge Schott)

5. "[Whittaker] Chambers was a short, pudgy, unattractive, intelligent, and intensely self-conscious man." (Thomas Reeves, *The Life and Times of Joe McCarthy*)

6. "In any hut in any village on the planet, one world leader is *honored* and *loved* above all others. Spoken in a thousand dialects his name is still George Bush." (Phil Gramm, "Had the Congress Said Yes")

★ 7. "Reagan's obsession with tax cuts went back to the days when he and others like him in Hollywood made the kind of money that placed them in the highest tax bracket." (William C. Berman, *America's Right Turn*)

8. "Mr. Clinton better watch out if he comes down here. He'd better have a bodyguard." (Senator Jesse Helms, quoted in *The News & Observer*)

9. "I can only assume you are in an extremely challenged mental state or suffered a serious head injury." (letter to Ellen Goodman, cited in her "Schools Can Teach About Religion Role in Society")

★ 10. "So there it [his radio show] was, this unique blend of humor, irreverence, and the serious discussion of events with a conservative slant." (Rush Limbaugh, *The Way Things Ought to Be*)

11. "These hip outlaws made revolution look like fun." (Todd Gitlin, *The Sixties*)

12. *Ed:* "I hear that you're mentally ill."

    Fred: "I am not!"

    Ed: "Won't even admit it, huh? You're sicker than I ever imagined!"

★ 13. "Andrea Dworkin is a lunatic fringe queen." (Cathy Young, "Should Women Be More Modest?" in *Slate*)

14. "If you commit a crime, you are guilty." (Rush Limbaugh, *35 Undeniable Truths*)

15. I'm not going to forgive her whether she apologizes or not.

★ 16. "You call me a conservative? Well, you're a McCarthy-loving, fascist reactionary."

EXERCISE 6.9

For each of the following, identify the fallacy.

★ 1. They're out to get me. I don't have any evidence, but all these people are just pretending to be nice to me, but they are really out to get me.

2. "Thick-headed." (Description in a commercial of both a popular kind of root beer and an individual who keeps wondering aloud about bills from his bachelor party in his new wife's presence.)

3. "Neither of my parents went to high school and yet my momma had a dream. . . . (Phil Gramm)

★ 4. "The homicide rate in North Dakota went up 38% last year."

5. Why did we attack Moldavia? It's simple: they attacked us first.

6. Whenever Sally gets a cold, she also gets a fever. She now believes that the cold is the cause of the fever.

★ 7. "In the military he [Alexander Haig] was the ultimate perfumed prince who brown-nosed his way to the top by always being a horse holder to a top guy." (David Hackworth)

8. Nine out of ten doctors endorse Snooz-all.

9. "From 1992 to 1998, prosecutions have been cut almost in half." (Charlton Heston, "Truth and Consequences")

★ 10. "All of them [blacks] are bad news."

11. Over 95% of people polled favored this proposal.

12. "It's time for choosing: their way of more taxes or our way of more opportunity." (Phil Gramm)

★ 13. "We do not believe that it is right to keep the Indians out of civilization in order that certain picturesque aspects of savagery and barbarism may continue to be within reach of the traveler and the curious, or even of the scientific observer. In the objectionable 'Indian dances' which are breaking out at many points we see not a desirable maintenance of racial traits, but a distinct reversion toward barbarism and superstition." (Frederick M. Binder and David M. Reimers, *The Way We Lived*)

14. "This obsession with abortion and lesbian rights became entrenched in the women's movement in about 1978. . . . I date it from the 1978 conference that was chaired by Congresswoman Bella Abzug of New York." (Rush Limbaugh, *The Way Things Ought to Be*)

15. "All liberals eat lunch. Cathy Young eats lunch. Therefore, Cathy Young is a liberal." (argument pattern attributed to Cathy Young by Wendy Shalit, "Should Women Be More Modest?" in *Slate*)

★ 16. "Who's to blame? Who do you believe started the fire at the Branch Davidian compound at Waco? The Branch Davidians? Law enforcement? Not sure?" (*Time*)

17. "What we should change is a Democratic Congress that wastes precious time on partisan matters of absolutely no relevance to the needs of the average American." (Ronald Reagan)

18. "A dental rinse was described as reducing 'plaque on teeth by over 300%.' Now that's effective!" (cited in *The New York Times*)

★ 19. "You pinko liberal." (Archie Bunker)

EXERCISE 6.10

For each of the following, identify the fallacy or fallacies.

★ 1. "The old southern voice that made the Negroes jump and run to their holes like rats, is told to shut up, for the Negro of today is not the same as Negroes were thirty years ago. So it is no use talking about how Negroes ought to be kept at the bottom where God intended them to stay; the Negro is not expected to stay at the bottom." (Ida Wells, quoted in Leon Litwack, *Trouble in Mind: Black Southerners in the Age of Jim Crow*)

2. "We have to raise the car-rental tax as high as we can possibly do it. . . . We have to look at opportunities like that to just screw them [visitors to the 2002 Winter Olympics]" (Jim Bradley, mayoral candidate, Salt Lake City)

3. "And that, ladies and gentlemen, is the legacy of the Bush years: the slowest economic growth for any four-year presidential term since World War II. An economy crippled by debt and deficit. The fading of the American dream. Working-class families sliding back down toward poverty, deprivation, inexplicable violence." (Mario Cuomo, "Nominating Address")

★ 4. "The Klan, therefore, has now come to speak for the great mass of Americans of the old pioneer stock. We believe that it does fairly and faithfully represent them, and our proof lies in their support." (Homer Evans, "The Klan's Fight," in *The Twenties*)

5. Some believe that if Johnson is elected, then the economy will improve. But the economy will not improve, since Johnson will not get elected.

6. "By January of 1989, the Reagan-Bush economic program had created 19 million new jobs." (Phil Gramm)

★ 7. "Under the Reagan Doctrine, one by one, it was the communist dominos that began to fall. First, Grenada was liberated by U.S. airborne troops and the U.S. Marine Corps. Then, the mighty Red Army was driven out of Afghanistan with American weapons. In Nicaragua, that squalid Marxist regime was forced to hold free elections—by Ronald Reagan's contra army—and the communists were thrown out of power. Fellow Americans, we ought to remember, it was under our party that the Berlin Wall came down, and Europe was reunited. It was under our party that the Soviet Empire collapsed and the captive nations broke free." (Pat Buchanan)

8. "Mortimer Adler, associate editor of the Great Books of the Western World—part of the classics, for those of you in Rio Linda—explains that in the great tradition of Western thought, from Plato right down to the nineteenth century, it was almost universally held that man and man alone is a rational animal." (Rush Limbaugh, *The Way Things Ought to Be*)

9. "We should offer lump-sum payments to terminally ill patients who agree to commit suicide. But why stop with the terminally ill? The same bribe could be offered to any medically costly citizen." (John Leo, *U.S. News & World Report*)

★ 10. "This Administration is the 'Barnum & Bailey' of American law enforcement. It's all about the show and the spotlight of the news media circus, and nothing about enforcing existing federal laws to take armed criminals, one by one, off the streets of America." (Wayne LaPierre, news release from the NRA)

11. "[There is] no question that an admission of making false statements to government officials and interfering with the FBI and CIA is an impeachable offense." (Bill Clinton)

12. "The [Black] Panthers are still being punished for the violence of a decade of struggle in which crimes were committed on both sides. Policemen were killed, it is true (though far more Panthers were killed *by* police). But it is no secret that violence and criminality by police was a desperate issue in the Black community, then as now." (Terry Bisson, "The Black Panthers: Where Are They Now?" in *New York Newsday*)

★ 13. "You share some of their less commendable traits, such as a highly one-sided view of male-female relations and a cavalier attitude toward evidence." (Cathy Young, *Slate*)

14. "We've got to have some common sense about a disease [AIDS] transmitted by people deliberately engaging in unnatural acts." (Jesse Helms)

15. "Babbling bimbos and financial chicanery surround him, old cronies rot behind bars, new accusations explode almost daily—but America is just wild about Bill [Clinton]. (John Blosser, "Why America Still Loves Bill!" in *National Enquirer*)

★ 16. "This eminently reasonable approach, as thoughtful as it is fair, has produced a student body with a significant minority component whose record of academic success is outstanding." (Gerald Ford, "Inclusive America, Under Attack," in *The New York Times*).

17. The plane never crashed, it simply made "tragic unavoidable contact with the ground."

18. If you are a genius, then I am an alien from outer space. Since you are not a genius, then I am not a space alien.

EXERCISE 6.11

For the following two passages, identify each fallacy.

★ 1.   I read rapidly through what he gave me. Then I read it a second time, more carefully. When I'd finished the second reading, I was certain the Senator had just selected the wrong document. I no longer recall just what was in it, but it was a letter from one Army officer or government official to another, and it didn't seem to prove anything about anything. I told [Senator Joseph] McCarthy that as far as I could see, it was a pretty routine piece of correspondence.

"You're certainly right about that," he said. "Don't get me wrong, now. I didn't mean you'd find the whole story there. Standing alone it doesn't mean much. I know that just as well as you do. But it's a link in a chain. It's one piece in a jigsaw puzzle. When you've seen some of these other documents, you'll know what I mean."

This was reassuring. In fact, I felt a bit ashamed of myself for expecting to master a complex situation in a few minutes. I read the next document McCarthy handed me. "Now, when you put these two together," he said, "you get a picture." The second document was mainly a listing of names. None of them meant anything to me. I tried to think what connection they might have with the letter I'd just read or with Senator Baldwin. I tried to "put them together," as McCarthy had advised, and "get a picture." No picture came. I confessed this to McCarthy.

"Exactly," he said. "That's exactly my point. Those names mean nothing to you. They didn't mean anything to me, either, when I began to look into this conspiracy. But they're going to mean something to you—I can guarantee you that." (Richard Rovere, *Senator Joe McCarthy*)

★ 2. Dear Editor,

 I am writing in response to Buford Olson's letter which was written in support of the view that animals have the same rights as human beings. Well, I think Buford is a tree-hugging, bleeding-heart, California wacko. From what egg was he hatched? I argue that if animals are intelligent, then they have rights, and since they are not intelligent, they don't have any rights, period. He says he's interested in the welfare of animals, but we all know that the American welfare system is royally messed up. The only reason he supports animals rights is because his mother works at the local animal shelter (an appropriate place for her). If you grant Buford's claim that animals have the same rights as humans, the next thing you know animals will want social security, want to run for political office, get elected, and our cherished traditions will go down the drain. Everyone knows the animal rights wackos are nuts and shouldn't be taken seriously. If Buford and his fellow mental midgets don't shape up, then me and the boys will boycott Buford's place of business (that'll learn him). I recently read that Bill Clinton is against animal rights, and I think all god-fearing Americans should stand up to these dress-wearing granola eaters. Either we stand up to Buford and his fellow hatch-lings, or our country goes to the dogs! I conclude by calling on my fellow Americans to take a stand against this insidious plot to corrupt and destroy all that we hold dear to our hearts. And if Buford happens to meet an un-timely end, then I won't lose any sleep.

Articulately yours,

Iggy Norant

GLOSSARY

fallacy A flawed or defective argument that may still be persuasive and even convincing.

affirming the consequent A formally invalid pattern of reasoning that takes this form: If A, then B; B [affirming the consequent]; therefore, A.

denying the antecedent A formally invalid pattern that takes this form: If A, then B; not A [denying the antecedent]; therefore, not B.

appeal to pity A fallacy of relevance whereby the claimant shifts the focus away from the supporting reasons to the potential negative consequences for the claim-ant. Some appeals to emotion (including pity) can be legitimate, but many are not; context is the crucial factor.

appeal to authority A form of reasoning that is fallacious if the claimant strays outside his or her area(s) of expertise; it is perfectly acceptable if the claimant actually is an authority in the area in question.

appeal to popular opinion A fallacy of relevance whereby, even if everyone believes X to be true, this in no way guarantees that X is true or that it is reasonable to believe that X is true.

abusive ad hominem A fallacy of relevance whereby claimants are personally attacked, rather than having the supporting reasons for their claim called into question.

"you, too" ad hominem   A fallacy of relevance whereby person A, who has been accused of being guilty of X by person B, responds by claiming that person B is even worse with respect to X than A is. Person A completely ignores whether he or she actually is guilty of X.

appeal to force   A fallacy of relevance whereby someone threatens force (physical, economic, political) if the other person does not agree with his or her view on a particular matter. Such an approach completely ignores the reasons offered in support of the claim in question.

two wrongs make a right   A common form of fallacious reasoning that involves fundamental issues in ethics. The fact that person A has wronged person B is hardly grounds for B to treat A in an immoral or otherwise unacceptable fashion.

appeal to ignorance   A fallacy of relevance whereby not knowing whether X is true does not count as evidence in favor of either X or ~X. It merely encourages us to withhold or suspend judgment until and unless more evidence is forthcoming.

false confidence   A fallacy of relevance whereby the fact that someone boldly asserts X does not count, by itself, as evidence for believing in X. Self-confidence may well be relevant to psychological well-being, but it has no direct bearing on the central issues of truth and rationality.

prejudicial language   A fallacy of language whereby emotionally charged language (either positive or negative) is used in an attempt to influence how someone perceives a claim.

equivocation   A fallacy of language whereby words or phrases in an argument are used in two or more senses, thus making the argument invalid.

straw man   A fallacy of misrepresentation whereby an opponent's argument is (often intentionally) distorted or caricatured and so made to look weaker than it actually is. The degree of distortion or exaggeration may range from slight to severe.

slippery slope   The claim that event A, seemingly inevitably, leads to event B and ultimately to event F, which is a particularly bad or undesirable state of affairs. This mode of arguing is fallacious if there is no close causal connection between event A and the subsequent events.

complex question   A fallacy of misrepresentation whereby two questions are rolled into one rather deceptive question.

false dilemma   A fallacy of misrepresentation whereby two options are presented when there are actually more than two; should not be confused with genuine dilemmas, of which there are many in life.

begging the question   A fallacy of poor reasoning whereby the premise(s) of an argument merely states (or assumes) the conclusion the claimant is trying to establish. Whenever we can state the premise(s) and the conclusion with the same words, there is good reason to think this fallacy has been committed.

common cause   A fallacy of poor reasoning whereby the fact that event C always follows event B does not necessarily mean that B is the cause of C. The two events may be accidentally related, or they may both be the effect (result) of another event A.

hasty generalization   A fallacy of poor reasoning whereby a broad or general conclusion is based on a relatively small and/or limited sample or on what might well be stereotypes, whims, or prejudices.

misleading statistics A fallacy whereby statistics are used in a deceptive or misleading fashion. Among other things the statistics cited may be out of context, distorted, or based on a limited sample; or they may be based on faulty questions or sampling techniques.

untestable claims A fallacy whereby claims that have the appearance of sanity are in fact essentially untestable.

CHAPTER 7

Knowledge and Worldview

He wouldn't know a good argument if it bit him.
—Emmett Kelly

In this chapter we will look at a number of issues related to arguments and their evaluation. The sources of knowledge, the conditions for accepting premises as reasonable, the concept of rationality (or reasonability), the importance of background knowledge, and the concept of worldview will all be examined. This will help us to see that arguments and their evaluation do not occur in a vacuum, but always in some larger context.

THE SOURCES OF KNOWLEDGE

How do we know what we know? That is, what are the sources of our knowledge? Consider the following four claims, which are fundamentally different because they involve appeals to four different sources of knowledge.

1. I was in Kalamazoo yesterday. (memory)
2. I see a green plant. (sense perception)
3. I am presently thinking. (introspection)
4. 2 plus 2 equals 4. (reason)

Let's examine these sources in more detail.

Memory

We know that many things occurred in the past because we remember them happening. And given that generally our memories are fairly reliable, especially about the recent past, they are justifiably seen as a source of knowledge.

To illustrate, look at these claims:

1. I watched the Masters golf tournament yesterday.
2. I remember John Kennedy's assassination.
3. I watched the Beatles on television in 1964.
4. My wife and I were married in 1979.

In each case I am appealing to a knowledge of the past that is established by my ability to remember the past. And given that other people also have memories, if I doubt whether a particular event actually happened or happened in a certain way, then I can cross-check my memories with theirs.

Even though memory is a generally reliable source of information, it does not *generate* or *create* new beliefs the way that, say, sense perception does. For example, if I go to a soccer match in 1982, my original belief is that I am seeing a soccer match. Years later I may remember this event, but my memories merely put me in touch with the original event; they do not shape it in any way. So, even though memory connects us to our past, it does not make knowledge possible the way the other three sources do.

As helpful as memory is, it is by no means infallible. In other words our memories are not perfect but may be mistaken for many reasons:

1. The event remembered happened a long time ago.
2. We never had a good grasp of the event in the first place (maybe it was foggy or dark).
3. We sometimes confuse one event with another (Was it Bob or Eddie who had the red suspenders on?).
4. We have a poor memory in general.
5. We have an unfortunate tendency to remember the past in the way most favorable to us.

In short, though our memory claims are often accurate, they are far from infallible and should not be viewed as such. At one time or another, we have all said something along the lines of, "I'm so certain that I parked in Lot 58 that I will bet you $20 that this is so." And almost all of us have later found out that in some cases we were mistaken!

Sense Perception

Another possible source of knowledge claims is sense perception. Many of our everyday claims are based on our five senses: sight, hearing, smell, taste, and touch. Look at these examples:

1. I saw Paula at the grocery store.
2. I feel the chair on which I am sitting.
3. I smell pizza.

4. I hear Garth Brooks singing.

5. I taste Cheerios.

All of these claims are tied to one or more of our five senses. But can we trust our senses all the time? Unfortunately, as with memory, claims based on the five senses are not infallible.

Consider the following examples:

1. In the fog Eddie thought he saw a black car go by.

2. Otis heard what sounded like thunder.

3. Without her glasses on, Bonnie mistook the cat for a skunk.

In the first example the car actually was dark blue, but the poor visibility made it difficult to know this. In the next example, what Otis actually heard was a jet plane breaking the sound barrier. As for Bonnie, her less-than-perfect eyesight makes such misperceptions far more likely. As the philosopher Descartes and many others have pointed out, even though our senses may be generally reliable, this hardly represents the level of certainty we would like to have.

Introspection

For those of your currently reading what I'm writing, is it true that you are also currently thinking? We are inclined to answer in the affirmative. But how do we *know* (1) that we are presently thinking and (2) what we are presently thinking? None of our five senses gives us the answer to either question, but we clearly seem able to answer both. How is this possible?

The answer is that we have another source of knowledge, namely, introspection. **Introspection** can be roughly defined as looking inward, not in a literal sense but in a figurative or nonliteral sense. Whenever we think about ourselves and our lives, we are being introspective. For example, if Darcy is currently thinking about a red sweater, it is obvious to her that what she is thinking about is a red sweater, because introspection provides her with immediate access to what is going on in her mind. Just as our five senses enable us to perceive much of the world around us, so introspection enables us to perceive our "inner" world.

Thinkers like John Watson and B. F. Skinner have questioned whether introspection is a legitimate source of knowledge. Watson and Skinner thought that appealing to introspection suffers from two defects: (1) there is no way to verify or prove what someone else is thinking, and (2) focusing on what individuals are thinking is excessively subjective. But most philosophers accept it as a valuable source of knowledge—one of the few ways to truly know what is going on in one's own mind.

Reason

We have yet another source of knowledge: our ability to reason. We know that 2 plus 2 equals 4 and that triangles have three sides. These are widely held to be truths of reason. Our ability to think, logically and abstractly, gives us access to truths such as these.[1] Philosophers like Immanuel Kant and, more recently, Noam Chomsky have argued that we have natural abilities to organize and structure the data that our five senses provide. Ideally we need to gather information from all four sources of knowledge if we are to organize our view of the world around us. Though being familiar with the four sources of knowledge is important, it is also important to be aware of the concept of reasonability (or rationality).

EXERCISE 7.1

With the four sources of knowledge in mind, do the following:

1. Write two sentences that make claims involving memory (for example, "I saw my mother last Sunday").

2. Write two sentences that make claims involving sense perception (for example, "I see a computer monitor").

3. Write one sentence that appeals to something known through introspection (for example, "I am presently thinking about the words I am typing").

4. Discuss what kinds of knowledge human reason might provide.

REASONABILITY

Obviously we all have beliefs. Even if someone says, "I have no beliefs," we might ask, "Well, what about that claim?"—for even the claim "I have no beliefs" itself involves at least one belief.

Given that we have beliefs, is it true that some of our beliefs may be more reasonable than others? The answer seems to be yes. Let's consider some possibilities:

1. 2 plus 2 equals 5.
   Comment: This belief is certainly false.

2. Elvis is still alive.
   Comment: This belief is false with a very high degree of probability.

3. Jesse Ventura will win the presidency someday.
   Comment: This belief is likely to be false.

4. There are an even number of grains of sand on the beaches of New Jersey.
   Comment: This claim has 50% probability, making it equally reasonable for us to believe it or not believe it.

---

[1] One is encouraged to consult, for example, Roderick Chisholm, *Theory of Knowledge* (Englewood Cliffs, NJ: Prentice-Hall, 1977), and Richard Foley, *The Theory of Epistemic Rationality* (Cambridge, MA: Harvard University Press, 1986), for a more sophisticated treatment of this issue.

Calvin and Hobbes   by Bill Watterson

There are many things about which we cannot have 100% certainty. CALVIN AND

HOBBES © Watterson. Reprinted with permission of UNIVERSAL PRESS SYNDICATE. All rights reserved.

5. The Los Angeles Lakers will make the playoffs this year.
   Comment: The experts think this is more likely to happen than not, though there is a significant chance that they could be wrong.

6. Physical objects exist.
   Comment: This belief has a very high level of probability attached to it. But it is not guaranteed because we cannot prove that we are not being deceived all the time by a powerful and hidden cosmic deceiver.

7. 2 plus 2 equals 4.
   Comment: This belief is certainly true.

Clearly some of our beliefs are more reasonable than others. And we need to know not only what our beliefs are but also how reasonable they are. We would not want to invest all our life savings in a venture that had only a 62% success rate; even though the odds would be in our favor, the chance of significant and catastrophic failure would be much too high. Similarly, if you have a headache and take medication for it, there is no guarantee of pain relief, though there is a good probability that you will get some relief. Life offers few certainties, but reasonable people generally will gear their practices to the probability of the beliefs involved.

Many philosophers urge that all our beliefs be reasonable—or, to put it another way, that none of our beliefs be unreasonable. But what would be so bad about acting on unreasonable beliefs? Let us consider two scenarios:

Scenario 1: Pam is looking for a place to invest her life savings. The Fly by Night Investment Company contacts her and assures her that her investment has a good chance (better than 50%) of losing money. Should Pam invest in this company? Certainly not, because she would unreasonably endanger her life savings.

Scenario 2: Alan is considering asking Abby to marry him. But he believes with high probability that Abby is immature, prone to be unfaithful, and domineering. Should he make a lifelong commitment to Abby in the belief that he will be happy? The answer is a definite no.

These scenarios illustrate some of the problems that can arise if we act on unreasonable beliefs. Given that reasonable beliefs are based on evidence of some sort, we need to have some way of determining what to accept as true and what to reject as untrue. One way involves knowing some conditions for accepting premises.

CONDITIONS FOR ACCEPTING PREMISES

In an earlier chapter we discussed sound arguments, which have both validity and rationally acceptable premises. The challenge here becomes: How can we know that any given premise is rationally acceptable? In other words, what standards or criteria help us separate rationally acceptable premises from rationally unacceptable ones?

Recall that premises are simply claims that are either true or false. Some premises are more reasonable than others, and we should only believe those that are more likely to be true than not. The four conditions under which it is acceptable to believe a particular premise involve common knowledge, reliability, legitimate authorities, and supporting arguments.

Condition 1: The Claim Is a Matter of Common Knowledge

By this we do not mean that the premise is widely believed. If we accepted a premise solely for that reason, we would be guilty of accepting a fallacious appeal to popular opinion. To be a matter of common knowledge, a premise or claim must be widely believed and have no widely known objections to it.

For example, all of the following would count as examples of common knowledge:

1. The United States is a country.
2. Soccer is a sport.
3. China has many people.
4. The Holocaust happened.

All of these claims can safely be regarded as facts, and the overwhelming majority of able-minded adults believe them. Of course, a few people deny that the Holocaust happened, but these claimants face considerable problems. First, there is a huge body of evidence supporting the belief that it happened, much of it based on reliable eyewitness testimony by Germans and Jews. Second, contrary to what some of these deniers claim, there is no credible evidence to suggest that it did not happen. Given these two facts and the fact that belief in the existence of the Holocaust is widespread, it can safely be considered a matter of common knowledge.

Condition 2: The Claim Is Based on Reliable Testimony

Here we need to evaluate two particular aspects of the claim: its believability and its reliability. With regard to the former, for example, consider the following three claims:

1. I saw a dog yesterday.

2. I met with the president yesterday.

3. I had lunch with Genghis Khan last Tuesday.

The first claim involves a very common occurrence and is therefore very believable.

The other two examples are more problematic. Some people meet every day with the president, and it is not unheard of for him to meet with average American citizens. However, given that very few American citizens ever meet the president, it would be helpful here to have some supporting evidence, such as an autographed picture. In short, we should be open to claims like this, but we should also require more evidence than we would for the first sort of claim.

Finally, seeing as how Genghis Khan has been dead for hundreds of years, we would need some extraordinary evidence to make this claim believable. If we could establish either that humans never died or that some people lived on in other people's bodies (roughly corresponding to the idea of reincarnation), this would make the claim more believable than it would otherwise be. But given that neither of these matters has been established, we should reject the claim.

With regard to the reliability of claims, not all people are equally trustworthy. Unfortunately some may have a history of making claims that turn out to be either partially or entirely false. For example, if I read in the *National Enquirer* that space aliens have settled in New Jersey, I should be inclined to reject the claim. But if three or four established experts made such a claim, then I would have to at least be open to the possibility of the claim being true.

Condition 3: The Claim Is Supported by Appeals to a Legitimate Authority

Suppose Henrik claims that X is true and appeals to Abe, a supposed authority in the appropriate field. Here we should be interested in learning all of the following:

1. **That Abe is a genuine authority in this area.** For example, Abe's having a Ph.D. or similar degree would be a good start. Genuine authorities usually have credentials of some sort, and Abe's credentials need to be evaluated to determine whether he truly is an expert.

> ### *Four Conditions for Accepting Premises*
>
> 1. The claim is a matter of common knowledge.
> 2. The claim is based on reliable testimony.
> 3. The claim is supported by appeals to a legitimate authority.
> 4. The claim is adequately argued for elsewhere.

2. **That Abe is an honest and dependable person.** This tells us that he will make every effort to present information fairly and accurately and that he conducts research in a careful manner.

3. **That Abe's belief concerning X is generally accepted by other experts in the field.** Here we are making an appeal to popular opinion, but only within the context of the experts in this particular field. This will not guarantee that Abe is correct, but it will increase the probability that he is. If there is a divergence of opinion among the experts, then appealing to Abe's expertise will carry far less weight than it would if there were a general consensus.

Condition 4: The Claim Is Adequately Argued for Elsewhere

If the claim in question has been addressed by the claimant or by someone else in another book, article, or the like, then this information can be passed on to readers so that they can evaluate the source cited. Using either a footnote (at the bottom of the page) or an endnote (either at the end of the chapter or the end of the book) is the standard way to pass on such source information to readers.

BACKGROUND KNOWLEDGE

Also relevant to evaluating premises is an awareness of the importance of background knowledge. Various people may evaluate claims differently in light of their own unique experiences in life. **Background knowledge** refers to the sum total of our experiences, including those related to the acquisition of knowledge, up to the present. Given that we all are different and have had different experiences in life, no two people possess the same background knowledge. What might background knowledge include? Here are just a few possibilities:

Your relationship with your parent(s)

Your relationship with your siblings

Your relationship with your friends and peers

Your undergraduate school experiences

Significant events that occurred during childhood, both good and bad

College and/or graduate school

Significant adult relationships with others

Your reaction to significant events

Your work experiences

The way all these were filtered through your personality

The information from these areas make up our background knowledge. And we rely on this background knowledge to make an initial assessment of a claim that we read or hear. So if we hear something that is inconsistent with our background knowledge, we should initially assign it a low probability of being true, at least until we can investigate further.

To illustrate, consider these claims:

1. A boy was electrocuted by a lightning bug.

2. A woman ran the mile in 45 seconds.

3. A man ran the mile in 3 minutes 43 seconds.

4. UFOs have been stealing our top scientists.

First, though I am not an entomologist (insect expert), I do know that lightning bugs do not electrocute people, so I assign this claim a very low initial probability (approaching zero). Similarly, given what we know about current human capabilities, the second example fares no better. The current world record for the mile is around 3 minutes 44 seconds. No human under any conditions could possibly run the mile four times faster than anyone else in history, so this is another candidate for a very low initial probability.

The third example is a bit more difficult. If we find out that the man who supposedly ran a 3:43 mile has run a 3:48 twice before, then we should at least be open to the possibility that he clocked a 3:43. Again, though, it would be helpful to have some supporting evidence: a videotape or reliable witnesses or the like. Five seconds may not seem like a lot of time, but to run the mile five seconds faster than one has ever run it before is highly unusual in track and field. So, though initially we should not assign it the same low probability as the first two claims, we are entitled to remain skeptical pending further evidence.

The fourth example obviously is laughable. Given that the existence of UFOs has hardly been established and that most experts deny their existence, we should assign the claim a very low initial probability. Low-probability events cry out for more evidence, and unless that additional evidence is forthcoming, we clearly are justified in rejecting them. This claim about UFOs abducting scientists is possible in the broadest sense of the word—what philosophers often call a **logical possibility**—but there is absolutely no evidence that anything of this sort has ever happened.

EXERCISE 7.2

★ 1. Carefully consider the following claims. Then rank them in order from most likely to be true (most reasonable) to least likely to be true. Be sure to give reasons for the level of probability you assign to each claim. It might be helpful to assign tentative probabilities (such as 85%) to each claim.

   a. Elvis was alive as of 2000.
   b. If I flip this coin, it will come up heads.
   c. Michael Jordan is one of the ten best basketball players ever.
   d. God exists.
   e. Humans have free will, which involves the ability to choose between options.
   f. Intelligent life exists elsewhere in the universe.
   g. The beaches in New Jersey have an even number of grains of sand.
   h. Abortion is morally right if the mother's life is in danger.
   i. There is an afterlife of some sort.
   j. Material possessions can bring genuine happiness.
   k. Important things in life do not come easily.
   l. The Mets will win a World Series in the next fifty years.
   m. John F. Kennedy was murdered by space aliens.
   n. Physical objects exist.
   o. 2 plus 2 equals 7.
   p. Abraham Lincoln was a good president.
   q. Jesus existed.
   r. Mozart was a musical genius.
   s. Humans need other humans for companionship.

2. Consider the following sets of claims. Then state which item in each set is more reasonable, and why.

   ★ a. 1. Human beings exist.
        2. Dinosaurs exist.

   b. 1. Perseverance pays off in the long run.
      2. Good people get what they deserve in life.

   c. 1. All New Yorkers are nice.
      2. All the New Yorkers I have met are nice.

   ★ d. 1. Miracles are not possible.[2]
        2. Belief in miracles is reasonable.[3]

---

[2] Rudolf Bultmann, a famous twentieth-century New Testament scholar, clearly affirmed this position in his *Kerygma and Myth* (New York: Harper & Row, 1967), p. 5.
[3] This is an accurate summary of the view of Richard Swinburne, a twentieth-century philosopher. See Chapter 12 of his *Existence of God* (Oxford: Clarendon Press, 1979).

e. 1. Belief in God is not reasonable.[4]
   2. Belief in God is reasonable.[5]
f. 1. The environment is the key factor in shaping human personality and behavior.[6]
   2. Free will is the key factor in shaping human destiny.[7]
   3. Biology is the dominant factor in shaping human destiny.[8]

WORLDVIEW

Just as our background knowledge influences how we evaluate things, so does our worldview. Every person has a **worldview:** a comprehensive way of looking at the world that involves attempting to answer some fundamental questions. A worldview is a conceptual scheme or a lens through which everything an individual encounters is filtered. This helps explain why two educated people may have two very different explanations of the same event—because they have two very different worldviews. Humans "have a deep-seated need to form some general picture of the total universe in which they live, in order to be able to relate their own fragmentary activities to the universe as a whole in a way meaningful to them."[9] A well-rounded worldview involves personal beliefs in at least five different areas: God, reality, knowledge, morality, and human nature. Let's take a brief look at each.

The Existence of God

Is there a supreme being of any sort? This question has intrigued and challenged philosophers, theologians, and others for centuries. In Western civilization the question is often asked, "Is there a god?"—with God typically defined as an eternal, all-loving, all-powerful, and all-knowing being. Indeed, Plato, Aquinas, Descartes, Hume, Kant, Marx, Nietzsche, and other prominent philosophers have grappled with the many thorny issues that this question involves, and even today there is little consensus as to what the most reasonable answer might be.

Some philosophers suggest that on the whole it is reasonable to believe that God exists. Some argue that, since the universe is a **contingent** entity—

---

[4]J. L. Mackie clearly advances this claim in his *Miracle of Theism* (Oxford: Clarendon Press, 1982).

[5]Just as there are many twentieth-century atheists, there are also many twentieth-century theists. One example would be Stephen Evans, who defends the reasonability of belief in God in his *Philosophy of Religion* (Downers Grove, IL: InterVarsity Press, 1985).

[6]B. F. Skinner may be the best-known advocate of this view. See his *Beyond Freedom and Dignity* (Harmondsworth: Penguin Books, 1973) for his development of this view.

[7]The French thinker Jean-Paul Sartre develops this view in his *Existentialism and Human Emotions* (New York: Citadel Press, 1957).

[8]Sigmund Freud is probably the best-known advocate of this position. See James Strachey, ed., *New Introductory Lectures on Psychoanalysis,* by Sigmund Freud (New York: Norton, 1999), for more on this.

[9]William Alston, "Problems of Philosophy of Religion," in *The Encyclopedia of Philosophy* (New York: Macmillan, 1972), 6:286.

that is, it exists, but it might not have—and since all events, including the origin of the universe, need a cause to explain their coming into existence, then it is reasonable to believe that God is that cause. This sort of argument, called the cosmological argument, works backward from an effect (the universe or cosmos) to the cause (God).

Other thinkers propose something called the design argument to explain the existence of the universe. They suggest that the universe contains many conditions favorable to the existence of life and that the odds of all these conditions occurring by chance are slim. Thus it is more reasonable to believe that the "design" is the intentional result of a wise and powerful being, namely, God.

In recent years a number of prominent philosophers have argued for the existence of God by appealing to human experience. These thinkers suggest that human experience, carefully considered, can provide us with evidence that points toward the existence of God.

At the same time a number of prominent philosophers have argued for the reasonableness of either atheism (God does not exist) or agnosticism (God may or may not exist). A. J. Ayer[10] and others have proposed that the concept of God is meaningless in that we cannot possibly establish God's existence by appealing to any one or more of our five senses. And since Ayer believed that we acquire all knowledge through our five senses, it logically follows that knowledge of God is not possible and so fruitless to pursue. It is widely believed today that Ayer's approach unreasonably restricts the scope of human knowledge to sense experience, though the controversy remains as to whether belief in the existence of God is reasonable.

Another longstanding objection to belief in God's existence revolves around what has been called the "problem of evil." This argument may be summarized as follows:

1.   There is evil (for example, undeserved suffering) in the world.

2.   Such evil is inconsistent with the existence of an all-loving, all-knowing, and all-powerful being.

∴   It is reasonable to conclude that God does not exist.

This argument has many variations, including this popular one:

1.   There is gratuitous, or pointless, evil in the world (for example, the Holocaust).

2.   There is no reason for God to allow gratuitous evil.

∴   It is reasonable to conclude that God probably does not exist.

---

[10] Ayer's classic work here is his *Language, Truth and Logic* (New York: Dover Books, 1956).

In short, philosophers may disagree as to whether God exists, but they generally agree that it is an issue worth investigating.[11]

The Nature of Reality

A second key component of worldviews involves the nature of reality: Is the universe ultimately physical (material) in nature? Materialists believe that everything that exists is physical matter, while dualists believe the universe is made up of both material objects and immaterial or spiritual entities such as God and the human soul. Another issue concerns the origins of the universe: Was it caused to come into existence? Or did it simply appear at some time, making it a "causeless" fact? Still another relevant issue is whether the universe is eternal or came into existence at some time.

Part of the debate concerning the nature of reality focuses on human consciousness and whether it can be explained by appeal to the (entirely physical) brain or whether it is also reasonable to believe in a nonphysical soul. In this sense human consciousness is a very complex phenomenon. Metaphysical materialists suggest that human consciousness and all that it involves ultimately is reducible to physical matter; metaphysical dualists claim that it is evidence for the existence of a nonphysical human soul. When thinkers reflect on the nature of reality, a key question is, How do we acquire knowledge of the world? This leads us to the third major component of a worldview: the nature of knowledge.

The Nature of Knowledge

With regard to worldviews and the nature of knowledge, several issues are of interest here. First, is knowledge about the world possible, and if so, are there reliable methods that tend to produce genuine knowledge? Second, what are the sources of human knowledge? (We touched on this previously.) Third, is there such a thing as truth? Should we make a distinction between how we think things are (appearance) and how they really are (reality)? If we do this, can we ever be sure that how we view the world reflects the way things actually are?

Religion and religious beliefs provide an interesting example of how difficult it can be to "know" something. Religious beliefs involve both faith and reason. But what exactly is the relationship between these two concepts? For example, is it even possible to have a faith based on reason or evidence of any sort? What about the common twentieth-century belief that faith and reason are mutually incompatible—that you can have one or the other but never

---

[11] The interested reader is encouraged to investigate Richard Swinburne, *The Existence of God* (Oxford: Oxford University Press, 1979), William Rowe, *The Cosmological Argument* (Princeton, NJ: Princeton University Press, 1975), J. L. Mackie, *The Miracle of Theism* (Oxford: Clarendon Press, 1982), and Michael Peterson, *Evil and the Christian God* (Grand Rapids, MI: Baker Book House, 1982). All of these books will challenge persons new to philosophy, but a thoughtful reading should prove rewarding.

THE FAR SIDE   By GARY LARSON

The gods play with Ted and Jerry

A bad day in the making. THE FAR SIDE © FARWORKS, INC. Used by permission. All rights reserved.

both at the same time? Are there good reasons for believing this to be true? Thomas Aquinas, the great thirteenth-century Dominican philosopher and theologian, thought that belief in God can be shown to be rationally probable. In other words, he believed that faith in God can be shown to be a reasonable faith. Other theists, such as Søren Kierkegaard, thought that although God exists faith is more properly a matter of the heart and not the head. Still others, not inclined to believe in God, thought that faith and reason are mutually exclusive—you can have one or the other but not both.

Morality

People seem to be more aware of this aspect of their worldview than any other. The vast majority of adults have some concept of moral right and wrong, as the following common claims suggest:

1. What he did was wrong.

2. She is a bad person.

3. Addictive drugs are not a good thing to dabble in.

4. It is better to give than to receive.

All of these claims are moral claims, in that they all assume a standard by which to judge the things they do. It makes no sense to claim "What he did was wrong" unless there is some moral standard that his behavior fell short of. Imagine how the person who claims that there are no moral standards would feel if you took her car without permission; presumably she would feel that some moral wrong had been committed. Even Meursault, the central character in Albert Camus's *The Stranger,* periodically makes value judgments (such as "I don't like cops") despite his stated belief that we live in a world without values.[12] In other words, the things that we all do every day commit us to certain beliefs about the realm of values, whether we are aware of it or not.

Precisely what makes an action morally right or wrong is a notoriously difficult question. Some have suggested that morality is determined by the culture or society one lives in. According to this view, called **ethical relativism**, moral right and wrong are always relative to a particular culture. Note that ethical relativism comes in both an individual version, in which moral right and wrong are relative to each person, and a cultural version, in which moral right and wrong are relative to one's culture. (This issue will be addressed in more detail in Chapter 8). Others have suggested that at least one moral standard cuts across all cultures and societies, regardless of whether members acknowledge it. According to this view, called **ethical objectivism**, one or more moral principles are binding on all people and all cultures. One possible example of such a principle would be "Do not intentionally kill innocent people."[13]

Ethics also includes what is sometimes called applied ethics. This involves the application of moral theory to specific ethical issues, such as capital punishment, abortion, affirmative action, euthanasia (mercy killing), and gun control. Given the complexity of ethical theory and the strong emotions associated with many of these issues, not surprisingly, such issues are highly controversial.

Human Nature

As with the other components of our worldviews, a discussion of human nature quickly involves us in a host of sticky issues, like the following:

1. Do humans have free will?

2. Are humans merely physical beings, or do they also have a soul?

3. Are humans fundamentally unselfish creatures?

---

[12] Nihilism (from the Latin *nihil,* meaning "nothing") is the belief that we live in a valueless world, one in which nothing is good and nothing is bad. So nihilists believe that there is no such thing as moral right or wrong. Albert Camus (1913–1960) was a great French writer whose novels from the 1930s and 1940s capture the spirit of nihilism.

[13] For a defense of ethical relativism, see William Graham Sumner, *Folkways* (Boston: Ginn, 1906), and J. L. Mackie, *Ethics: Inventing Right and Wrong* (New York: Penguin Books, 1976). For a defense of ethical objectivism, see Louis Pojman, *Ethics: Discovering Right and Wrong,* 2nd ed. (Belmont, CA: Wadsworth, 1995), and James Rachels, *The Elements of Moral Philosophy,* 3rd ed. (Boston: McGraw-Hill, 1999).

4. Is there any sort of life after physical death?

5. Do humans have a basic need to interact with other humans?

Each of these questions is connected to a number of other issues we have discussed here. For example, many thinkers have observed that if humans do not have free will (which can be defined as the ability to do as one pleases) then life will be far less worthwhile than it otherwise would be. If one has no free will, then the idea of autonomy—of being significantly in control of one's life—becomes meaningless. In other words being autonomous means being self-directed as opposed to being controlled by something outside of oneself. Free will is also closely connected to the idea of responsibility, and many have argued that holding someone responsible for an action assumes that the action was done freely. But if there is no free will, then holding people responsible for their actions makes little sense.

PULLING IT ALL TOGETHER

As reflective people we will address each of the five components of a worldview just discussed. Doing so will foster Socrates' idea of the examined life and also help us better understand why we each believe what we do.

We have covered a variety of issues, and it may not be clear how they all tie together. To illustrate, let's consider a few examples.

Worldview and the Problem of Evil

Look at the following argument:

1. There is much evil in the world.

2. There is no life after death.

3. Much of the evil in the world clearly is gratuitous—that is, no greater good occurs.

∴ Belief in God is unreasonable.

How might we respond to this? Let us imagine that this argument is among three people: (1) Thelma, a theist, (2) Andrew, an atheist, and (3) Sean, a skeptic or agnostic. These three individuals probably have different worldviews, given that they have different answers to the question "Does God exist?"

For openers, then, how do they respond to the first premise of the argument? Perhaps surprisingly, all three agree that, however we measure evil, there is a considerable amount of it in the world. How do they know this? Their experiences and those of people they have read or heard about consistently testify to this fact. Given this appeal to experience and their knowledge of

A Worldview

A worldview is a comprehensive way of looking at the world that involves answering some fundamental questions concerning the following:

1. The existence of God

2. The nature of reality

3. The nature of knowledge

4. Morality

5. Human nature

human history, they quite reasonably conclude that premise 1—that there is much evil in the world—is true. So far, so good.

What about the second premise? Here Thelma, Andrew, and Sean might well have three different ideas as to how reasonable this claim is. Suppose Thelma is a Christian theist who believes that death does not bring human existence to an end. For evidence she cites four things: (1) the Bible, especially the New Testament, (2) Christian tradition (Augustine, Aquinas, Luther, and many others believed in an afterlife), (3) the evidence for the resurrection of Jesus, and (4) evidence from cases such as the Edgar Vandy story.[14] Thelma concludes that her belief is a rational one and that the evidence for it outweighs the evidence against it.

For his part the atheist Andrew, not being a Christian, is hardly committed to the veracity of the Scriptures or the evidential value of Christian tradition. Furthermore Andrew rejects the claim that Jesus rose from the dead, citing works by Crossan and Ludemann.[15] And as to the strange case of Edgar Vandy's unusual circumstances, other interpretations of the evidence are possible, and the existing evidence hardly proves the reality of some kind of postmortem existence. So Andrew believes himself rational in endorsing the second premise of the argument.

Not surprisingly the agnostic Sean inhabits a middle ground between the other two. That is, regarding life after death, he neither believes as Thelma does nor disbelieves as Andrew does. Sean is familiar with the evidence cited

[14] See William Rowe, *Philosophy of Religion* (Belmont, CA: Wadsworth, 1978), pp. 45–50. Edgar Vandy was an inventor who died under mysterious circumstances in 1933. His brothers then contacted mediums (psychics), who gave amazingly accurate details concerning his death. The only possible source of this information was (1) Edgar Vandy himself—from the other side of the grave—or (2) the brothers' minds, which the mediums "read"—even though the brothers did not actually meet with the mediums.

[15] See John Dominic Crossan, *The Historical Jesus* (San Francisco: Harper, 1993), and Gerd Ludemann, *What Really Happened to Jesus* (Philadelphia: Westminster, 1993), for more on this.

Calvin and Hobbes   by Bill Watterson

School is tough enough even if life is meaningful. CALVIN AND HOBBES © Watterson. Reprinted with permission of UNIVERSAL PRESS SYNDICATE. All rights reserved.

by both sides, and he is open to both positions, but he finds none of it sufficiently compelling. So, for now at least, he remains skeptical.

Given the disagreement on this key premise, that there is also disagreement about the third premise is not surprising. Thelma believes that there is no gratuitous, or pointless, evil. She concedes that there are some horrendous evils, such as the Holocaust, but she also claims that there is an afterlife. So what is the connection here? She believes that all individuals have the opportunity to have faith in God and that those with true faith will spend eternity in heaven with God. Accordingly she believes that an eternity in a very good place, heaven, more than compensates for any horrendous, and seemingly gratuitous, evil.[16] For Thelma, then, the existence of an afterlife is a key ingredient in her response to the problem posed by the large amount of evil in the world.

Andrew is far from convinced. Given his rejection of any sort of afterlife, Andrew believes there is no greater good, such as the Christian heaven, and that the horrendous evils we know of are not "canceled out" by an afterlife or any other sort of good. For Andrew the belief in horrendous evil combined with the absence of an afterlife or any other possible compensating good means that some evils are genuinely gratuitous and therefore that belief in God is also unreasonable.

Once again, Sean thinks neither side is entirely persuasive. He is not convinced by Thelma's claim that an afterlife in heaven is a response to the reality of horrendous evil, nor is he persuaded by Andrew's claim that gratuitous evil exists. Sean realizes how limited and finite human beings are, and that the issues under discussion are quite complicated. Thus he is not sure he is in any position to know whether horrendous evil is ultimately gratuitous, as Andrew claims, or whether it is overcome or defeated, as Thelma believes. Again, he

---

[16]Thelma's argument here is indebted to one developed by Marilyn Adams, "Horrendous Evils and the Goodness of God," in *The Problem of Evil*, ed. Marilyn Adams and Robert Adams (New York: Oxford University Press, 1990), pp. 209–221.

has read and considered the evidence, but for now he believes the most reasonable stance is skepticism. Of course, he remains open to future evidence and to the possibility of changing his mind.

This imaginary debate is not unlike many of the discussions that take place in the real world. Notice that each claimant bases his or her claims on evidence or reasons, that all are open to the possibility of being mistaken, and that they treat each other with respect and courtesy. Let us now consider one more example.

Worldview and the Trial of President Clinton

Imagine that it's 1998 and the Senate trial of impeached President Clinton is under way. Look at this argument:

1. President Clinton is guilty of high crimes and misdemeanors.

2. He deserves to be punished.

3. His wrongdoings are of a serious nature.

∴ He should be convicted.

For our second imaginary debate our three participants are (1) Urban, a utilitarian, (2) Dana, a deontologist, and (3) Rhonda, a relativist. (These differing ethical orientations are discussed in detail in Chapter 8.) All three are committed to searching out the truth, to basing their beliefs on the evidence, and to treating their fellow debaters with respect. Despite their shared commitments, however, their differing ethical orientations significantly impact their outlook on the Clinton trial.

Let's begin with Urban. Utilitarians focus on the consequences of an action as the key element in determining its rightness or wrongness. They believe that we have a moral duty to perform the act that produces the most happiness or the greatest benefit for the group as a whole. In other words they take an approach along these lines:

1. Determine what the situation or problem is. In this case many people are upset with President Clinton's behavior and believe that he should be punished accordingly.

2. Figure out what the possible courses of action are.

3. Calculate how each action would affect each member of the group involved.

4. Perform the action that maximizes the good of the group.

With respect to step 1, the problem/challenge is whether the Senate should convict President Clinton. As such, the possible courses of action seem to be limited to these:

1. Find the president not guilty.

2. Find the president guilty.

3. Do neither of the preceding, but instead censure the president.

The last option is not grounded in the Constitution as such but is clearly an option available to the Senate. There is the historical precedent of President Andrew Jackson being censured in the 1830s (though this decision was later rescinded).

Calculating how each of the three courses of action might impact the various parties is no easy matter. For openers, what parties would be affected? There seem to be (at least) four such parties:

1. The president himself

2. The office of the presidency

3. Congress

4. The American people

The general consensus seems to be that, given the seriousness of the charges against the president, censure and conviction are the main options before the Senate. Urban is committed to encouraging the Senate to choose the option that maximizes the good for the various parties involved, and a good case could be made for either censure or conviction.

What about Dana? As a deontologist she focuses on doing her duty and on treating everyone involved fairly; she also believes that certain actions are intrinsically wrong (as opposed to focusing on the consequences of those actions). Dana's approach might be along these lines:[17]

1. What is President Clinton guilty of?

2. What is an appropriate punishment for these particular charges/ crimes? Here the emphasis is on the punishment "fitting" the crime.

3. What is the constitutional standard for impeachment and conviction by the Senate?

Dana focuses on whether President Clinton's conviction (by the House of Representatives) for perjury and obstruction of justice meets the level of seriousness ("high crimes and misdemeanors") spelled out in the Constitution. Unfortunately the Constitution does not tell us exactly what "high crimes and misdemeanors" means. Dana might reason in one of two ways (among others):

---

[17] There is no such thing as a single, unified deontological position (the same is true with respect to utilitarianism). What I'm suggesting is one possible deontological approach.

Calvin and Hobbes

by Bill Watterson

We can always hope for the unlikely to occur. CALVIN AND HOBBES © Watterson. Reprinted
with permission of UNIVERSAL PRESS SYNDICATE. All rights reserved.

ARGUMENT 1

1. President Clinton is guilty of serious wrongdoing.

2. Legal scholars are not at all sure his crimes are of the "high crimes and misdemeanors" variety.

∴ The Senate could reasonably err on the side of caution and not vote to convict.

ARGUMENT 2

1. President Clinton is guilty of serious wrongdoing.

2. Legal scholars are not at all sure his crimes are of the "high crimes and misdemeanors" variety.

3. Censure (including a stiff fine, a public apology, and so on) is an appropriate punishment for the crimes committed.

∴ The Senate should vote to censure the president.

It is important to point out that Dana's two arguments are not mutually exclusive. One could agree with her first argument and see it as pointing toward censure, while the second argument is an explicit (rather than implicit) argument for censure. Given the current state of affairs and Dana's deontological commitments, a vote for censure would be the one she is most comfortable with.

We still need to consider Rhonda. As a relativist Rhonda believes that issues of morality are decided by individual cultures and that there are no universal moral standards for judging human behavior. (This view will be developed in the next chapter.) Though American culture is far from perfect, there is a general belief that lying is morally wrong and that perjury is an especially significant kind of lying. But according to most of the polls, the

American public, though generally agreed that President Clinton was guilty of something, did not believe that this guilt was sufficient for removing him from office. Remember that the key issue for ethical relativists is what the majority believes, and not whether the majority is well informed or justified in their belief. So, given popular sentiment (which is certainly subject to change), Rhonda is bound by the general consensus of the people, namely, that President Clinton should not be convicted and removed from office by the Senate.

As this debate shows, reasoning about some matters involves complex considerations, and thoughtful, intelligent people often disagree. This does not mean that there are no good ways of discussing, and perhaps resolving, the various differences. Though our three claimants approached the matter from three different ethical viewpoints, the viewpoints themselves can and should be critically examined.[18] How we all decide to live our lives is important, and we all need to carefully and rationally consider the various possibilities before choosing a set of guiding principles.

SUMMARY

We have various sources of knowledge, including the senses, reason, memory, and introspection. According to the concept of rationality, some beliefs are more reasonable than others, and rationality is a matter of degrees. Understanding several conditions for accepting premises helps us to assess rationality. Complete human objectivity is not possible, but it is important to understand how both background knowledge and worldview shape and influence the way we look at the world. The problem of evil and the Senate trial of President Clinton show how differing perspectives (worldviews) might result in a different understanding of important issues. And even though different worldviews often result in different conclusions, it is possible—and desirable—to discuss and evaluate the underlying worldviews themselves.

EXERCISE 7.3

With the material on worldviews in mind, you are now going to be challenged to begin developing your own worldview or evaluating the one you already have. For each of the five components of a worldview, answer the accompanying questions.

---

[18] Some good introductory texts in ethics include the following: Louis Pojman, *Ethics*, 2nd ed. (Belmont, CA: Wadsworth, 1995), Emmett Barcalow, *Moral Philosophy*, 2nd ed. (Belmont, CA: Wadsworth, 1996), James Rachels, *The Elements of Moral Philosophy*, 3rd ed. (Boston: McGraw-Hill College, 1999), and Fred Feldman, *Introductory Ethics* (Englewood Cliffs, NJ: Prentice-Hall, 1978).

God/Nature of Reality

1. Does God exist?

   a. Consider what might be regarded as arguments for God's existence, and evaluate them for validity and soundness. For example, the cosmological argument posits God's existence along these lines:
      1. The universe exists.
      2. It has not always existed.
      3. So it came into existence.
      4. This coming into existence was either caused (to happen) or uncaused.[19]
      5. But there are no uncaused events (things that happen).
      6. So it was caused to come into existence.
      7. That cause is a first cause (an uncaused cause).
      8. That first cause is God.[20]

   b. Now consider what are regarded as arguments for God's nonexistence. For example, the problem of evil may be stated as follows:
      1. There exist great and awful evils (events which are never balanced out by good), such as the Holocaust.
      2. An all-powerful, all-loving, and all-knowing God could and would stop such evils.
      3. But this sort of evil exists.
      4. So it is unreasonable to believe in God (as defined here).[21]

2. What are the best (most important) things in life? For example, if you had to rank money, health, and friends in order of importance, what would be ranked first, and why?

3. Do humans have free will? Are you able to do as you please? Do you have the ability to choose between options?

4. Is there an afterlife?

5. Do humans have a soul? This and the preceding question are generally thought to be closely related.

Nature of Knowledge

1. What do you know with certainty? Remember that this means there is no possibility of your being mistaken. (Hint: your list should be fairly short.)

2. Are faith and reason compatible, at least in theory? Is it ever reasonable to put faith (trust) in someone else?

3. What are the obstacles to human knowledge?

---

[19] Many philosophers regard this as the most controversial of the premises here. For more on this, see the Rowe book cited below.

[20] For an enthusiastic defense of the cosmological argument, see William Lane Craig, *The Cosmological Argument from Plato to Leibniz* (New York: Macmillan, 1980).

[21] William Rowe is probably the most articulate defender of this view. See his *Philosophy of Religion* (Belmont, CA: Wadsworth, 1978).

Morality

1. Are there any universal moral principles?

2. Are there good reasons to adopt ethical relativism?

3. What is the Good (the most important thing or goal in life)?

4. What are the standards for determining moral right and wrong?

5. Is it ever morally OK to steal a loaf of bread?

Human Nature

1. Are humans basically good and unselfish?

2. What are the basic human needs—the things we must have to both survive and flourish?

3. Why are meaningful human relationships difficult to establish and maintain?

EXERCISE 7.4

How does your worldview help shape or influence your view of each of the following?

1. Gun control

2. Communism

3. God's existence

4. Abortion

5. Civil rights

6. Violence

EXERCISE 7.5

Now consider some recent television commercials and some popular sayings, and see if you can figure out what worldview, or aspect of a worldview, underlies the particular claim. Then ask yourself whether you agree with the particular perspective, and defend your position.

★ 1. "He who dies with the most toys wins."

2. "Image is everything."

3. "It doesn't get any better than this."

★ 4. "You only go around once in life, so grab for all the gusto you can."

5. "Just do it."

6. "You deserve a break today."

★ 7. "Have it your way."

8. "Try it, you'll like it."

9. "Don't knock it unless you've tried it."

★ 10. "The great pleasure in life is doing what people say you cannot do." (Walter Bagehot)

11. "All the things I like to do are either illegal, immoral, or fattening." (Alexander Woolcott)

12. "Take short views [be open-minded], hope for the best, and trust in God." (Sydney Smith)

★ 13. "Turn on, tune in, drop out." (Timothy Leary)

14. "Do what you like." (François Rabelais)

15. "Our life is frittered away by detail . . . simplify, simplify." (Henry David Thoreau)

★ 16. "Life is just a bowl of cherries." (Lew Brown)

17. "All that matters is love and work." (Sigmund Freud)

18. "There's no need to worry—whatever you do, life is hell." (Wendy Cope)

★ 19. "Man cannot live by bread alone." (Jesus)

20. "A belief in a supernatural source of evil is not necessary; men alone are quite capable of every wickedness." (Joseph Conrad)

21. "There is nothing good or bad, but thinking makes it so." (William Shakespeare)

★ 22. "Life is meaningless." (many nihilists)

23. "To find a friend one must close one eye. To keep him—two." (Norman Douglas)

24. "God is love, but get it in writing." (Gypsy Rose Lee)

★ 25. "God is dead." (Friedrich Nietzsche)

26. "It's not death that I mind; it's the hours." (Woody Allen)

GLOSSARY

introspection The process or act of "looking inward" to gain access to what we are presently thinking or conscious of and thus to acquire knowledge.

reasonability To think or act in accordance with rules of reasoning; also known as "rationality."

background knowledge   All of our experiences, including those relating to the acquisition of knowledge, up to the present.

logical possibility   Any claim that is possibly true, in the broadest sense of the word *possible*.

worldview   A comprehensive way of looking at the world that involves answers to five questions: (1) Is there a supreme being? (2) What is the nature of reality? (3) What is knowledge? (4) How should we live? and (5) What is human nature? A worldview provides the lens through which we look at the world.

contingent   Anything that could have been different or happened differently.

ethical relativism   The belief that there are no universal moral principles and that moral right and wrong are decided by individual cultures or societies.

ethical objectivism   The belief that certain moral principles are universal and objective—for example, the duty not to intentionally kill innocent persons.

CHAPTER 8

Thinking about Values

If it was so, it might be; and if it were so, it would be, but as it isn't, it ain't. That's logic. —*Lewis Carroll,* Through the Looking Glass

DESCRIPTIVE VERSUS PRESCRIPTIVE CLAIMS

The things we say can be categorized in many ways. One helpful sort of categorization involves the difference between descriptive and prescriptive claims. A **descriptive claim** is one that tells us how things are; it describes the world as it is—or at least how we think it is. For example, all of the following are descriptive claims:

1. I am forty-four years old.

2. It is cold today (as I write this).

3. I like cheese.

4. Jonathan Edwards lived in the 1700s.

5. Rock 'n' roll pioneer Buddy Holly was from Texas.

All of these claims are put forward as correct descriptions, or "pictures," of reality. But even a descriptive claim that turns out to be false is still a descriptive claim. So, for example, all of the following are false descriptive claims:

1. Today (as I write this sentence) is Monday.

2. Teddy Roosevelt lived in the 1300s.

3. The Minnesota Vikings have won a Super Bowl.

4. Johann Sebastian Bach is a modern composer.

5. Los Angeles is in Indiana.

Prescriptive claims are different. A **prescriptive claim** gives advice; it says what we *ought* to do. Just as a medical prescription gives us directions or commands ("Take two tablets four times a day with food"), so does a prescriptive claim. Prescriptive claims come in many forms and often include value judgments. **Value judgments** are assertions that something is good or bad, or right or wrong. Examples of prescriptive claims include the following:

1. Don did the wrong thing.
2. E. B. White was a gifted writer.
3. The president should ask forgiveness for his wrongdoings.
4. Otis is a bad dog.
5. Eduardo's is an excellent restaurant.

Prescriptive claims typically include words like the following:

ought	right
should	wrong
good	excellent
bad	awful

EXERCISE 8.1

For each of the following claims, state whether it is descriptive or prescriptive.

★ 1. Grace's car is red.

2. You should do that.

3. Lisa's homework is excellent.

★ 4. That is a big tree.

5. The president ought to act in a dignified manner.

6. I feel sad.

★ 7. Rosalita is pretty.

8. Take two of these and call me in the morning.

9. Please make your bed.

MATTERS OF TASTE

Many have claimed that all value judgments are merely matters of taste (such as "I like such-and-such"). Let's take a brief look at matters of taste; later, we'll address value judgments.

All of the following are claims involving matters of taste:

1. Winnie likes crab.

2. Irma prefers Pepsi to Coke.

3. Jamal favors McDonald's over Burger King.

4. I dislike eggplant.

5. Ahmad loves chocolate.

6. Koko loves sushi.

All of these claims are literally matters of taste—claims about which foods are pleasing or displeasing to individual palates. And we can make a fairly good case that there are no truly "good" or "bad" foods, only countless individual preferences.

However, even claims like these can be interpreted in too relative a manner. To illustrate, think about these four claims:

1. Steak is better than hamburger.

2. Almond macaroons are better than coconut macaroons.

3. Water is better to drink than gasoline.

4. Bread tastes better than dirt.

Most of us are comfortable with the first two claims. Even if we disagree with the specific claims, we recognize that they are literally matters of taste. But what about claims 3 and 4? Given that properly treated water is almost universally liked and that gasoline tastes horrible by most accounts and is unhealthy, is it entirely a matter of taste? We may not want to pass final judgment on what are truly matters of taste, but these examples suggest there may well be some limits to claims along those lines. We would certainly have doubts about someone who truly preferred gasoline to water, or dirt to bread—not only about their health but also about their general mental well-being. In short, even in matters of taste we can discern broad boundaries between matters of taste and commonsense notions.

AESTHETIC JUDGMENTS

Everyone has opinions about movies, TV shows, songs, performers, and so on. The issue here is whether such claims are merely matters of taste, as with food, or whether more objective elements are involved. Consider these examples:

1. Jamie Wyeth is a better artist than I am.

2. The Beatles are musically superior to The Partridge Family.

3. *Schindler's List* is an excellent movie.

Calvin and Hobbes

by Bill Watterson

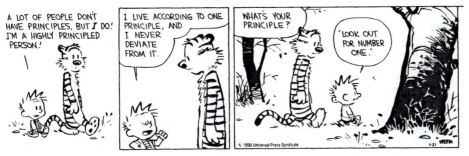

This principle reflects one very popular value. CALVIN AND HOBBES © Watterson. Reprinted
with permission of UNIVERSAL PRESS SYNDICATE. All rights reserved.

4. *Plan 9 from Outer Space* is a really bad movie.

5. Pete Seeger is the greatest American folk singer ever.

Here we have examples from art, film, and music. Are there any objective
standards for evaluating such claims? The answer seems to be a carefully qualified yes, keeping two points in mind:

1. There are broadly agreed-upon criteria for judging various media.

2. It is important to take genre into account.

Suppose we begin with the first claim. Jamie Wyeth is an artist who might
be described as a realist. Among other things realists must accurately portray
reality. So, if Jamie Wyeth painted a pig and I painted a pig, one relevant
standard for evaluating the two paintings would be "Does it look like a pig?"
In fact Wyeth has done a justly famous painting of a pig, while if I tried to
paint a pig there's no doubt that it could just as easily be mistaken for a dog,
rat, or hippopotamus. This is a simple but relevant point: though there may
be no universal standards as to what constitutes a "good" or "master" artist,
there are some generally agreed-upon standards when we bring the idea of
genre (or type) into play—in this case, realism.

What about movies? Are there any sort of standards by which we might
reasonably judge and evaluate them? Again, the answer is a qualified yes. It is
not merely my opinion that *Plan 9 from Outer Space*, by the legendary director
Ed Wood, is a "really bad" movie. The movie is lacking in a number of areas:

1. The script is poorly written.

2. The dialogue is terrible.

3. The special effects are laughable.

4. The acting is amateurish.

5. The movie does not accomplish what it sets out to.

The net result is that the movie at times is excruciatingly funny, though not due to any intent on the director's part. So, by any reasonable standard, when compared with other movies of any genre, *Plan 9* comes up short. Rational and informed people may disagree about whether, say, *Casablanca* is better than *Gone with the Wind,* but even here they could agree on some criteria. Of course the evaluative criteria need to be properly weighted, because not all criteria are of equal importance. Also, consensus concerning criteria does not guarantee that even two people who agree will apply those criteria in the same manner, but it does give us a starting point of sorts.

Concerning example 5 on p. 205, it is controversial to say that Pete Seeger is the best folk singer ever. But it does not necessarily follow that this claim is entirely a matter of personal opinion. For example, all of the following (among others) might be viewed as contenders for the title of best American folk singer (or folk group) ever:

Bob Dylan (in his early years)

Peter, Paul, and Mary

The Weavers

The Kingston Trio

Nanci Griffith

Tracy Chapman

The Chad Mitchell Trio

John Denver

Joan Baez

Emmylou Harris

Kate Wolf

Simon and Garfunkel

Someone familiar with the history of American folk music might choose any of these and be able to make a decent, if not necessarily persuasive, case for his or her choice. But all of the following would be excluded from consideration:

Duke Ellington (wrong genre)

Mozart (wrong genre again)

Cheryl Wheeler (good, but not good enough to merit consideration here)

John Gorka (a good writer, but only a pleasant voice)

Woody Guthrie (a gifted songwriter, but again only a pleasant voice)

Phil Ochs (the voice is not good enough)

This is hardly an exhaustive list, but it is a start. But what if William Shatner of *Star Trek* fame put out a folk album or even went into folk full-time? We can safely say that he would not be a serious contender for the designation of best singer. Anyone who has ever heard Shatner sing "Mr. Tambourine Man" or "Lucy in the Sky with Diamonds" knows that he does not possess a great singing voice—to put it kindly. In short, although rational and informed people may legitimately disagree as to who the best is, there is still a limit to the number of viable contenders.

ETHICS

The most important kinds of issues involving value judgments are ethical issues. Ethical issues address how we should live and seek to determine what is most important in life. The issue of how we should live our lives is both relevant and controversial. Are there moral standards that transcend cultural and societal values, or are all moral standards simply the choice of each culture and society? What is the best thing in life? Is abortion morally justifiable? All these questions are central to ethics (or morality). In this section, as we discuss a few of the key issues in ethics, keep in mind that these issues are highly controversial, and many fine ethicists disagree on one or many points.

Ethical Relativism

The first issue that needs to be addressed concerns whether ethical relativism is true. Recall from Chapter 7 that ethical relativism has two components:

1. Moral right and wrong are decided by each individual culture—presumably by the majority of members.
2. There are no universal or objective moral standards—no standards that apply to all people at all times in all places.

A popular belief is that ethical relativism promotes tolerance, is anti-ethnocentric, and allows for human diversity and individuality. If all this were true, then it would constitute a decent argument in favor of ethical relativism. But many contemporary philosophers (including William Frankena, Louis Pojman, James Rachels, Philippa Foot, and Alan Gewirth, to name but a few) argue that ethical relativism, however defined and qualified, suffers from a number of serious deficiencies. The key question remains, Are there good reasons for rejecting ethical relativism, which is immensely popular in Western culture? For the sake of brevity, let's focus on five main challenges to ethical relativism, using the hypothetical country of Wahoozia as an example.

The first problem is that, contrary to what is often claimed, ethical relativism does not guarantee or promote tolerance. Suppose the inhabitants of Wahoozia think that significant individual differences should not be tolerated and so vote to establish standards for singling out and torturing anyone who is significantly different. But given that the majority has approved of this, in Wahoozia it is now morally right to be intolerant and morally wrong to be tolerant! In other words, ethical relativism allows individual societies to establish their own moral and legal guidelines, and whether each society is tolerant is entirely up to the majority in that society. Clearly, then, there is no guarantee of tolerance if ethical relativism is adopted.

A second problem is even more serious. Suppose the Wahoozians are not only intolerant but also rabidly anti-Semitic (anti Jewish). The majority firmly believes that Jews are either second-class humans or not human at all, and that it is morally permissible to single them out for ridicule, persecution, and even death. One might object that the Wahoozians are fictional, and this is true. But anyone familiar with twentieth-century history and the Holocaust knows that Hitler and Nazi Germany took an approach to the Jews very much like the one adopted by the Wahoozians. Are we prepared to say that the persecution and killing of Jews is morally permissible? The answer is a resounding no. Rather, the Nazis were morally mistaken, as well as morally corrupt, in their attitude toward and treatment of the Jews. And since ethical relativism permits the moral justification for such barbaric and inhumane actions, it is a significantly flawed view of ethics.

More formally this argument might be laid out as follows:

1. If a view of ethics makes it possible to justify clearly immoral actions (such as anti-Semitism), then it is significantly flawed and worthy of our rejection.

2. Ethical relativism in theory justifies clearly immoral actions.

∴ Ethical relativism is significantly flawed and worthy of our rejection.

This is a valid argument, as it is an example of modus ponens (If A then B; A; so B). We have already shown premise 2 to be true, and premise 1 is one that any rational and informed person should accept.

A third problem with ethical relativism actually is an argument for ethical objectivism. Recall from Chapter 7 that ethical objectivism has two components:

1. Ethical relativism is false.

2. There is at least one universally binding moral principle.

According to ethical objectivism moral rightness and wrongness depend not on social approval but on independent considerations such as whether an act promotes human well-being or lessens human suffering.

So can we now come up with one moral principle that all rational and informed people should accept? Here's one possibility:

It is morally wrong to torture people for the fun of it.[1]

---

[1] The example is from Louis Pojman, *Ethics: Discovering Right and Wrong*, 2nd ed. (Belmont, CA: Wadsworth, 1995), p. 48.

All actions have consequences. CALVIN AND HOBBES © Watterson. Reprinted with permission of UNIVERSAL PRESS SYNDICATE. All rights reserved.

Are there any circumstances that would ever justify torturing someone just for the fun of it? Most philosophers can't think of any. Of course this does not guarantee that no such reasons exist, but it does put the burden of proof on those who disagree. Even if the notorious Wahoozians unanimously thought it was OK to torture people for the fun of it, it would hardly follow that it was morally justified. We should think, then, that the Wahoozians would be morally mistaken—indeed, morally barbaric—if they believed and practiced along these lines. If people can make mistakes concerning mathematics, history, science, and grammar, why can't ethical claims be mistaken as well?

A fourth problem with ethical relativism relates to the issue of moral progress. We can say that a person or a society makes moral progress when, according to objective moral standards, there is either an increase in moral virtue and/or a decrease in moral wrongdoing. The United States no longer practices slavery, nor does it withhold from women the right to vote. Both of these are examples of moral progress. But if ethical relativism is true, then this claim of moral progress is not well founded. Remember, ethical relativism

Five Problems with Ethical Relativism

1. Ethical relativism in no way guarantees tolerance; rather, each individual society decides what it wants to be tolerant about.

2. Ethical relativism can justify brutal and inhumane actions.

3. There is at least one universal moral principle.

4. Genuine moral progress requires a transcultural moral standard, but ethical relativism rules out there being such a standard and so cannot account for the moral progress that has in fact taken place.

5. If we leave decisions about moral right and wrong up to the majority of each society, then on issues for which the vote is close, the rightness of an action, such as capital punishment, could vary from day to day.

dictates that each culture or society be judged by the standards of its own people in its own time. This, then, rules out the possibility of there being one or more standards by which we can legitimately judge cultures over time. Given that moral progress clearly seems both a possibility (we can imagine it) and a reality (we have knowledge of it), and that ethical relativism cannot account for or make sense of this progress, then we have yet another problem with ethical relativism.

A final problem for ethical relativism revolves around the concepts of belief and moral rightness. According to ethical relativism, if the majority in society S believe that action X is morally wrong, then it is morally wrong. Suppose that Wahoozia has been decimated by illness and now has only 23 able-minded adult survivors—and thus, only 23 people to vote on any given ethical standard. Suppose further that the issue of capital punishment comes before the voters on Monday and that 12 endorse it as morally justifiable while 11 reject it. So on Monday capital punishment is morally justified in Wahoozia. But the Wahoozians love to vote, and they vote every day of that week on that issue. But when they vote on Tuesday, Fred Fickel changes his mind from pro to con, resulting in a 12-11 vote against capital punishment. This means that capital punishment is morally justified on Monday but is unjustified on Tuesday! To make matters worse, Fred changes his mind every day that week, with the result that capital punishment is morally justifiable on Monday, Wednesday, and Friday, and morally unjustifiable on Tuesday, Thursday, and Saturday! And to cap things off, a fatigued Fred decides to flip a coin on Sunday. Obviously the idea that an action could be morally right or wrong depending on the day of the week is ludicrous. Indeed it is widely believed that any view that leads to ridiculous consequences is seriously flawed. This method of arguing is called reductio ad absurdum, or "reduction to the absurd." So the fact that ethical relativism can have such crazy consequences counts as yet another strike against it.

For these five reasons (and there are others), ethical relativism does not seem to be an approach to ethics worth adopting. But what should we pursue in its place? Philosophers offer a wide range of (often competing) possibilities, the three most prominent of which are (1) virtue ethics, the approach taken by many of the ancient Greek philosophers, (2) utilitarianism, a view first formulated in Britain in the early 1800s, and (3) deontologism, a view developed by Immanuel Kant in the late 1700s.

Virtue Ethics

Virtue ethics, which dates back to the ancient Greeks, and especially to Aristotle, emphasizes developing moral virtue in order to become a person of good moral character. Let us begin with a simple example: a person performing an action. Various philosophers have viewed these factors as relevant to the study of ethics:

1. The character (or "heart") of the person
2. The motive behind the action—the reason the person performed the action
3. The consequences of the action, for both the individual and the larger group

According to virtue ethics motives and consequences are not unimportant, but they should not be our primary focus. Rather, we should focus on human character—the sum total of our moral habits, tendencies, and dispositions. A morally good person is one who has firmly established good moral habits and accordingly now performs morally right actions naturally and even spontaneously. Virtue ethics focuses more on *being* a good person (the internal) than on *doing* a particular action (the external).

Aristotle believed that continually performing good actions would produce two results: (1) we would gradually learn to do good as a matter of habit, and (2) we would greatly increase our chances of being happy, as the ancient Greeks believed that virtue promotes happiness, while vice promotes unhappiness. The virtues thus can be seen as "excellences of character, trained behavioral dispositions that result in habitual acts."[2] Note, too, that these habitual acts should be ones sought; otherwise the definition could apply to bad habits.[3] As Pojman points out, these virtues have traditionally been divided into two types: moral and nonmoral.[4] The moral virtues are thought to include these:

---

[2] Pojman, p. 166.
[3] See Edmund L. Pincoffs, *Quandaries and Virtues: Against Reductionism in Ethics* (Lawrence: University of Kansas Press, 1986), for more on this point.
[4] Pojman, p. 166.

Honesty	Kindness
Benevolence (doing good for others)	Conscientiousness
Nonmalevolence (avoiding doing bad to others)	Gratitude
Fairness	

The nonmoral virtues include the following:

Courage	Patience
Optimism	Endurance
Rationality	Industry
Self-control	Wit

Now that we have some idea of what the virtues are, the question still remains, Why should we seek to be virtuous? Let us briefly consider three possibilities:

1. **Courage.** Life is difficult and full of obstacles. We all need courage to "run the good race" and to give life our best effort even when we don't feel like it. Without courage many of us would be overcome by life's difficulties.

2. **Honesty.** We are social creatures: we need to interact with others and to develop relationships and friendships. Meaningful communication with others, at both the business and interpersonal levels, would not be possible without a significant amount of honesty. Communication would break down, and positive things like trust would be undermined.

3. **Fairness.** Fairness is connected to the belief that all humans are intrinsically valuable and that they are equally valuable. It also involves treating like cases alike. Suppose I give Moe a raise for doing X under circumstances Y, and Larry and Curly and Shemp are also doing X under circumstances Y; fairness dictates that they also receive a raise. We clearly violate the moral idea of fairness when we follow racist or sexist practices.

Its many strengths notwithstanding, virtue ethics also has some problems.[5] Here we will focus on a key one. It is generally thought that any worthwhile system of ethics should provide us with, among other things, a prescriptive or action-guiding principle. Ethical relativism, for all it shortcomings, does just this: we should always act according to the wishes of the majority in our culture or society. By contrast, with virtue ethics the answer to the question of what we should do is whatever action will improve our character. The problem is that it is often not clear *which* action that might be. And

---

[5] See Pojman, *Ethics,* and James Rachels, *The Elements of Moral Philosophy,* 3rd ed. (New York: McGraw-Hill, 1999), for a balanced critique of virtue ethics.

any ethical theory that leaves us without a clear prescriptive principle is deficient. So, though it has many strengths, virtue ethics still suffers from at least one significant defect.

Utilitarianism

Another of the main traditions in ethics, **utilitarianism** refers to the idea that the morally right action is the one that maximizes utility. There are two main branches of utilitarianism—act and rule—but here I will focus on a broad and generic version, one that fairly represents the version put forth by Jeremy Bentham himself, the founder of utilitarianism. Utilitarians thus focus on the consequences of actions and believe that carefully weighing the possible consequences of a course of action is crucial if we are to properly morally evaluate it. To illustrate, consider the following scenario: Bonnie wishes to play her music (mostly heavy metal) loud, though she has five neighbors living within earshot of her apartment. Is it morally right for Bonnie to play her music loud? Given her preferences, she has three basic options: (1) crank it, (2) play it with the headphones on, or (3) don't play it at all. We already know who is involved (Bonnie and her neighbors), and we have established that she has three options. Now we need to create a scale for measuring how much happiness/unhappiness each of the three options might produce. Suppose we agree that +100 units means that someone is very happy, −100 units means that someone is very unhappy, and 0 means someone is neutral. We can now map out Bonnie's options as follows:

	1 BONNIE CRANKS IT	2 BONNIE USES HEADPHONES	3 BONNIE DOESN'T PLAY MUSIC
Bonnie's happiness score	+80	+60	−70
The five neighbors' happiness score	−300 (−60 each)	0	0
Totals	−220	+60	−70

According to utilitarianism, Bonnie has a moral duty to choose option 2, which, at +60 units, makes the most people the happiest. And she would have a moral duty to avoid option 1, which causes the most unhappiness for the group as a whole.

Utilitarianism is initially attractive in that it enables us to map out our options, figure the cost/benefit of each option, and then choose the one that produces the most happiness for the group as a whole. Utilitarianism also clearly has a number of good features: (1) it promotes a good thing, happiness; (2) it takes everyone's interests into account, which makes it a democratic approach; (3) it provides us with a relatively clear action-guiding principle; and (4) it seems to work pretty well, at least most of the time. Unfortunately there is more to it than this. Philosophers have raised a number of objections to utilitarianism and its various claims;[6] here we will focus on one in particular.

Pojman asks us to imagine the following:

> Suppose that a rape and murder is committed in a racially volatile community. As the sheriff of the town, you have spent a lifetime working for racial harmony. Now, just when your goal is being realized, this incident occurs. The crime is thought to be racially motivated, and a riot is about to break out that will very likely result in the death of several people and create long-lasting racial antagonism. You see that you could frame a tramp for the crime so that a trial will find him guilty and he will be executed. There is every reason to believe that a speedy trial and execution will head off the riot and save community harmony. Only you (and the real criminal, who will keep quiet about it) will know that an innocent man has been tried and executed. What is the morally right thing to do? The utilitarian seems committed to framing the tramp, but many would find this appalling. . . .
>
> This cavalier view of justice offends us. The very fact that utilitarians even countenance such actions . . . seems frightening.[7]

Does the utilitarian have an adequate response to this objection raised by Pojman and others? Can the utilitarian plausibly claim that on rare occasions it is right to sacrifice one innocent person for the good of the group? Put another way, can the anti-utilitarian plausibly defend the claim that the right to life of innocent humans always overrides the public good? This is a difficult issue, and I will leave it to you to ponder its implications.[8] But keep in mind that it is generally believed that unless an adequate response is available to the utilitarian here, then the view is in serious trouble.

Deontological Ethics

Immanuel Kant is widely acknowledged as one of the greatest philosophers of all time. He wrote on a number of topics, but here we will briefly consider his approach to ethics. Kant was a deontologist. According to **deontologism**, as human beings we have a duty to do the right thing whether or not it benefits us or the group. In other words Kant does not consider the probable consequences of an action to be a factor in determining whether the action is morally right. Kant instead asks us to focus on the motive behind an action as the ethical focal point.

---

[6] See Pojman, pp. 105–132, for a good overview of utilitarianism and its problems.
[7] Pojman, p. 122.
[8] J. J. C. Smart defends utilitarianism by questioning our ordinary ideas of justice and argues that we should not be committed to the ordinary ("intuitive") conception of justice. See his "An Outline of a System of Utilitarian Ethics," in *Utilitarianism: For and Against*, ed. J. J. C. Smart and Bernard Williams (Cambridge: Cambridge University Press, 1973), pp. 3–74.

Kant was searching for a universal moral principle, one that would be applicable to all people at all times. Does such a principle exist? Kant believed it does. He developed a principle that he called the **categorical imperative**— literally, "exceptionless command." This principle is not only objectively true (true independent of what anyone thinks), but also absolute in that it allows for no exceptions and can never be overridden by another principle. Thus it is an example of **ethical absolutism.** Note that this view should not be confused with ethical objectivism. Although all ethical absolutists are ethical objectivists, not all ethical objectivists are ethical absolutists. Ethical objectivists believe that universal moral principles exist but that many of these principles allow for exceptions. For example, "Do not lie" is a universal standard but not an absolute one. If it conflicted with the universal moral principle "Do not murder," we would honor the latter principle, as it can be reasonably argued that human life has more value than truth telling. Most philosophers who reject ethical relativism are more accurately characterized as ethical objectivists than as ethical absolutists.

Kant offered more than one version of the categorical imperative, but we will focus on only one here. Kant claimed that one should "act only according to the maxim by which [one] can at the same time will that it should become a universal law."[9] Many of you may wonder, "What exactly does that mean?!" Before we answer that question, we need to define what Kant means by "maxim" and "universal law." A **maxim** is "a personal rule specifying how and why one will behave in certain circumstances."[10] For example, a maxim might say, "In circumstances C, I will do action A for purpose P." To determine whether the particular maxim is justified (that is, should be followed), we need to ask ourselves, "If I do action A under circumstances C for purpose P, am I willing for everyone else in the world [this is the **universal law** part] to do the same thing for the same reason under the same circumstances?" If the answer is yes, it means that the maxim is morally justified. If the answer is no, it means that the maxim is morally wrong and so should not be acted upon.

The observant reader may notice that what Kant is getting at sounds a lot like the Golden Rule: do unto others as you wish them to do unto you. Indeed, Kant's view emphasizes fairness. To illustrate, suppose that Alyssa and Karen are getting ready to play one-on-one basketball. Karen says that they need to establish some rules before they can play. Alyssa responds that she would like to set the rules. Karen counters that, whatever set of rules Alyssa chooses, those rules will apply equally to Karen and to Alyssa. So will Alyssa pick a set of rules that favor her? No, because she knows that in the interest of fairness all the rules must apply equally to everyone involved. Kant believed that his test, sometimes called the test of **universalizability,** would

---

[9] Immanuel Kant, "Metaphysical Principles of the Doctrine of Right," in *The Metaphysics of Morals,* trans. Mary Gregor (New York: Cambridge University Press, 1991), p. 38.
[10] Emmett Barcalow, *Moral Philosophy* (Belmont, CA: Wadsworth, 1994), p. 374.

A Gallery of Quotes

The following are some well-known thoughts on the nature of morality.

"Cum finis est licitus, etiam media sunt licita." (The end justifies the means.) (Herman Busenbaum)

"Morality is the herd-instinct in the individual." (Friedrich Nietzsche)

"It is always easier to fight for one's principles than to live up to them." (Alfred Adler)

"The nation's morals are like its teeth; the more decayed they are the more it hurts to touch them." (George Bernard Shaw)

"Would that we had spent one whole day well in this world!" (Thomas à Kempis)

"Virtue she finds too painful an endeavor, Content to dwell in decencies forever." (Alexander Pope)

"Few things are harder to put up with than the annoyance of a good example." (Mark Twain)

"The greatest offence against virtue is to speak ill of it." (William Hazlitt)

"Terrible is the temptation to be good." (Bertolt Brecht)

"I used to be Snow White . . . but I drifted." (Mae West)

effectively weed out all maxims that are immoral, as no one could consistently wish that everyone adopt such maxims.

Let us briefly consider two maxims to see what Kant might have to say about them. First, suppose that Chan and Lee are roommates. Chan is low on money, so when Lee leaves for work, Chan takes Lee's stereo to the local pawn shop, gets $8,000 for it, and uses the money to buy a used car for himself. After returning home from work, Lee notices that his stereo is missing. Chan immediately pipes up that he sold it because he needed the money for a car. Given that both Chan and Lee readily admit they are committed to being morally fair, Lee poses the following challenge to Chan: "Isn't your maxim in this case something like the following: Whenever I need money, it is morally OK to take someone else's property, sell it, and keep the money?" Lee concedes that this is the maxim behind what he did. Lee then asks Chan if he is willing for everyone (the universal law application) to steal whenever they need money? Chan admits that this would result in serious social instability, if not chaos. Chan recognizes that it would also allow Lee to steal Chan's stuff and sell it if he needed the money! Chan gets the point: the maxim behind his action is not universalizable, so what he did is morally wrong. In other words maxims of actions that are not universalizable are self-defeating in that if everyone adopted them the results would be contrary to what performers of the actions want. Kant believed that his categorical imperative ruled out not only stealing, but also murder, rape, and many other actions that harm people and society.

Consider one more example. Suppose it is a cold, snowy winter night and Jamal is driving home from work. He notices a car stuck in a snow bank, with the lights still on and a woman inside. Jamal is tired and cold, but he wants to do the morally right thing. What should he do? Supposes he reasons as follows: Whenever circumstances are like this, I will stop to see if I can help because it is a good thing to help people in need. Can Jamal consistently desire that everyone do the same thing under the same circumstances? The answer seems to be a resounding yes. It is good to help people in need, and the world would be a much better place if people as a rule helped others in need. So, with its emphasis on universalizing, Kant's approach seems to support morally right actions and to undermine morally wrong ones.

Most philosophers view Kant's approach to ethics as problematic. We will briefly touch on a popular challenge to Kant's approach, one that zeros in on Kant's claim that all moral principles are absolute and thus exceptionless. Suppose we begin with this moral principle: always tell the truth. Many philosophers would agree with Kant that this principle is morally justified, but they would disagree with his claim that there should never be any exceptions to this principle.

To illustrate, imagine that it is 1943 and World War II is in full force. You are living in western Europe, and you are hiding a Jewish family in your attic. You know that the Nazis are looking for all Jews and that if this family is caught there is a high probability that one or more of them will die in the concentration camps. One night the Nazis pound on your door and ask if you know the whereabouts of this family. Should you tell the truth or should you lie, or is there some other alternative?

Kant's moral absolutism would require that you tell the truth here, but is that the morally right thing to do? Most philosophers think that telling the truth is not the right thing to do here—in fact, it is the morally wrong thing to do. By telling the truth you are allowing innocent human beings to be captured, and probably murdered, by the Nazis, who have no good (morally persuasive) reason for wanting to know where this family is. Sometimes in life we have serious moral conflicts. In this case there are at least two duties in force: (1) tell the truth, and (2) protect innocent human life. Unfortunately we simply cannot act in accordance with both duties; we must choose one or the other. How do we do this? We can make a good case that protecting innocent human life has more value than telling the truth, so it is a higher-ranking duty. And if a higher-ranking duty comes into conflict with a lower-ranking duty, we should always act in accordance with the higher-ranking duty. So telling the truth is *not* the morally right thing to do here; one could even make a good case that telling the truth makes us an accessory to murder! Kant's absolutist tendencies thus make his view unfit for handling some kinds of serious moral conflict.

MORAL REASONING

As this brief overview shows, ethics is sometimes a complicated business, and philosophers and nonphilosophers alike sometimes have fundamental disagreements over important issues. Moral reasoning can help us work our way through such thorny issues.

Moral reasoning has two basic components:

1. Knowledge of what moral principle is involved

2. Evidence of some sort indicating that the action in question is morally required, morally permitted, or morally prohibited

Moral Judgments

When we have a moral principle in place and sufficient evidence, we are then in a position to make a moral judgment. A **moral judgment** involves determining whether an action is morally right or wrong in light of the relevant moral principles. For example, consider the following scenario:

Moral Principle	+	**Factual Information**	=	**Moral Judgment**
Murder is morally wrong.		Ray has intentionally killed Don.		Ray has acted immorally.

The moral judgment that Ray has acted immorally is simply an application of the relevant moral principle to the facts surrounding Ray's actions toward Don.

Note that many serious moral disagreements revolve around the *factual* component, and not the *principle* component. For example, consider the abortion controversy. Many pro-abortion and anti-abortion advocates alike claim that it is morally wrong to intentionally kill an innocent human. So here, perhaps surprisingly, we have agreement with respect to principle. One of the key disagreements is whether the fetus at, say, three months is a human; this is a disagreement over facts. And even if we resolved such factual disputes, there is no guarantee that we would settle the abortion controversy. In sum, controversies in ethics may revolve around either differences in principle or a different understanding of the facts involved.

Characteristics of Mature Moral Thinkers

Given the controversy surrounding the domain of ethics, we should say a few words about the characteristics of people who think well about moral matters. These people could be described as being morally responsible and having good moral character. And they would possess many or all of the following characteristics:[11]

---

[11] The following list is adapted from William Hughes, *Critical Thinking* (Ontario: Broadview Press, 1992), pp. 213f. Copyright © 1992 William Hughes. Reprinted with permission of Broadview Press.

It's important to base our beliefs on the evidence at hand. Peanuts reprinted by permission of United Feature Syndicate, Inc.

1. **Independence of judgment.** We believe what we believe on the basis of (hopefully good) reasons, and not because it is fashionable, convenient, or the like. In this sense, the individual should be morally autonomous.

2. **Justification by appeal to principles.** All moral judgments are ultimately answerable to appropriate moral principles. In other words, if no particular moral principle supports our moral judgment, then we need to rethink our moral reasoning process.

3. **Generalization of moral judgments.** We believe that, whenever it is morally wrong for someone to do something under a particular set of circumstances, then it is morally wrong for everyone else to do that action under those same circumstances. (This is Pojman's test of universalizability.)

4. **Consistency.** First, we need to live according to the principles we have adopted. People who consistently fail to live up to their own standards are guilty of hypocrisy and will lose the respect of mature members of the moral community. Second, we should apply our principles consistently across the board. If we believe that it is morally wrong to break the law with respect to murder, but morally OK with respect to speeding laws, we need either to show that the two cases are relevantly different or to change our thinking about one of the two matters. Finally, the principles we adopt should be consistent among themselves. For example, suppose Lou adopts two moral principles: (1) it is morally wrong to eat meat, and (2) it is morally right to do as we wish as long as it gives us physical pleasure. The problem here is that many people get physical pleasure from eating meat, so it would be impossible for them to obey these two conflicting principles.

5. **Awareness of complexity.** We recognize that life/reality is complicated and that applying the relevant moral principle and gathering all the relevant facts can be complicated and even perplexing. Reality is often not as simple as we make it out to be.

Eight Characteristics of Mature Moral Thinkers

1. Independence of judgment
2. Principled moral beliefs
3. Generalization of moral judgments
4. Consistency
5. Awareness of complexity
6. Knowledge of the relevant facts
7. Recognition of our fallibility
8. Tolerance

6. **Knowledge of the relevant facts.** We do not make moral judgments until we have all the relevant facts in hand. For example, for emotionally volatile issues such as euthanasia, abortion, and affirmative action, much arguing takes place even though the facts are either lacking or distorted.

7. **Recognition of our fallibility.** Humans are finite and limited creatures. There is much we do not know, we tend to believe what we want to believe, and many thoughtful and morally informed people will disagree with us on any moral judgment we might make. To think that a moral judgment is correct simply because it is our own is to display a form of arrogance (the Greeks called it *hubris*) that is not justified.

8. **Tolerance.** We should always respect the moral judgments of individuals who have made the effort to gather the facts and carefully apply the proper moral principle. We can significantly disagree with others yet treat them with the respect and dignity they deserve as fellow human beings.

Note that the morally mature individual may not have full possession of all eight characteristics; rather, moral maturity, like many good things, is a matter of degree. The fact that few if any will ever attain moral perfection does not mean that these are not worthy ideals for which we should strive.

SUMMARY

Descriptive claims merely describe things, while prescriptive claims tell us what we ought to do. It is difficult, if not impossible, to move from a descriptive ("is") statement to a prescriptive ("ought") statement. Unlike matters of taste, aesthetic judgments are not entirely subjective. Four common approaches to ethics are ethical relativism, virtue ethics, utilitarianism, and Kant's deontological ethics. Ethical relativism has some serious problems and so is widely rejected in the philosophical community. But none of the other three views is entirely satisfactory, though some combination of virtue ethics and Kant's approach may give us a workable approach to ethics and the challenges it presents. Finally, the characteristics of the morally mature person are suitable ideals to strive for, even though we may never entirely live up to all of them.

EXERCISE 8.2

For each of the following, determine whether it is a matter of taste, an aesthetic judgment, or a moral judgment.

★ 1. I love pizza.

2. Murder is wrong.

3. Picasso's *Guernica* is a great painting.

★ 4. *Schindler's List* is an excellent movie.

5. Yogurt is OK, but hamburger is better.

6. "You've Lost That Lovin' Feeling" is a great song.

★ 7. She treated her sister poorly.

8. Breyer's vanilla ice cream is the best.

9. *Plan 9 from Outer Space* is a lousy movie.

★ 10. You shouldn't have done that.

EXERCISE 8.3

Write a brief essay (150–200 words) about any two of the following:

1. What are the criteria for judging a movie? Does the genre of the movie matter?

2. What separates your favorite musicians from all the others?

3. What are the most important virtues in life?

4. What is your favorite movie, and why?

5. Are there any standards for comparing musicians from different genres: jazz, folk, country, rock 'n' roll, classical, blues, gospel, and pop?

EXERCISE 8.4

1. For each of the following, state whether the action in question is morally right or wrong, and give reasons in support of your claim.
   a. Swatting houseflies
   b. Catching flies and pulling their wings off
   c. Cheating on an exam when you know you won't get caught
   d. Tattling on a sibling who has broken a cardinal rule of the household
   e. Getting an abortion at three months into the pregnancy
   f. Executing a convicted murderer
   g. Scratching another car and not leaving a note
   h. Going faster than the speed limit
   i. Having an extramarital affair
   j. Wasting time
   k. Making fun of someone else if it makes you feel good and no one else knows about it
   l. Not taking care of our minds and/or bodies
   m. Having unprotected sex with a new partner

2. For each of the following moral scenarios, indicate how you would respond.
   a. Your good friend Tara has talked about committing suicide for years. She is neither depressed nor on mood-altering drugs. She asks you to help her commit suicide, arguing that it is a long-term and thoughtful decision on her part.
   b. Your friend Bobby is HIV positive, but only you and he know this. He is about to begin having sexual relations with his friend Janna. Given that he has already refused to tell her, do you have an obligation to do so? Would it matter if Janna were also a good friend of yours?
   c. You are engaged to be married to a wonderful person. The two of you have talked about your undying love for each other and how committed you are to each other. But your true love is in a serious car accident and is paralyzed from the waist down. Does this affect your relationship with this person? Should it?
   d. If you murder an innocent person, it will end world hunger.[12] Should you do it?
   e. If you cut off your foot, you will win $1 million. Do you do it?
   f. You are a campaign worker for Senator Jones, who is in a neck-and-neck race for reelection. In the final days of the campaign, her opponent has resorted to sleazy tactics, which have resulted in the opponent inching ahead of her in the polls. You are tempted to use sleazy tactics yourself, knowing that they will probably be effective and may well put Senator Jones over the top. Should you resort to "dirty tricks"? Give detailed support for your choice.
   g. A person in your state has been convicted of first-degree murder in the death of an eight-year-old boy. Should he receive capital punishment? Who or why not? Is the issue of whether capital punishment acts as a deterrent relevant here? Why or why not?

---

[12]This example is from Gregory Stock, *The Book of Questions* (New York: Workman, 1987), p. 31.

GLOSSARY

descriptive claim   A claim that depicts or portrays something as it is; a listing of characteristics.

prescriptive claim   A claim that tells or commands what ought to be done.

value judgment   Any claim asserting that something (a person, action, phenomenon) is good or bad, or right or wrong—for example, "Murder is wrong" or "Van Gogh was a great painter."

virtue ethics   An approach to ethics that emphasizes developing moral virtue in order to become a person of good moral character. This approach was first developed by Plato and, especially, Aristotle.

utilitarianism   The idea that the morally right action is the one that maximizes utility, or the one that makes the most people the happiest (though some utilitarians focus on things other than happiness).

deontologism   A view of ethics that emphasizes doing one's duty because it is the right thing to do, not because it has the most beneficial consequences for individuals or society.

categorical imperative   A concept in Kantian ethics, it is a command (the "imperative" part) that allows for no exceptions. Kant's version of the categorical imperative amounts to a somewhat souped-up version of the Golden Rule.

ethical absolutism   A view in ethics stating that whatever is morally right is *always* morally right, with no exceptions whatsoever.

maxim   A general rule or principle indicating how an agent intends to act.

universal law   A law whereby individuals are willing for everyone to act as they did under the same circumstances for the same reason.

universalizability   A method for testing maxims in Kantian ethics whereby only if you are willing for all people in the same situation to do the same thing for the same reasons is it a morally right action.

moral judgment   The process of applying a moral principle to the act of an agent.

CHAPTER 9

Putting It All Together

It is one thing to show a man that he is in error, and another to put him in possession of the truth.
—*John Locke*, Essay Concerning Human Understanding

A SEVEN-STEP PROCESS FOR ANALYZING ARGUMENTS

In this chapter we review a sequence of steps for analyzing arguments and then apply them to the controversial issue of capital punishment; the accompanying chart summarizes the process. Note that, as with any controversial issue, many thoughtful and informed people may see things differently than you or me. In any case here are the seven steps:

1. **Read the passage carefully.** You cannot properly analyze an argument unless you first know that there is an argument. Many passages contain no argument, while many others contain more than one argument, in which case you need to identify all the arguments.

2. **Identify all explicit premises and conclusions.** Many passages contain explicit arguments: both premises and conclusion are stated. When you write out the argument, you can either copy the relevant part of the passage verbatim or put it into simpler or more precise language. Be careful, though, not to leave out something crucial to the argument.

3. **Identify all implicit premises and conclusions.** Many passages leave crucial claims (premises or conclusions) unstated. It is your job to "read between the lines" and include all implicit claims when you reconstruct the argument. But note that there is a fine line here between reading too much into the passage and leaving out an implicit premise or conclusion.

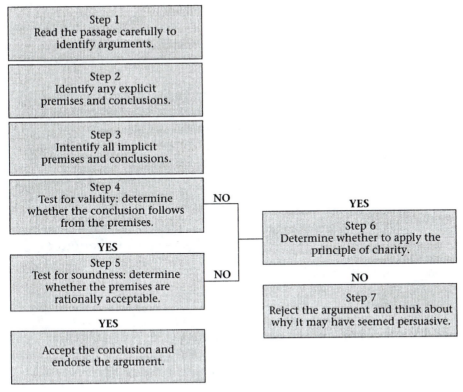

A seven-step flow chart

4. **Determine whether the conclusion follows from the premises.**
   Remember that the conclusion does not follow if all the premises
   can be true and the conclusion still be false. Good (valid) arguments
   are truth preserving in the sense that if all the premises are true then
   so is the conclusion—with the word *if* being the key here.

5. **Determine whether the premises should be accepted.** Conclusions are never any stronger than the premises on which they are
   based, so if the premises are questionable then so is the conclusion.
   Chapter 7 discussed some guidelines for evaluating premises, and
   you should keep them in mind when working through this particular step.

6. **Determine whether to apply the principle of charity.** While the
   conclusion may not follow from the premises, or one or more of the
   premises may be questionable, it still remains to be seen whether
   you can interpret the argument more charitably. This kinder interpretation may well avoid some of the pitfalls and problems of the
   earlier version. You may even be surprised to find out that this version is worthy of your acceptance, though you would not have

thought so previously. Remember that applying the principle of charity can benefit not only the author of the argument under scrutiny but also you as the evaluator. Thus putting an argument in the most favorable light may help you come closer to the truth that we all seek.

7. **Reject the argument, and think about why it may have seemed persuasive.** Here you need to consider why an argument that is worthy of rejection seemed persuasive in the first place. A thorough knowledge of the various fallacies (discussed in Chapter 6) is indispensable here. Remember that many flawed arguments may still have elements that are fairly reasonable or persuasive. For example, suppose a particular flawed argument has three premises. Two of the premises are perfectly reasonable, and even insightful and full of wisdom, but the third premise has an objectionable element in it that renders the entire argument defective and thus worthy of rejection.

APPLYING THE PROCESS TO AN ACTUAL ARGUMENT

Now let's apply the seven-step procedure to the following essay.

The Death Penalty

MICHELLE LOCKE

Former California governor Edmund G. "Pat" Brown has a favorite story   1
about why he doesn't think capital punishment works: the prisoner who built his own death chamber. In his book, "Public Justice, Private Mercy," Brown recalls how a plumber serving time for robbery was among those drafted to build the San Quentin gas chamber in 1937. He helped install the complicated device and watched test pigs executed.

But the grisly task didn't have much impact. Within a year, the plumber was paroled, killed three members of his family, was sentenced to death, and breathed his last in the contrivance he helped construct.

Does the death penalty work?

It's a debate that's taken on new urgency in California as double murderer Robert Alton Harris is scheduled on Tuesday to become the 195th person to die in the green chamber.

Governor Pete Wilson conducted a closed-door clemency hearing for   5
Harris Wednesday. There was no indication when he planned to release his decision.

During two terms in office, Brown granted clemency to 23 people and saw 59 people executed. In his 1989 book, written with Dick Adler, he tells how many of the reprieved went on to lead blameless lives, while one murdered a woman and was executed.

Eventually, Brown decided the death penalty was a bad idea. "I just don't believe the death penalty is a civilized treatment of a crime," the former governor said by telephone from his Southern California home.

But proponent Walter Burns of the Washington, D.C.–based American Enterprise Institute says capital punishment is necessary. "We want a population that is morally outraged, angry when confronted with heinous crimes," he said.

In his book, Brown said that in 1966 in California, when there were no executions, there were 4.7 homicides per 100,000 population. In 1967, when Aaron Mitchell, the last man to die in the gas chamber, was executed, there were 5.4 homicides per 100,000.

Burns conceded evidence over whether the death penalty is a deterrent is 10
inconclusive.

But he said a society that doesn't get angry about wrongdoing runs the risk of apathy. He cited the 38 New Yorkers who ignored the cries of Kitty Genovese as she was stabbed to death. "To some extent we punish in order to foster a kind of population that would come to the help of the Kitty Genoveses," he said.

Death penalty opponents point out that many Western countries have abandoned the practice.

"It's playing God, and I'm not willing to do that," said Laura Magnani of the Northern California Coalition Against the Death Penalty.

Harris was convicted in the 1978 abduction and murder of two 16-year-old San Diego boys, Michael Baker and John Mayeski, whose car he wanted for a bank robbery.

"Quit crying and die like a man," Harris later boasted he told the teenager, 15
a cellmate testified. "God can't help you now, boy. You're going to die."

Harris has admitted the murders, but says he doesn't know why he killed. He denies taunting the teenager or, as his brother testified, eating the boys' hamburgers after the killings.

Those pushing for clemency say jurors haven't heard the full story of Harris's childhood, a litany of abuse that began literally before he was born, when his father kicked his pregnant mother in the stomach, forcing a premature birth.

But Steven Baker, a San Diego police detective and Michael's father, doesn't have much sympathy for what he calls "the devil-made-me-do-it" defense. "It's real easy to blame all of your actions on something or someone else."

The death of Harris would "mean the end of that particular chapter finally after 14 years. Not only to me, but to the rest of the people of California," Baker said, noting that a recent California poll indicated 80 percent of residents support the death penalty.

In his book, [Pat Brown] wrote, "the longer I live, the larger loom those   20
59 decisions about justice and mercy that I had to make as governor. They
didn't make me feel godlike then. Far from it; I felt just the opposite. It as an
awesome, ultimate power over the lives of others that no person or government should have, or crave."

Associated Press

Analysis of the Argument

Step 1 mandates that we read the passage carefully. It is usually a good idea to
read a passage twice—once rapidly to get an overview, and once carefully so
as to understand what is being said. Clearly a careful analysis assumes that we
first understand what we are thinking about.

Steps 2 and 3 involve clearly identifying all explicit and implicit premises.
Former California governor Pat Brown makes the first argument, in paragraphs 1–3. It can be written as follows:

ARGUMENT 1

1. If capital punishment worked, then it would deter people from
   murdering. (paragraph 2)

2. If it deterred people from murdering, then convicted
   offenders would not commit murder. (implicit)

3. But one offender did commit such a murder after being
   paroled. (paragraph 2)

   ∴   Capital punishment does not work.

This is a valid argument having the following argument pattern:

1. If A, then B.

2. If B, then C.

3. Not C.

∴   Not A.

Of the three premises, the third one clearly is true—it is a matter of fact. But
the first two premises are less straightforward. The appeal in premise 1 will be
far more persuasive to those who take a utilitarian approach to ethics. Though
consequences are certainly not unimportant, as was argued in Chapter 8, it is
not at all clear that a utilitarian approach to ethics is the best one. Other
philosophers, such as Kant, have argued that criminal justice should be more
concerned with retribution and just deserts than with consequences. Retribution involves the idea of having the punishment fit the crime; it is less

concerned with whether the "fair" or "just" punishment is the one with the best consequences. For Kant the issue is whether certain crimes ever merit the extreme punishment of death. If someone told Kant that capital punishment did (or did not) deter others from murdering, his response would be that such claims are secondary to the main issue: what punishment best fits the specific crime committed. This is an area of longstanding controversy, and, at the least, the advocate of deterrence as a key issue in the debate needs to offer a supporting argument.

What about the second premise? Even if we grant that deterrence should be at the heart of the capital punishment debate, would it logically follow that premise 2 is true? It does not seem so. Capital punishment could well have a general deterrent effect while still allowing for individual exceptions to the norm. So the fact that it did not deter in one case is interesting, but by itself it hardly undermines the general deterrent value of such a practice. So the second premise is at best unconvincing.

Given that premises 1 and 2 are far from persuasive as they stand, we can reasonably conclude that this argument falls short of the goal of having rationally acceptable true premises.

A second argument, found in paragraph 6, might be reconstructed as follows:

ARGUMENT 2

1. If convicted murderers are given a second chance, then the vast majority will go on to lead "blameless lives."

2. Many have been given a second chance (clemency).

∴   They went on to lead blameless lives.

This argument is a classic example of modus ponens and is therefore clearly valid. It is also true that the second premise is a true statement—it is a matter of fact. So the success of the argument hinges on the truth of the first premise. Suppose we grant, for the sake of argument, that premise 1 seems reasonable. Is the author of the article content merely to establish what this argument offers as its conclusion? Probably not. Rather, she apparently intends for the argument to bear more weight than I have suggested thus far. Suppose we see the conclusion from argument 2 as offering support for a third argument, along these lines:

ARGUMENT 3

1. If convicted murderers can be rehabilitated (be granted clemency and then lead productive lives), then capital punishment should not be practiced.

2. Generally convicted murderers can be rehabilitated.

∴   This is good reason to think that capital punishment should not be practiced.

Suppose we concede that premise 2 is reasonable—though I have some serious doubts about it. Why do I grant the truth of a premise about which I have significant doubts? Because I believe that premise 1 is also flawed, and if I can show that the first premise should not be accepted, then it really does not matter whether the second premise is reasonable.

How do we even begin to think about the first premise? One starting point is to focus on the ongoing debate between the utilitarians and their opponents. If the utilitarians' approach to ethics is the most reasonable one, then the sort of claim contained in premise 1 will have significant appeal. This is because the first premise focuses on the possible consequences of giving convicted murderers a second chance, and the author notes that the results are very good—indeed twenty-two of twenty-three go on to lead "blameless" lives, with the only exception being noted. But as many philosophers sympathetic to the Kantian approach to ethics have noted, why should the bottom line here be consequences? Why not focus instead on whether the prescribed punishment—in this case death—is appropriate to the crime committed? If the bottom line is giving the criminal what he or she deserves, then whether the criminal is "rehabilitatable" is at best of secondary importance. Kant could grant that all convicted murderers can be rehabilitated but then claim that the key issue is whether the punishment fits the crime, and not the possible consequences of giving convicted murderers another chance. At the least the author needs to give us an argument as to why convicted murderers being "rehabilitatable" is as important as or more important than the concepts of retribution and just deserts. So argument 2 is at best unconvincing.

Paragraphs 8 and 9 give us three more arguments. In paragraph 8 we can glean the following sort of argument, attributable to Walter Burns, an advocate of capital punishment:

ARGUMENT 4

1. If we want a certain [good] kind of society [one that is caring, responsible, and so on], then we should practice capital punishment.
2. We do want such a society.

∴   We should practice capital punishment.

The second premise makes a claim that most people would assent to, and as I know of no good reason to reject it, let us turn our attention to the first premise. Here we need to ask ourselves whether the practice of capital punishment is the best, or even a good, way to achieve this particular goal. And it is not at all clear that it is. For example, what about this proposal: we could achieve the same goal by promoting mandatory life imprisonment instead of the practice of capital punishment. Can we imagine a society in which the homicide rate is low, people respect human life and property, and capital punishment is nonexistent? It would certainly seem so. What this shows is that capital punishment is not the only means for achieving the desired goal. So we need further reasons to think that capital punishment is either the sole or the best way of making progress toward this goal. The result, then, is that this argument is also inconclusive.

Our fifth argument, found in paragraph 13, can be written as follows:

ARGUMENT 5

1.   If all other Western countries have abandoned capital punishment, then so should the United States.

2.   All other Western countries have abandoned capital punishment.

∴   The United States should abandon the practice of capital punishment.

This argument could be construed as an appeal to either popular opinion (an "everyone is doing it" sort of argument) or authority ("they are all reasonable and they are not practicing it, so neither should we"). If it is an appeal to the majority (*argumentum ad populum*), then the key question is: Are there good reasons to think the majority is right in this case? We all know that the majority is not always right, so we should only follow the majority if there are good reasons for doing so. And thus far in this passage we have not encountered any such reasons. That having been said, what about the appeal to authority angle? The other Western countries certainly have many intelligent people, but this hardly means that these countries are somehow experts on the issue of capital punishment. Given that there is no good reason to consider them a genuine authority on this matter, then the appeal to authority fails here.

A sixth argument, found in paragraph 14, can be summarized as follows:

ARGUMENT 6

1.   If we decide who lives and dies (as Governor Brown did), then we are playing God.

2.   We should not play God.

∴   We should not decide who lives and dies.

This is clearly a valid argument, as it is an example of modus tollens. For the sake of argument, let us grant that the second premise is true, or at least acceptable. But what about the first premise? This is not so obvious. Is it true that deciding that one person should be executed while another should be granted clemency is playing God? There seem to be at least two lines of critique open to us here. The first is to suggest that the connection between executive decisions by the governor and playing God is not an obvious one, and that the author needs to offer an argument establishing that connection. The president of the United States (in conjunction with Congress) has the authority to decide whether the United States should go to war, but I doubt the author would equate this with "playing God," even though many deaths may result. The challenge to her, then, is to spell out why the presidential decision is not an example of playing God (and thus permissible), while the governor's executive decision is. There may be such an argument, but I do not know of it.

A second line of attack is to engage the author on her own terms. Suppose we grant that God exists and that God has a will. It follows, then, that either there is a revealed will of God or there is not. If the latter, then she has no ground for criticizing what Governor Brown was doing. I am assuming here that if the author criticizes people for playing God, then she is committed to the following beliefs:

1. God exists.

2. God has revealed himself (expressed his will).

3. The governor's executive decisions are contrary to God's will.

For the sake of argument, I am perfectly willing to grant her the first two beliefs, but the third belief is another matter. If we follow the traditional Christian practice of appealing to the Bible as the primary source of God's revelation, then the author's case does not get the support it requires. The Old Testament states that if one commits murder then his life will be forfeit. This establishes a prima facie case for capital punishment, at least for those who take the traditional Christian commitment to the Scriptures seriously. At the least it again shifts the burden of proof to the author. So for these two reasons we are justified in concluding that the author has failed to establish her claim that making executive decisions regarding life and death amounts to "playing God."

The author presents two more arguments in support of capital punishment. Paragraph 18 gives us this argument:

ARGUMENT 7

1. If the murderer had an unbelievably abusive childhood, then we should show compassion and not sentence him to death.

2. The murderer did have such a childhood.

∴   We should not sentence him to death.

Premise 2 is not objectionable. The accused clearly had an awful childhood, and I am willing to grant that it was as bad as was described. But is this enough to lessen his responsibility for his crime or reduce the punishment he receives? If we believe that humans have free will (which can be understood to mean either "the ability to do other than one did" or "the ability to do as one pleases") and are therefore responsible for their behavior, this suggests that we should hold individuals responsible for their behavior—unless there is some exceptional reason for thinking otherwise. And it is not at all clear that coming from an awful childhood qualifies here. If all the people who grew up in a significantly or even moderately dysfunctional home were not held accountable for their behavior as adults, then many people (probably the majority!) would not be accountable. We all know that trying circumstances can make it more difficult to be a virtuous person, but we also know that humans have the ability to respond well to even the most difficult of circumstances. We expect adult humans to behave in a responsible fashion regardless of their background. Although Harris's past is a sad one, he still *chose* to do what he did.

An eighth argument can be found in paragraph 20:

ARGUMENT 8

1. If the vast majority of the people are for capital punishment, then we should practice it.

2. The vast majority (80%) of Californians are for capital punishment.

∴   We should practice capital punishment.

Thinking back to Chapter 6, this is a straightforward appeal to popular opinion. If "everyone is doing (or believing) it," is it any more likely to be true or reasonable than if it is a minority view? Probably not. Many times throughout history the majority, even the overwhelming majority, has been mistaken in its beliefs, as these examples show:

1. People in the Middle Ages thought the earth was flat.

2. In 1951 the majority of Americans thought Senator Joe McCarthy was a good guy.

3. The majority of people in the 1700s, including doctors, thought it was medically wise to bleed people when they were sick so as to get rid of the "bad blood."

4. The majority of people in 1300 thought the sun revolved around the earth, and not the other way around.

5. The majority of Greeks in 400 B.C. thought women were weak and unstable and not capable of voting intelligently.

This hardly means that the majority is never right, but there seems to be no necessary connection between a belief being popular and its being reasonable or true. The bottom line here is whether the majority of Californians have good reason to believe as they do, and not how many of them believe it. It is better to side with one person who has good reasons for her belief as opposed to millions who have poor or no reasons for their belief to the contrary.

There is a final, implicit argument, contained in paragraph 21, that might be reconstructed as follows:

ARGUMENT 9

1. If one has the power to make decisions concerning life and death, then one has too much power.

2. Governor Brown had that much power.

∴   Governor Brown had too much power.

The second premise is not objectionable—Governor Brown did have that much power, at least over those who had been convicted of murder. So the key to this argument is the first premise. It certainly seems true that if one has that much power then one has a great deal of power. But the first premise claims more than that. It claims that this much power is too much power, which may or may not be true.

To establish the reasonableness of this premise, we need to ask, What is the power standard or barrier beyond which one would have too much power? In other words, where do we draw the line between having an acceptable amount of power and having too much of it? Suppose the author responds by saying that anyone who has life-or-death power over others, as Governor Brown did, has too much power.

At least two lines of argument can be developed here. The first is that claiming that something is true is not the same as giving a good reason for believing that to be true. The author still needs to give us a good reason for thinking that someone with that much power has too much power. I am open to that possibility, but I need to be persuaded by one or more good reasons in support of the claim.

The second line of argument is a little more sophisticated. Suppose we grant the author that anyone who has life-or-death power over others has too much power. Would accepting this claim as true have acceptable consequences? It is not at all clear that it would. For example, consider the following: in the world of medicine, advisory committees make decisions concerning who will get an organ transplant and who will not. Given that there are often not enough organs to go around, these committees, in a very real sense, have the authority to make life-or-death decisions concerning people's lives. Do these people have too much power? Probably not. But if we grant the author's claim that anyone with this much power has too much power, then presumably the transplant advisory committees should be disbanded or have their authority greatly weakened.

Since acceptance of the author's main claim results in perfectly legitimate undertakings being undermined, if not done away with completely, her main principle, as it stands, deserves to be rejected. What possible response could she make? First, she might modify her main principle so that it excludes the kind of authority over life and death that Governor Brown had but leaves intact the authority wielded by the organ transplant committee. Second, she might maintain that the principle is a reasonable one and that perhaps the organ transplant committees should be disbanded. Finally, she could admit that the main principle is seriously flawed and should be rejected. It is not clear which of three options is the best one, but given that organ transplant committees are necessary for a number of reasons, the main options seem to be the first and third ones.

A SUMMARY OF THE ARGUMENTS

We can summarize the author's arguments as follows:

Argument 1: This argument is against capital punishment. Though the argument is a valid one, both the first and second premises fail to be persuasive, making the entire argument unconvincing.

Arguments 2 and 3: These arguments are inseparable, in that the second argument points beyond itself to the third. For her third argument to succeed, the primary focus of ethical theory should be the consequences of actions. The author needs to offer reasons we should think this, or at least reasons we should think rehabilitation is more important than retribution and just deserts.

Argument 4: Here the argument in favor of capital punishment hinges on whether the practice of capital punishment is a good way to promote the goal of a caring and kind society. But it is unclear whether capital punishment does indeed promote such a society, let alone whether it is a good means toward that end.

Argument 5: This anti–capital punishment argument involves either an appeal to authority or an appeal to the majority (of countries). As was argued previously, the majority can and has been wrong in the past. The bottom line is whether there are good reasons to abandon the practice of capital punishment, and not whether it is shunned by many countries.

Argument 6: This is another anti–capital punishment argument. Though valid this argument also fails in that there are not persuasive reasons for thinking that having some authority over the life and death of others (as with the president and organ transplant committees) is a bad or undesirable thing.

Argument 7: This is yet another anti–capital punishment argument. This argument fails because we believe, rightly so, that even people from significantly dysfunctional childhoods should be held accountable for their behavior as adults. Such a childhood might be grounds for some leniency, but it alone would not be sufficient to absolve the perpetrator from responsibility for the murder of the two boys.

Argument 8: This is an appeal to popular opinion offered in favor of capital punishment. As was discussed in Chapter 6 on fallacies, there is never a guarantee that the majority is right, so we take the majority seriously only if it has good reasons for its belief. And since no such reason is offered, the argument deserves to be rejected.

Argument 9: This final argument, offered against capital punishment, is also unsuccessful. Even if someone has the amount of power (over life and death) that Governor Brown had, it still is not clear that such power is somehow wrong or inappropriate.

Even though a variety of arguments were presented both for and against capital punishment, none of them was convincing, and all of them suffered from one or more serious defects. Of course, even though none of the arguments was rationally persuasive, this does not mean that no such arguments concerning capital punishment exist. It simply means that we have not yet discovered any such argument.

Let us briefly consider a similar situation. Many students, upon finding out that a particular argument (we'll call it PA) for the existence of God is unsuccessful, will draw one of two conclusions:

1. That there are no good arguments for God's existence (and if one is inclined to believe in God, then it must be on faith alone)

2. That not only are there no good arguments for God's existence, but in fact it is thus reasonable to believe that God does not exist

Neither one of these conclusions is justified given the evidence at hand. The only reasonable conclusion we can draw is that PA itself fails to show belief in God to be reasonable, not that there are no such arguments. Similarly, if I believe that Michael Jordan is the greatest basketball player of all time because (I say) a little green space alien told me, it will follow that any belief based on such a claim will be unreasonable. But the belief that Michael Jordan is the greatest basketball player ever is still a reasonable one, for other, better reasons. In short, the fact that a particular argument for God's existence or nonexistence fails simply shows that that argument fails, and not that *all* arguments of that kind fail.

SUMMARY

As this chapter shows, a number of arguments exist both for and against capital punishment, but none of them are fully persuasive or convincing. The challenge to you here becomes applying your newfound critical thinking skills first to the essays in Chapter 10 and then to the everyday arguments found in real life.

EXERCISE 9.1

To practice your critical thinking skills, do the following:

1. Choose a controversial issue such as one of these:
   a. Capital punishment
   b. Abortion
   c. Euthanasia (mercy killing)
   d. Surrogate motherhood
   e. Handgun control
   f. Gay marriage
   g. Affirmative action
   h. Censorship of books, music, art, and so on
   i. Universal health care
   j. Animal rights

2. List all the arguments—good and bad—for and against the issue.

3. Determine which arguments, both pro and con, are the strongest (the most persuasive).

4. Develop the two strongest arguments for each side. This involves doing this:
   a. Present each argument.
   b. Check each for validity.
   c. Evaluate the premises:
      1. If you think each premise is rationally acceptable, then offer reasons in support of each premise.
      2. If you think one or more premises are rationally unacceptable, then offer reasons for doubting/rejecting those premises.

5. Give a reasoned conclusion, stating which side has the better arguments, and why. Note that in some cases the reasons pro and con may genuinely counterbalance each other, with the most reasonable position being neither pro nor con.

6. Present your findings to the class (from steps 4 and 5).

7. Get feedback from the class.

8. Modify your argument where necessary.

9. Practice these skills on a regular basis. Letters to the editor in your local newspaper, editorials in newspapers and magazines, and articles in magazines are good sources.

CHAPTER 10

Essays for Analysis

Read the following essays carefully, and then analyze them using the seven-step procedure discussed in the previous chapter. Some of the arguments involve controversial matters, so be sure to lay out the various arguments as fairly as possible. The discussion questions following each essay will get you started.

Rutgers Senior Finds His $7 How-To Is in Demand Among College Students

ANTHONY FLINT

One of the hottest books on college campuses isn't the latest collection of   1
Calvin and Hobbes—it's a book about cheating.

"Cheating 101" is a how-to guide on shortcuts to a degree—effective places to hide crib sheets, systems of foot signals for sharing multiple-choice answers, places to buy term papers and dozens of other tips.

Michael Moore, 24, a Rutgers University senior and author of the book has sold 5,000 copies, mostly at Rutgers, Ohio State and the University of Maryland. He recently returned from a marketing road trip to Penn State. And he plans to go to Boston, home to 11 colleges and universities, to hawk the $7 book around spring break.

"We're going to Boston right after we hit Daytona Beach in March."

Moore, a journalism major, contracts with a printer to produce the 86-   5
page book and sells it mostly out of his home in Hopewell, N.J. But because of the book's popularity, he takes sales operations on the road from time to

time. Sometimes aided by a pre-visit article in a student newspaper, he sets up a table in a fraternity house or a room on campus and watches the money roll in.

"Students love it," said Moore, who described his weekend selling session at Penn State University and St. Francis College as a "mob scene." The trip was good for 1,150 copies.

Moore said that in addition to students snapping up the guide, college administrators, lawyers, and clinical psychologists have ordered it too—presumably as a form of counterintelligence.

Moore makes no excuses about the profits he reaps from the book, and acknowledges that he set out to make money. But he also considers "Cheating 101" to be a commentary on the shortcomings of higher education: ill-prepared professors more concerned with research, dreary required courses and the lack of training for real-world applications.

"I thought it would be a good opportunity to point out what I believe are the permanent problems in education," said Moore, who said his experience in college has been sour. "It's an indictment of the system. Maybe somebody will make some changes, to curb cheating and make college a better place."

Cheating, Moore said, is a response to the shortcomings that students   10
see. It flourishes because often professors are not interested or look the other way, he said.

"Students just don't cheat because they're lazy or hung over," he said. "They see a professor who's not interested in what they're doing, so students aren't going to be interested in learning. That's a natural defense mechanism."

Rutgers officials, while praising Moore's entrepreneurial skills, have sharply criticized "Cheating 101" as a blatant violation of academic ethics. Some have drawn parallels to Michael Milken and Ivan Boesky, describing the book as the scholar's quick-and-dishonest route to success.

The penalties for cheating vary from school to school, but frequently include suspension or expulsion. Most colleges spell out the rules against cheating or plagiarizing in student codes provided to all freshmen.

Some educators are using the book as an opportunity to teach about ethics. Carol Oppenheim, a communications professor at Boston's Emerson College, recently led a discussion with students on whether student newspapers should run an advertisement for the book.

"It's an interesting teaching opportunity about a real ethical dilemma,"   15
Oppenheim said.

Moore said the wrath of college administrators is to be expected. "It's a manual about their mistakes, their shortcomings and failures. It's like a bad audit."

But he denies that he is engaging in anything dishonest or unethical.

"I don't think that people that are buying the book have never cheated before. They already know a lot of the methods. I'm not making a cheater out of anybody," he said.

"There's 'Final Exit,' a book on how to get out of drunk driving, a book on how to get out of speeding tickets," Moore said. "I'm making an honest living. I'm not dealing drugs. I'm just exercising my First Amendment rights."

Boston Globe, February 3, 1992

Questions for Discussion

1. What, if anything, makes cheating morally wrong?
2. Moore says cheating is in response to "the shortcomings [of classes] that students see." Does this justify it? Why or why not?
3. Is Moore "making an honest living"?
4. What advice, along with supporting reasons, would you give to individuals who asked you if they should cheat in college?

The Real Opiate of the Masses

GEORGE WILL

In the escalating war against smoking—a habit that has taken many more lives than all of America's wars combined—some states are seeking compensation from tobacco companies for medical expenses for smoking-related injuries and prosecutors are contemplating perjury and conspiracy charges against tobacco executives who testified to disbelief in the obvious—the addictive nature of nicotine. In this war, ironies and paradoxes abound.

Smokers shiver outside their workplaces, pariahs in a country the father of which was a tobacco farmer. Probably the most powerful disincentive for smoking—peer pressure—is also the most powerful incentive for people to start smoking. Most smokers start before age eighteen and start because of peer pressure in the search for status and glamour. However, smoking now seems dumb and déclassé.

Cigarettes are the world's most heavily taxed consumer product. U.S. state taxes range up to Washington's 81.5 cents a pack, and in twenty industrialized nations cigarette taxes are even higher, sometimes five times higher. The ideal revenue yield from such taxes would be zero.

By some calculations, the social costs of smoking (in health care, lost productivity from illness and shortened lives, and fire damage) about equal the sum produced by cigarette taxes plus the savings that smoking produces in the form of reduced spending for Social Security, pensions, and nursing home care for smokers. If every smoker quit today, that would be a crisis for Social Security and all pension plans that incorporate actuarial assumptions about millions of smokers dying before they can receive benefits they otherwise would collect.

Cigarettes generate interesting product liability because cigarettes are   5
harmful when used as intended. The fact that cigarettes are harmful has been
broadly understood for several generations and today is almost universally
acknowledged. (The one-fourth of smokers who die prematurely because of
smoking lose on average twenty years of life expectancy, or twenty-nine
minutes per cigarette.) The consensus about this, combined with the warning
labels on cigarette packs and advertising, has helped immunize tobacco companies against liability for damage their products do. Juries have spurned
plaintiffs who have said they deserve recompense from tobacco companies
because "everyone knows" smoking is harmful.

Government subsidizes tobacco farming and the treatment of illnesses
tobacco causes. Government pays for these things from a Treasury diminished
by revenues lost because of productivity lost as a result of 1,164 smoking-
related deaths a day. Think of three jumbo jet crashes, 365 days a year. Or
think of three smoking-related deaths in the time it takes to read this column.
Yet the cigarette war is a substantial government success.

In the mid-1950s half the nation's adults smoked. Today one-quarter do.
Democracy presupposes the efficacy of information. Regarding tobacco, more
people are behaving reasonably, largely because of government's most cost-
effective activity, the dissemination of public health information. Is there in
all of government in the last three decades a life-enhancing success comparable to the stigmatizing of smoking since the 1964 surgeon general's report
affirmed a causal connection between smoking and cancer?

In *Ashes to Ashes*, Richard Kluger's Pulitzer Prize–winning history of
America's tobacco industry, he writes that there long has been an intuitive,
commonsense consensus that filling one's lungs with smoke is unhealthy. So
why do a quarter of Americans over eighteen smoke, and smoke heavily—
twenty-five cigarettes a day on average, which means about 70,000 nicotine
"hits" per year?

Smoking, says Kluger, is a highly sensual experience costing about a
penny a minute. No wonder it is the century's preferred pacifier, "the truest,
cheapest, most accessible opiate of the masses" as they cope with "the careen-
ing velocity of life." Yes, smoking kills, but, says Kluger, the smoker's cate-
chism is: Smoking hastens the death of only one in four smokers, so the odds
are on the particular smoker's side, you must die of something, so the something might as well be a pleasure; smoking takes years off the end of life,
which is not quality time; life is risky, so seize pleasure whenever possible.

Recently the Liggett Group Inc., which has less than 3 percent of Amer-   10
ica's cigarette market, agreed, under the pressure of a class action suit from
smokers, to accept various government regulations and fund some programs
to help smokers kick the habit. A small advance in the war.

It is a war with a long past that suggests a long future. A Russian czar used
torture, Siberian exile, and executions to discourage smoking, a Mogul em-
peror of Hindustan had smokers' lips split, and a Turkish sultan, convinced
that careless smoking caused a conflagration in Constantinople, made an

example of some smokers by having pipes driven through their noses, some-times just before, sometimes just after beheading them. "And yet," writes Kluger, "the custom thrived."

Questions for Discussion

1. How much damage has smoking done to the health of Americans?
2. In what sense is smoking an "opiate"?
3. Should there be restrictions on smoking in public? Why or why not?
4. What approach should the government take toward smoking?

A Tough but Responsible Solution

BOB DOLE

While no longer a member of Congress, as the Republican presidential candidate in 1996 I do have more than a passing interest in the im-pending impeachment proceeding [of President Clinton].

Without rehashing that election, suffice it to say that any chance of suc-cess I may have had was wiped out by an avalanche of negative advertising paid for with money raised through questionable fund-raising tactics by the President and Vice President. Attorney General Janet Reno has buried her head in the sand on this serious matter, but let's hope that someone in Con-gress will hold the Attorney General accountable and pursue the alleged ille-gal fund-raising activities.

Having said that, let me lay out what might be an imperfect but tough and reasonable solution to the pending impeachment matter.

I have reminded myself that to impeach or accuse is the constitutional responsibility of the House; to convict or acquit is the constitutional respon-sibility of the Senate. I seriously doubt that half the American people under-stand the complex impeachment process.

Let me also note, at the outset, that many large and small details would have to be worked out by constitutional leaders working with the House and the Senate parliamentarians and legal counsels. I've been there and know how much work putting all this together will entail, including all the proce-dural hurdles.

So, here goes:

Step No. 1: Vote in the House of Representatives on any or all of the four articles of impeachment reported by the House Judiciary Committee.

Step No. 2: Regardless of the outcome of the House vote on any of the four articles, the Senate majority leader would, at the earliest possible time, introduce in the Senate a joint resolution (numbered 1600 if possible). The resolution would contain the essence or "guts" of all articles of impeachment considered by the House, plus any other necessary language, as determined by the Senate majority leader.

Step No. 3: After suspending or amending the rules governing impeachment proceedings, the Senate would take up and consider the joint resolution under a time agreement. The Vice President (President of the Senate) would preside at all times. No amendments except technical amendments offered by the majority leader would be in order. All points of order would be waived.

Step No. 4: Upon final action by the Senate, the House of Representatives 10 would take up the joint resolution: no amendments in order, except technical amendments offered by the Senate or his designee. Points of order would be waived.

The resolution would be considered under a time agreement.

Step No. 5: If a House-Senate conference is necessary, the conference report would be considered under a time agreement in both the House and the Senate.

Conditions, Etc.

1. The president announces his intention to support and sign the joint resolution before any action on the resolution by the Senate.

   a. The president agrees to sign the joint resolution at a public signing ceremony attended by the Vice President, Congressional leadership and other appropriate members of the House and Senate recommended by Democratic and Republican leaders; the President's Cabinet; the Chief Justice of the Supreme Court, and others as recommended by House and Senate leaders.

   b. White House, Senate and House media—television, radio, print and photographers—shall be present.

   c. The site, date and hour of the ceremony is to be determined by the House Speaker, or his designee, and the Senate majority leader.

   d. Copies of the signed joint resolution, with an appropriate Presidential letter, are to be forwarded to members of the Cabinet, members of Congress and heads of other Government agencies. This is to be completed within seven days of signing the joint resolution.

2. The overall agreement is to be determined by the Speaker, or his designee, and the Senate majority leader. Possible items:

   a. *All Congressional action completed and the President's signature affixed on or by Jan. 2, 1999.*

   b. *Bipartisan.* Any agreement in the House or Senate with reference to the proceedings shall be inoperative if the President, Vice President and Democratic Congressional leaders fail to publicly and actively support the joint resolution. Support is to be demonstrated by the President, Vice President and Democratic leadership in House and Senate, prior to and throughout consideration of the joint resolution. Republican leaders also agree to publicly and actively support.

c. The Speaker, or his designee, and the majority leader shall outline procedure, rules, time and any and all other matters pertaining to debate and disposition of the joint resolution, and could, if appropriate, include provisions relating to the President's legal obligations upon leaving office.

3. Penalties. Any penalty imposed must be in accordance with the Constitution and could require the voluntary agreement by the President to overcome the prohibition against bills of attainder.

Summary

These are my ideas. They are offered in good faith. I have consulted with no one.

They may not be worthy of a second thought, but I believe the suggestion   15
could lead to a fairly broad bipartisan result.

There is scarcely anyone who believes that the required 67 Senators would vote to convict the President on any of the four articles of impeachment approved by the House Judiciary Committee, notwithstanding what the full House might do.

I hope these suggestions will be seen as a blending of responsibility and justice, which will permit an expeditious disposition of the entire matter before the new 106th Congress begins work in January 1999.

It is also my hope that pursuing the above suggested outline, or a modified version thereof, would demonstrate to the vast majority of Americans that Republican Congressional leaders will fulfill their constitutional responsibilities, clear the decks and move forward when the 106th Congress convenes on Jan. 6, 1999.

I cannot imagine a better way for Republicans to start the new year than by taking charge, and producing results, at this historic moment. It is a time for a *tough* but *responsible* conclusion. Maybe these ideas will be a starting point for a bipartisan ending.

Questions for Discussion

1. Does Dole's proposal strike you as a *fair* one? Give reasons for your answer.
2. How does Dole's proposal differ from those of most Republicans in the Senate?
3. Is what Dole says in the second paragraph relevant to the topic at hand?
4. Give your overall assessment of Dole's proposal ("I generally agree/disagree with it because . . .").

Dissenting Opinion in Gregg v. Georgia *(1976)*[1]

THURGOOD MARSHALL

The two purposes that sustain the death penalty as nonexcessive in the Court's view are general deterrence and retribution. In *Furman*, I canvassed the relevant data on the deterrent effect of capital punishment. The state of knowledge at that point, after literally centuries of debate, was summarized as follows by a United Nations Committee:

> It is generally agreed between the retentionists and abolitionists, whatever their opinions about the validity of comparative studies of deterrence, that the data which now exist show no correlation between the existence of capital punishment and lower rates of capital crime.

The available evidence, I concluded in *Furman*, was convincing that "capital punishment is not necessary as a deterrent to crime in our society.". . .

. . . The evidence reviewed in *Furman* remains convincing, in my view, that "capital punishment is not necessary as a deterrent to crime in our society." The justification for the death penalty must be found elsewhere.

The other principal purpose said to be served by the death penalty is retribution. The notion that retribution can serve as a moral justification for the sanction of death finds credence in the opinion of my Brothers STEWART, POWELL, and STEVENS. . . . It is this notion that I find to be the most disturbing aspect of today's unfortunate [decision].

The concept of retribution is a multifaceted one, and any discussion of its role in the criminal law must be undertaken with caution. On one level, it can be said that the notion of retribution or reprobation is the basis of our insistence that only those who have broken the law be punished, and in this sense the notion is quite obviously central to a just system of criminal sanctions. But our recognition that retribution plays a crucial role in determining who may be punished by no means requires approval of retribution as a general justification for punishment. It is the question whether retribution can provide a moral justification for punishment—in particular, capital punishment—that we must consider.

My Brothers STEWART, POWELL, and STEVENS offer the following explanation of the retributive justification for capital punishment:

> The instinct for retribution is part of the nature of man, and channeling that instinct in the administration of criminal justice serves an important purpose in promoting the stability of a society governed by law. When people begin to believe that organized society is unwilling or unable to impose upon criminal offenders the punishment they "deserve," then there are sown the seeds of anarchy—of self-help vigilante justice and lynch law.

---

[1] Gregg had been convicted of two counts of armed robbery and two counts of murder and then sentenced to death. On appeal his case eventually reached the Supreme Court.

This statement is wholly inadequate to justify the death penalty. As my Brother BRENNAN stated in *Furman,* "[t]here is no evidence whatever that utilization of imprisonment rather than death encourages private blood feuds and other disorders." It simply defies belief to suggest that the death penalty is necessary to prevent the American people from taking the law into their own hands.

In a related vein, it may be suggested that the expression of moral outrage through the imposition of the death penalty serves to reinforce basic human values—that it marks some crimes as particularly offensive and therefore to be avoided. The argument is akin to a deterrence argument, but differs in that it contemplates the individual's shrinking from antisocial conduct, not because he fears punishment, but because he has been told in the strongest possible way that the conduct is wrong. This contention, like the previous one, provides no support for the death penalty. It is inconceivable that any individual concerned about conforming his conduct to what society says is "right" would fail to realize that murder is "wrong" if the penalty were simply life imprisonment.

The foregoing contentions—that society's expression of moral outrage through the imposition of the death penalty pre-empts the citizenry from taking the law into its own hands and reinforces moral values—are not retributive in the purest sense. They are essentially utilitarian in that they portray the death penalty as valuable because of its beneficial results. These justifications for the death penalty are inadequate because the penalty is, quite clearly I think, not necessary to the accomplishment of those results.

There remains for consideration, however, what might be termed the purely retributive justification for the death penalty—that the death penalty is appropriate not because of its beneficial effect on society, but because the taking of the murderer's life is itself morally good. Some of the language of the opinion of my Brothers STEWART, POWELL, and STEVENS . . . appears positively to embrace this notion of retribution for its own sake as a justification for capital punishment. They state:

> [T]he decision that capital punishment may be the appropriate sanction in extreme cases is an expression of the community's belief that certain crimes are themselves so grievous an affront to humanity that the only adequate response may be the penalty of death.

They then quote with approval from Lord Justice Denning's remarks before the British Royal Commission on Capital Punishment:

> The truth is that some crimes are so outrageous that society insists on adequate punishment, because the wrong-doer deserves it, irrespective of whether it is a deterrent or not.

Of course, it may be that these statements are intended as no more than observations as to the popular demands that it is thought must be responded to in order to prevent anarchy. But the implication of the statements appears to me quite different—namely, that society's judgment that the murderer "deserves" death must be respected not simply because the preservation of order requires it, but because it is appropriate that society make the judgment and carry it out. It is this latter notion, in particular, that I consider to be fundamentally at odds with the Eighth Amendment. The mere fact that the community demands the murderer's life in return for the evil he has done cannot sustain the death penalty, for as Justices STEWART, POWELL, and STEVENS remind us, "the Eighth Amendment demands more than that a challenged punishment be acceptable to contemporary society." To be sustained under the Eighth Amendment, the death penalty must "comport with the basic concept of human dignity at the core of the Amendment"; the objective in imposing it must be "[consistent] with our respect for the dignity of [other] men." Under these standards, the taking of life "because the wrong-doer deserves it" surely must fail, for such a punishment has as its very basis the total denial of the wrongdoer's dignity and worth.

The death penalty, unnecessary to promote the goal of deterrence or to further any legitimate notion of retribution, is an excessive penalty forbidden by the Eighth and Fourteenth Amendments. I respectfully dissent from the Court's judgment upholding the [sentence] of death imposed upon the [petitioner in this case].

Questions for Discussion

1. What is Marshall's position on capital punishment?
2. What reasons does Marshall offer in support of his view?
3. To what extent do you agree with Marshall's view? What reasons can you give for your view?
4. How do the ideas of deterrence and retribution figure into the discussion?

Little Bessie (Chapter 3)

MARK TWAIN

Mamma, if a person by the name of Jones kills a person by the name of 1
Smith just for amusement, it is murder isn't it, and Jones is a murderer?
Yes, my child.
And Jones is punishable for it?
Yes, my child.
Why mamma? 5
Why? Because God has forbidden homicide in the Ten Commandments, and therefore whoever kills a person commits a crime and must suffer for it.

But mamma, suppose Jones has by birth such a violent temper that he can't control himself?

He *must* control himself. God requires it.

But he doesn't make his own temper, mamma, he is born with it, like the rabbit and the tiger; and so, why should he be held responsible?

Because God *says* he is responsible and *must* control his temper.   10

But he *can't* mamma; and so, don't you think it is God that does the killing and is responsible, because it was *He* that gave him the temper which he couldn't control?

Peace, my child! He *must* control it, for God requires it, and that ends the matter. It settles it, and there is no room for argument.

(*After a thoughtful pause.*) It doesn't seem to me to settle it. Mamma, murder is murder, isn't it? And whoever commits it is a murderer? That is the plain simple fact, isn't it?

(*Suspiciously*). What are you arriving at now, my child?

Mamma, when God designed Jones He could have given him a rabbit's   15 temper if He wanted to, couldn't He?

Yes.

Then Jones would not kill anybody and have to be hanged?

True.

But He chose to give Jones a temper that would *make* him kill Smith. Why, then, isn't *He* responsible?

Because He also gave Jones a Bible. The Bible gives Jones ample warning   20 not to commit murder; and so if Jones commits it he alone is responsible.

(*Another pause.*) Mamma, did God make the housefly?

Certainly, my darling.

What for?

For some great and good purpose, and to display His power.

What is the great and good purpose, mamma?   25

We do not know, my child. We only know that He makes *all* things for a great and good purpose. But this is too large a subject for a dear little Bessie like you, only a trifle over three years old.

Possibly, mamma, yet it profoundly interests me. I have been reading about the fly, in the newest science book. In that book he is called "the most dangerous animal and the most murderous that exists upon the earth, killing hundreds of thousands of men, women, and children every year, by distributing deadly diseases among them." Think of it, mamma, the most fatal of all the animals! by all odds the most murderous of all the living things created by God. Listen to this, from the book:

> Now the house fly has a very keen sense for filth of any kind. Whenever there is any within a hundred yards or so, the fly goes for it to smear its mouth and all the sticky hairs of its six legs with dirt and disease germs. A second or two suffices to gather up many thousands of these disease germs, and then off goes the fly to the nearest kitchen or dining room. There the fly

crawls over the meat, butter, bread, cake, anything it can find in fact, and often gets into the milk pitcher, depositing large numbers of disease germs at every step. The house fly is as disgusting as it is dangerous.

Isn't it horrible, mamma! One fly produces fifty-two billions of descendants in 60 days in June and July, and they go and crawl over sick people and wade through pus, and sputa, and foul matter exuding from sores, and gaum themselves with every kind of disease-germ, then they go to everybody's dinner table and wipe themselves off on the butter and the other food, and many and many a painful illness and ultimate death results from this loathsome industry. Mamma, they murder seven thousand persons in New York City alone, every year—people against whom they have no quarrel. To kill without cause is murder—nobody denies that, mamma.

Well?

Have the flies a Bible?   30

Of course not.

You have said it is the Bible that makes man responsible. If God didn't give him a Bible to circumvent the nature He deliberately gave him, God would be responsible. He gave the fly his murderous nature, and sent him forth unobstructed by a Bible or any other restraint to commit murder by wholesale. And so, therefore, God is Himself responsible. God is a murderer. Mr. Hollister says so. Mr. Hollister says God can't make one moral law for man and another for Himself. He says it would be laughable.

Do shut up! I wish that the tiresome Hollister was in H-amburg. He is an ignorant, unreasoning, illogical ass, and I have told you over and over again to keep out of his poisonous company.

Questions for Discussion

1. What are the main points that Bessie makes?
2. Why does Bessie find her mother's religious beliefs troubling and unconvincing?
3. What kind of relationship do Bessie and her mother have?
4. What do you think of Bessie's view?

Court Orders Treatment on Boy

ASSOCIATED PRESS

A cancer-stricken 13-year-old boy must undergo chemotherapy and possi-   1
bly have his leg amputated despite his wishes and those of his deeply religious parents, a Canadian judge ruled Thursday.

The case has sparked debate about the rights of parents and their children, and the responsibilities of the state, in deciding on appropriate medical treatment for minors.

The boy, Tyrell Dueck, had sought to halt his chemotherapy treatments for bone cancer and instead pursue alternative therapies such as vitamin and mineral injections coupled with prayer.

However, Judge Allison Rothery, after a series of hearings in Saskatoon, Saskatchewan, said Tyrell's views were based on misinformation provided by his father, Tim Dueck.

The judge said the father had screened the medical information reaching his son, and as a result Tyrell incorrectly believed that the alternative therapies available in Mexico had a 90 percent success rate. 5

"Tyrell has been misguided by his father into placing his hopes for recovery on a cure that does not exist," Rothery said. "This is simply cruel to Tyrell."

According to doctors who testified at the hearings, Tyrell will likely die within a year if his chemotherapy treatment is discontinued. The doctors said he had a 65 percent chance of recovery if he resumes the chemotherapy program and has his leg amputated above the knee.

Rothery ruled that Tyrell should remain with his parents, but that his medical treatment would be overseen by Saskatchewan's Social Services Department.

During the hearings, a psychiatrist testified that Tyrell had the emotional and intellectual capacity to make his own decision about treatment, but did not possess enough information to make an objective choice.

The psychiatrist, Dr. Donald Duncan, said the Duecks have a "fundamentalist, faith-healing view of the world, and place great trust in the power of prayer." 10

Rothery ordered that the parents not be present for further sessions of Tyrell's treatment.

"He is a boy deeply under the influence of his father," she said. "The information that his father gives to him is wrong and could place the child in medical peril."

Saskatchewan law allows the government to intervene when a child under 16 requires urgent medical treatment that their parents oppose. But there have been few previous cases anywhere in Canada where a relatively mature child joins the parent in refusing the treatment.

The lawyer for his parents, Owen Griffiths, said the family is considering an appeal.

Questions for Discussion

1. What reasons does the judge offer for her ruling?
2. How is religious liberty an issue in this case?
3. Should parents have absolute rights over the treatment of their own children? Why or why not?
4. Do you agree with the judge's ruling? Why or why not?
5. What issues make cases like this one emotionally charged?

Save African Children

RALPH DIAZ

I feel ashamed now remembering that when I first saw death among the   1
children laying on the cold earth I did not want to be affected by it. I held
my breath, lest I too inhale death. Close by, I noticed that others, much
stronger than myself, touched, and even smiled at, death. "See," one of them
seemed to say to me, "I can touch death and life takes on more vigor in me to
bring life to others."

Me? I was afraid to touch those small skeleton hands. I feared that the
reverse process would take place, that death would flow into life. All my
knowledge of human development was useless at that moment when I faced
death. There I was, standing, unable to move, wanting to go away, to wake up
in a different reality, in Geneva or Nairobi or some other place far from death
and the clutch of fear. So my mind started to rationalize. "What can you do
anyway? You are just one person representing one organization. It has air-
lifted 30,000 tons of wheat flour to a storage place nearby. Then what? It's too
late for most of the children, isn't it?"

The child nearby closed her eyes for the last time with a smile on her lips,
still holding the hands of the lady who dared to defy death. The lady had
managed to give something very precious to the child who had just died:
"You are dying as a person," she told her, "and not as an animal."

Moisture gathered in my eyes. The lady faced me. She read my thoughts.
She told me: "You are wrong. Not everyone is near death here. The force of
life is unbelievably strong in persons. With your help, many more children,
their mothers and others can be saved." Why had I not realized it before? First
fear, then rationalization: these are both instruments of death. I must break
away from them.

Let us do something now in Africa with our African brothers and sisters.   5
Together let us form a life bridge. Let us reverse death's harvest. There is still
time left for many children to be fully restored to life. Are you afraid? If so,
you too will become an instrument of death. Will you act now? If so, you too
can be a force of life.

New York Times, 6 January 1985

Questions for Discussion

1. Do we have any obligation to help other human beings in need? Why or
   why not?

2. Did any of the starving children do anything to deserve their situation
   in life?

3. Do the basic needs of others come before our desire for some of the
   luxuries (non-necessities) of life? Why or why not?

4. How would you respond to Diaz's essay?

We Aren't the World

NATIONAL REVIEW

The best way to experience the charity mega-hit "We Are the World" is by   1
means of the video, on which you can actually watch the collection of 45
pop stars, ranging from the hot (Bruce Springsteen) to the dead (Bob Dylan)
to the seemingly eternal (Ray Charles), shaking and singing for relief of Ethiopia. Musically, it's a good tune, astonishingly good for a committee effort;
and morally, it is better that the millions of dollars be raised with the intention of feeding the starving than of paying for the next few cocaine deals.

Intellectually, though, the musical effort leaves some things to be desired.
The last wave of concern for African misery, ten years ago, was stimulated by
the grinding Sahel drought. That drought was not an act of God. It was
caused, in large part, by overgrazing; which occurred because the nomads had
increased the size of their herds; which became possible because the local
governments, acting on the advice of Western "experts," had dotted the land-
scape with wells (which also, incidentally, lowered the water table). The suffering, in other words, was caused by misguided efforts to help. Since 20
percent of the profits of "We Are the World" is supposed to go for "long-term
development," the Sahel experience is not academic.

Or it would not be academic if the Marxist government of Ethiopia were
genuinely interested in ending the famine—which it is not. Most of the dying
are "rebels," and Addis Ababa is content to take food for its own hungry, and
let the rest eat sand. Relief organizations have been trying with difficulty to get
around the problem: by feeding refugees in Sudan; by going into rebel areas
illegally. But you won't learn this from "We Are the World." Men eat. They also
think; sometimes their thoughts lead them to cruelties not dreamt of in Bruce
Springsteen's philosophy. We aren't the world, and not all the world is like us.

Questions for Discussion

1. What is the main point of this essay?
2. How does it differ in tone and attitude from the previous essay?
3. To what extent do you agree with what is said here? What reasons can
   you give for your view?
4. Are we, in any sense, our brothers' and sisters' keeper? Why or why not?

Rich and Poor

PETER SINGER

Some Facts

Consider these facts: by the most cautious estimates, 400 million people lack   1
the calories, protein, vitamins, and minerals needed for a normally healthy

life. Millions are constantly hungry; others suffer from deficiency diseases and from infections they would be able to resist on a better diet. Children are worst affected. According to one estimate, 15 million children under five die every year from the combined effects of malnutrition and infection. In some areas, half the children born can be expected to die before their fifth birthday.

Nor is lack of food the only hardship of the poor. To give a broader picture, Robert McNamara, President of the World Bank, has suggested the term "absolute poverty." The poverty we are familiar with in industrialized nations is relative poverty—meaning that some citizens are poor relative to the wealth enjoyed by their neighbours. People living in relative poverty in Australia might be quite comfortably off by comparison with old-age pensioners in Britain, and British old-age pensioners are not poor in comparison with the poverty that exists in Mali or Ethiopia. Absolute poverty, on the other hand, is poverty by any standard. In McNamara's words:

> Poverty at the absolute level . . . is life at the very margin of existence.
> The absolute poor are severely deprived human beings struggling to survive in a set of squalid and degraded circumstances almost beyond the power of our sophisticated imaginations and privileged circumstances to conceive.
> Compared to those fortunate enough to live in developed countries, individuals in the poorest nations have:
> An infant mortality rate eight times higher
> A life expectancy one-third lower
> An adult literacy rate 60% less
> A nutritional level, for one out of every two in the population, below acceptable standards; and for millions of infants, less protein than is sufficient to permit optimum development of the brain

And McNamara has summed up absolute poverty as:

> a condition of life so characterized by malnutrition, illiteracy, disease, squalid surroundings, high infant mortality and low life expectancy as to be beneath any reasonable definition of human decency.

Absolute poverty is, as McNamara has said, responsible for the loss of countless lives, especially among infants and young children. When absolute poverty does not cause death it still often causes misery of a kind not often seen in the affluent nations. Malnutrition in young children stunts both physical and mental development. It has been estimated that the health, growing and learning capacity of nearly half the young children in developing countries are affected by malnutrition. Millions of people on poor diets suffer from deficiency diseases, like goitre, or blindness caused by a lack of vitamin A. The food value of what the poor eat is further reduced by parasites such as hookworm and ringworm, which are endemic in conditions of poor sanitation and health education.

Death and disease apart, absolute poverty remains a miserable condition of life, with inadequate food, shelter, clothing, sanitation, health services and education. According to World Bank estimates which define absolute poverty in terms of income levels insufficient to provide adequate nutrition, something like 800 million people—almost 40 percent of the people in developing countries—live in absolute poverty. Absolute poverty is probably the principal cause of human misery today.

This is the background situation, the situation that prevails on our planet all the time. It does not make headlines. People died from malnutrition and related diseases yesterday, and more will die tomorrow. The occasional droughts, cyclones, earthquakes and floods that take the lives of tens of thousands in one place and at one time are more newsworthy. They add greatly to the total amount of human suffering; but it is wrong to assume that when there are no major calamities reported, all is well.

The problem is not that the world cannot produce enough to feed and shelter its people. People in the poor countries consume, on average, 400 lbs of grain a year, while North Americans average more than 2000 lbs. The difference is caused by the fact that in the rich countries we feed most of our grain to animals, converting it into meat, milk and eggs. Because this is an inefficient process, wasting up to 95 percent of the food value of the animal feed, people in rich countries are responsible for the consumption of far more food than those in poor countries who eat few animal products. If we stopped feeding animals on grains, soybeans and fishmeal the amount of food saved would—if distributed to those who need it—be more than enough to end hunger throughout the world.

These facts about animal food do not mean that we can easily solve the world food problem by cutting down on animal products, but they show that the problem is essentially one of distribution rather than production. The world does produce enough food. Moreover the poorer nations themselves could produce far more if they made more use of improved agricultural techniques.

So why are people hungry? Poor people cannot afford to buy grain grown by American farmers. Poor farmers cannot afford to buy improved seeds, or fertilizers, or the machinery needed for drilling wells and pumping water. Only by transferring some of the wealth of the developed nations to the poor of the undeveloped nations can the situation be changed.

That this wealth exists is clear. Against the picture of absolute poverty that McNamara has painted, one might pose a picture of "absolute affluence." Those who are absolutely affluent are not necessarily affluent by comparison with their neighbours, but they are affluent by any reasonable definition of human needs. This means that they have more income than they need to provide themselves adequately with all the basic necessities of life. After buying food, shelter, clothing, necessary health services and education, the absolutely affluent are still able to spend money on luxuries. The absolutely affluent choose their food for the pleasures of the palate, not to stop hunger; they buy new clothes to look fashionable, not to keep warm; they move house to be in a better neighbourhood or have a play room for their children, not to keep out the rain; and after all this there is still money to spend on books and records, colour television, and overseas holidays.

At this stage I am making no ethical judgments about absolute affluence, merely pointing out that it exists. Its defining characteristic is a significant amount of income above the level necessary to provide for the basic human needs of oneself and one's dependents. By this standard Western Europe, North America, Japan, Australia, New Zealand and the oil-rich Middle Eastern states are all absolutely affluent, and so are many, if not all, of their citizens. The [former] USSR and Eastern Europe might also be included on this list. To quote McNamara once more:

> The average citizen of a developed country enjoys wealth beyond the wildest dreams of the one billion people in countries with per capita incomes under $200. . . .

These, therefore, are the countries—and individuals—who have wealth which they could, without threatening their own basic welfare, transfer to the absolutely poor.

At present, very little is being transferred. Members of the Organization of Petroleum Exporting Countries lead the way, giving an average of 2.1 percent of their Gross National Product. Apart from them, only Sweden, the Netherlands and Norway have reached the modest UN target of 0.7 percent of GNP. Britain gives 0.38 percent of its GNP in official development assistance and a small additional amount in unofficial aid from voluntary organizations. The total comes to less than £1 [1 pound] per month per person, and compares with 5.5 percent of GNP spent on alcohol, and 3 percent on tobacco. Other, even wealthier nations, give still less: Germany gives 0.27 percent, the United States 0.22 percent and Japan 0.21 percent. . . .

The Obligation to Assist

The Argument for an Obligation to Assist

The path from the library at my university to the Humanities lecture theatre passes a shallow ornamental pond. Suppose that on my way to give a lecture I notice that a small child has fallen in and is in danger of drowning. Would anyone deny that I ought to wade in and pull the child out? This will mean getting my clothes muddy, and either canceling my lecture or delaying it until I can find something dry to change into; but compared with the avoidable death of a child this is insignificant.

A plausible principle that would support the judgment that I ought to pull the child out is this: if it is in our power to prevent something very bad happening, without thereby sacrificing anything of comparable moral significance, we ought to do it. This principle seems uncontroversial. . . .

Nevertheless the uncontroversial appearance of the principle that we ought to prevent what is bad when we can do so without sacrificing anything of comparable moral worth is deceptive. If it were taken seriously and acted upon, our lives and our world would be fundamentally challenged. For the principle applies, not just to rare situations in which one can save a child from a pond, but to the everyday situation in which we can assist those living in absolute poverty. In saying this I assume that absolute poverty with its hunger and malnutrition, lack of shelter, illiteracy, disease, high infant mortality and low life expectancy, is a bad thing. And I assume that it is within the power of the affluent to reduce absolute poverty, without sacrificing anything of comparable moral significance. If these two assumptions and the principle we have been discussing are correct, we have an obligation to help those in absolute poverty which is not less strong than our obligation to rescue a drowning child from a pond. Not to help would be wrong, whether or not it is intrinsically equivalent to killing. Helping is not, as conventionally thought, a charitable act which it is praiseworthy to do, but not wrong to omit; it is something that everyone ought to do.

This is the argument for an obligation to assist. Set out more formally, it would look like this.

First Premise: If we can prevent something bad without sacrificing anything of comparable significance, we ought to do it.

Second Premise: Absolute poverty is bad.

Third Premise: There is some absolute poverty we can prevent without sacrificing anything of comparable moral significance.

Conclusion: We ought to prevent some absolute poverty.

The first premise is the substantive moral premise on which the argument rests, and I have tried to show that it can be accepted by people who hold a variety of ethical positions.   15

The second premise is unlikely to be challenged. Absolute poverty is, as McNamara put it, "Beneath any reasonable definition of human decency" and it would be hard to find a plausible ethical view which did not regard it as a bad thing.

The third premise is more controversial, even though it is cautiously framed. It claims only that some absolute poverty can be prevented without the sacrifice of anything of comparable moral significance. It thus avoids the objection that any aid I can give is just "drops in the ocean" for the point is not whether my personal contribution will make any noticeable impression on world poverty as a whole (of course it won't) but whether it will prevent some poverty. This is all the argument needs to sustain its conclusion, since the second premise says that any absolute poverty is bad, and not merely the total amount of absolute poverty. If without sacrificing anything of comparable significance we can provide just one family with the means to raise itself out of absolute poverty, the third premise is vindicated.

I have left the notion of moral significance unexamined in order to show that the argument does not depend on any specific values or ethical principles. I think the third premise is true for most people living in industrialized nations, on any defensible view of what is morally significant. Our affluence means that we have income we can dispose of without giving up the basic necessities of life, and we can use this income to reduce absolute poverty. Just how much we will think ourselves obliged to give up will depend on what we consider to be of comparable moral significance to the poverty we could prevent: colour television, stylish clothes, expensive dinners, a sophisticated stereo system, overseas holidays, a (second?) car, a larger house, private schools for our children. . . .

Objections to the Argument

Do people have a right to private property, a right which contradicts the view that they are under an obligation to give some of their wealth away to those in absolute poverty? According to some theories of rights (for instance, Robert Nozick's) provided one has acquired one's property without the use of unjust means like force and fraud, one may be entitled to enormous wealth while others starve. This individualistic conception of rights is in contrast to other views, like the early Christian doctine to be found in the works of Thomas Aquinas, which holds that since property exists for the satisfaction of human needs, "whatever a man has in superabundance is owed, of natural right, to the poor for their sustenance." A socialist would also, of course, see wealth as belonging to the community rather than the individual, while utilitarians, whether socialist or not, would be prepared to override property rights to prevent great evils.

Does the argument for an obligation to assist others therefore presuppose 20 one of these other theories of property rights, and not an individualistic theory like Nozick's? Not necessarily. A theory of property rights can insist on our right to retain wealth without pronouncing on whether the rich ought to give to the poor. Nozick, for example, rejects the use of compulsory means like taxation to redistribute income, but suggests that we can achieve the ends we deem morally desirable by voluntary means. So Nozick would reject the claim that rich people have an "obligation" to give to the poor, in so far as this implies that the poor have a right to our aid, but might accept that giving is something we ought to do and failing to give, though within one's rights, is wrong—for rights is not all there is to ethics.

The argument for an obligation to assist can survive, with only minor modifications, even if we accept an individualistic theory of property rights. In any case, however, I do not think we should accept such a theory. It leaves too much to chance to be an acceptable ethical view. For instance, those whose forefathers happened to inhabit some sandy wastes around the Persian Gulf are now fabulously wealthy, because oil lay under those sands; while those whose forefathers settled on better land south of the Sahara live in absolute poverty, because of droughts and bad harvests. Can this distribution be acceptable from an impartial point of view? If we imagine ourselves about to begin life as a citizen of either Kuwait or Chad—but we do not know which—would we accept the principle that citizens of Kuwait are under no obligation to assist people living in Chad?

Population and the Ethics of Triage

Perhaps the most serious objection to the argument that we have an obligation to assist is that since the major cause of absolute poverty is overpopulation, helping those now in poverty will only ensure that yet more people are born to live in poverty in the future.

In its most extreme form, this objection is taken to show that we should adopt a policy of "triage." The term comes from medical policies adopted in wartime. With too few doctors to cope with all the casualties, the wounded were divided into three categories: those who would probably survive without medical assistance, those who might survive if they received assistance, but otherwise probably would not, and those who even with medical assistance probably would not survive. Only those in the middle category were given medical assistance. The idea, of course, was to use limited medical resources as efficiently as possible. For those in the first category, medical treatment was not strictly necessary; for those in the third category, it was likely to be useless. It has been suggested that we should apply the same policies to countries, according to their prospects of becoming self-sustaining. We would not aid countries which even without our help will soon be able to feed their populations. We would not aid countries which, even with our help, will not be able to limit their population to a level they can feed. We would aid those countries where our help might make the difference between success and failure in bringing food and population into balance. . . .

In support of this view Garrett Hardin has offered a metaphor: we in the rich nations are like the occupants of a crowded lifeboat adrift in a sea full of drowning people. If we try to save the drowning by bringing them aboard our boat will be overloaded and we shall all drown. Since it is better that some survive than none, we should leave the others to drown. In the world today, according to Hardin, "lifeboat ethics" apply. The rich should leave the poor to starve, for otherwise the poor will drag the rich down with them. . . .

Putting aside the controversial issue of the extent to which food production might one day be increased, it is true, as we have already seen, that the world now produces enough to feed its inhabitants—the amount lost by being fed to animals itself being enough to meet existing grain shortages. Nevertheless population growth cannot be ignored. Bangladesh could, with land reform and using better techniques, feed its present population of 80 million; but by the year 2000, according to World Bank estimates, its population will be 146 million. The enormous effort that will have to go into feeding an extra 66 million people, all added to the population within a quarter of a century, means that Bangladesh must develop at full speed to stay where she is. Other

25

low income countries are in similar situations. By the end of the century, Ethiopia's population is expected to rise from 29 million to 54 million; Somalia's from 3 to 7 million, India's from 620 to 958 million, Zaire's from 25 to 47 million. What will happen then? Population cannot grow indefinitely. It will be checked by a decline in birth rates or rise in death rates. Those who advocate triage are proposing that we allow the population growth of some countries to be checked by a rise in death rates—that is, by increased malnutrition, and related diseases; by widespread famines; by increased infant mortality; and by an epidemic of infectious diseases.

The consequences of triage on this scale are so horrible that we are inclined to reject it without further argument. How could we sit by our television sets, watching millions starve while we do nothing? Would not that . . . be the end of all notions of human equality and respect for human life? Don't people have a right to our assistance, irrespective of the consequences?

Anyone whose initial reaction to triage was not one of repugnance would be an unpleasant sort of person. Yet initial reactions based on strong feelings are not always reliable guides. . . .

The question is: how probable is this forecast that continued assistance now will lead to greater disasters in the future?

Forecasts of population growth are notoriously fallible, and theories about the factors which affect it remain speculative. One theory, at least as plausible as any other, is that countries pass through a "demographic transition" as their standard of living rises. When people are very poor and have no access to modern medicine their fertility is high, but population is kept in check by high death rates. The introduction of sanitation, modern medical techniques and other improvements reduces the death rate, but initially has little effect on the birth rate. Then population grows rapidly. Most poor countries are now in this phase. If standards of living continue to rise, however, couples begin to realize that to have the same number of children surviving to maturity as in the past, they do not need to give birth to as many children as their parents did. The need for children to provide economic support in old age diminishes. Improved education and the emancipation and employment of women also reduce the birthrate, and so population growth begins to level off. Most rich nations have reached this stage, and their populations are growing only very slowly.

If this theory is right, there is an alternative to the disasters accepted as 30
inevitable by supporters of triage. We can assist poor countries to raise the living standards of the poorest members of their population. We can encourage the governments of these countries to enact land reform measures, improve education, and liberate women from a purely child-bearing role. We can also help other countries to make contraception and sterilization widely available. There is a fair chance that these measures will hasten the onset of demographic transition and bring population growth down to a manageable level. Success cannot be guaranteed; but the evidence that improved economic security and education reduce population growth is strong enough to

make triage ethically unacceptable. We cannot allow millions to die from starvation and disease when there is a reasonable probability that population can be brought under control without such horrors.

Population growth is therefore not a reason against giving overseas aid, although it should make us think about the kind of aid to give. Instead of food handouts, it may be better to give aid that hastens the demographic transition. This may mean agricultural assistance for the rural poor, or assistance with education, or the provision of contraceptive services. Whatever kind of aid proves most effective in specific circumstances, the obligation to assist is not reduced.

Questions for Discussion

1. According to Singer, how much hunger is there in the world?
2. Does Singer see the problem more as a matter of lack of food or poor distribution of existing food?
3. Why does Singer believe we have an obligation to the starving?
4. How does Singer respond to Hardin and others who disagree with his approach?
5. With whom do you more closely identify, Singer or Hardin? Give reasons for your choice.

Lifeboat Ethics: The Case against Helping the Poor

GARRETT HARDIN

Environmentalists use the metaphor of the earth as a "spaceship" in trying to persuade countries, industries and people to stop wasting and polluting our natural resources. Since we all share life on this planet, they argue, no single person or institution has the right to destroy, waste, or use more than a fair share of its resources. 1

But does everyone on earth have an equal right to an equal share of its resources? The spaceship metaphor can be dangerous when used by misguided idealists to justify suicidal policies for sharing our resources through uncontrolled immigration and foreign aid. In their enthusiastic but unrealistic generosity, they confuse the ethics of a spaceship with those of a lifeboat.

A true spaceship would have to be under the control of a captain, since no ship could possibly survive if its course were determined by committee. Spaceship Earth certainly has no captain; the United Nations is merely a toothless tiger, with little power to enforce any policy upon its bickering members.

If we divide the world crudely into rich nations and poor nations, two thirds of them are desperately poor, and only one third comparatively rich, with the United States the wealthiest of all. Metaphorically each rich nation can be seen as a lifeboat full of comparatively rich people. In the ocean outside each lifeboat swim the poor of the world, who would like to get in, or at least to share some of the wealth. What should the lifeboat passengers do?

First, we must recognize the limited capacity of any lifeboat. For example,   5
a nation's land has a limited capacity to support a population and as the current energy crisis has shown us, in some ways we have already exceeded the carrying capacity of our land.

Adrift in a Moral Sea

So here we sit, say fifty people in our lifeboat. To be generous, let us assume it has room for ten more, making a total capacity of sixty. Suppose the fifty of us in the lifeboat see 100 others swimming in the water outside, begging for admission to our boat or for handouts. We have several options: we may be tempted to try to live by the Christian ideal of being "our brother's keeper," or by the Marxist ideal of "to each according to his needs." Since the needs of all in the water are the same, and since they all can be seen as "our brothers," we could take them all into our boat, making a total of 150 in a boat designed for sixty. The boat swamps, everyone drowns. Complete justice, complete catastrophe.

Since the boat has an unused excess capacity of ten more passengers, we could admit just ten more to it. But which ten do we let in? How do we choose? Do we pick the best ten, the neediest ten, "first come, first served"? And what do we say to the ninety we exclude? If we do let an extra ten in our lifeboat, we will have lost our "safety factor," an engineering principle of critical importance. For example, if we don't leave room for excess capacity as a safety factor in our country's agriculture, a new plant disease or a bad change in the weather could have disastrous consequences.

Suppose we decide to preserve our small safety factor and admit no more to the lifeboat. Our survival is then possible, although we shall have to be constantly on guard against boarding parties.

While this last solution clearly offers the only means of our survival, it is morally abhorrent to many people. Some say they feel guilty about their good luck. My reply is simple: "Get out and yield your place to others." This may solve the problem of the guilt-ridden person's conscience, but it does not change the ethics of the lifeboat. The needy person to whom the guilt-ridden person yields his place will not himself feel guilty about his good luck. If he did, he would not climb aboard. The net result of conscience-stricken people giving up their unjustly held seats is the elimination of that sort of conscience from the lifeboat.

This is the basic metaphor within which we must work out our solutions.   10
Let us now enrich the image, step by step, with substantive additions from the real world, a world that must solve real and pressing problems of overpopulation and hunger.

The harsh ethics of the lifeboat become even harsher when we consider the reproductive differences between the rich nations and the poor nations. The people inside the lifeboats are doubling in numbers every eighty-seven years; those swimming around outside are doubling, on the average, every thirty-five years, more than twice as fast as the rich. And since the world's resources are dwindling, the difference in prosperity between the rich and the poor can only increase.

As of 1973 the U.S. had a population of 210 million people, who were increasing by 0.8 percent per year. Outside our lifeboat, let us imagine another 210 million people, (say the combined populations of Colombia, Ecuador, Venezuela, Morocco, Pakistan, Thailand, and the Philippines) who are increasing at a rate of 3.3 percent per year. Put differently, the doubling time for this aggregate population is twenty-one years, compared to eighty-seven years for the U.S.

Multiplying the Rich and the Poor

Now suppose the U.S. agreed to pool its resources with those seven countries, with everyone receiving an equal share. Initially the ratio of Americans to non-Americans in this model would be one-to-one. But consider what the ratio would be after eighty-seven years, by which time the American population would have doubled to a population of 420 million. By then, doubling every twenty-one years the other group would have swollen to 3.54 billion. Each American would have to share the available resources with more than eight people.

But, one could argue, this discussion assumes that current population trends will continue, and they may not. Quite so. Most likely the rate of population will decline much faster in the U.S. than it will in the other countries, and there does not seem to be much we can do about it. In sharing with "each according to his needs," we must recognize that needs are determined by population size, which is determined by the rate of reproduction, which at present is regarded as a sovereign right of every nation, poor or not. This being so, the philanthropic load created by the sharing ethic of the spaceship can only increase.

The Tragedy of the Commons

The fundamental error of spaceship ethics, and the sharing it requires, is that it leads to what I call the "tragedy of the commons." Under a system of private property, the men who own property recognize their responsibility to care for it, for if they don't they will eventually suffer. A farmer, for instance, will allow no more cattle in a pasture than its carrying capacity justifies. If he overloads it, erosion sets in, weeds take over, and he loses the use of the pasture.

If a pasture becomes a commons open to all, the right of each to use it may not be matched by a corresponding ability to protect it. Asking everyone to use it with discretion will hardly do, for the considerate herdsman who refrains from overloading the commons suffers more than a selfish one who says his needs are greater. If everyone would restrain himself, all would be well; but it takes only one less than everyone to ruin a system of voluntary restraint. In a crowded world of less than perfect human beings, mutual ruin is inevitable if there are no controls. This is the tragedy of the commons.

One of the major tasks of education today should be the creation of such an acute awareness of the dangers of the commons that people will recognize its many varieties. For example, the air and water have become polluted because they are treated as commons. Further growth in the population or per capita conversion of natural resources into pollutants will only make the problem worse. The same holds true for the fish of the oceans. Fishing fleets have nearly disappeared in many parts of the world, and technological improvements in the art of fishing are hastening the day of complete ruin. Only the replacement of the system of the commons with a responsible system of control will save the land, air, water and oceanic fisheries.

The World Food Bank

In recent years there has been a push to create a new commons called a World Food Bank, an international depository of food reserves to which nations would contribute according to their abilities and from which they would draw according to their needs. This humanitarian proposal has received support from many liberal international groups, and from such prominent citizens as Margaret Mead, U.N. Secretary Kurt Waldheim, and Senators Edward Kennedy and George McGovern.

A world food bank appeals powerfully to our humanitarian impulses. But before we rush ahead with such a plan, let us recognize where the greatest political push comes from, lest we be disillusioned later. Our experience with the "Food for Peace program," or Public Law 480, gives us the answer. This program moved millions of dollars worth of U.S. surplus grain to food-short, population-long countries during the past two decades. But when P.L. 480 first became law, a headline in the business magazine *Forbes* revealed the real power behind it: "Feeding the World's Hungry Millions: How It Will Mean Billions for U.S. Business."

And indeed it did. In the years 1960 to 1970, U.S. taxpayers spent a total   20
of $7.9 billion on the Food for Peace Program. Between 1948 and 1970, they also paid an additional $50 billion for other economic-aid programs, some of which went for food and food-producing machinery and technology. Though all U.S. taxpayers were forced to contribute to the cost of P.L. 480, certain special interest groups gained handsomely under the program. Farmers did not have to contribute the grain; the Government, or rather the taxpayers, bought it from them at full market prices. The increased demand raised prices of farm products generally. The manufacturers of farm machinery, fertilizers and pesticides benefitted by the farmers' extra effort to grow more food. Grain elevators profited from storing the surplus until it could be shipped. Railroads

made money hauling it to ports, and shipping lines profited from carrying it overseas. The implementation of P.L. 480 required the creation of a vast Government bureaucracy, which then acquired its own vested interest in continuing the program regardless of its merits.

Extracting Dollars

Those who proposed and defended the Food for Peace program in public rarely mentioned its importance to any of these special interests. The public emphasis was always on its humanitarian effects. The combination of silent selfish interests and highly vocal humanitarian apologists made a powerful and successful lobby for extracting money from taxpayers. We can expect the same lobby to push now for the creation of a World Food Bank.

However great the potential benefit to selfish interests, it would not be a decisive argument against a truly humanitarian program. We must ask if such a program would actually do more good than harm, not only momentarily but also in the long run. Those who propose the food bank usually refer to a current "emergency" or "crisis" in terms of world food supply. But what is an emergency? Although they may be infrequent and sudden, everyone knows that emergencies will occur from time to time. A well-run family, company, organization or country prepares for the likelihood of accidents and emergencies. It expects them, budgets for them, saves for them.

Learning the Hard Way

What happens if some organizations or countries budget for accidents and others do not? If each country is solely responsible for its own well-being, poorly managed ones will suffer. But they can learn from experience. They may mend their ways, and learn to budget for infrequent but certain emergencies. For example, the weather varies from year to year, and periodic crop failures are certain. A wise and competent government saves out of the production of the good years in anticipation of bad years to come. Joseph taught this policy to Pharaoh in Egypt more than 2,000 years ago. Yet the great majority of the governments in the world today do not follow such a policy. They lack either the wisdom or the competence or both. Should those nations that do manage to put something aside be forced to come to the rescue each time an emergency occurs among the poor nations?

"But it isn't their fault!" some kind-hearted liberals argue. "How can we blame the poor people who are caught in an emergency? Why must they suffer for the sins of their governments?" The concept of blame is simply not relevant here. The real question is, what are the operational consequences of establishing a world food bank? If it is open to every country every time a need develops, slovenly rulers will not be motivated to take Joseph's advice. Someone will always come to their aid. Some countries will deposit food in the world food bank, and others will withdraw it. There will be almost no overlap. As a result of such food shortage emergencies, the poor countries will not learn to mend their ways, and will suffer progressively greater emergencies as their populations grow.

Population Control the Crude Way

On the average, poor countries undergo a 2.5 percent increase in population   25 each year; rich countries, about 0.8 percent. Only rich countries have anything in the way of food reserves set aside, and even they do not have as much as they should. Poor countries have none. If poor countries received no food from the outside, the rate of their population growth would be periodically checked by crop failures and famines. But if they can always draw on a world food bank in time of need, their population can continue to grow unchecked, and so will their "need" for aid. In the short run, a world food bank may diminish that need, but in the long run it actually increases the need without limit.

Without some system of worldwide food sharing, the proportion of people in the rich and poor nations might eventually stabilize. The overpopulated poor countries would decrease in numbers, while the rich countries that had room for more people would increase. But with a well-meaning system of sharing, such as a world food bank, the growth differential between the rich and the poor countries will not only persist, it will increase. Because of the higher rate of population growth in the poor countries of the world, 88 percent of today's children are born poor, and only 12 percent rich. Year by year the ratio becomes worse, as the fast-reproducing poor outnumber the slow-reproducing rich.

A world food bank is thus a commons in disguise. People will have more motivation to draw from it than to add to any common store. The less provident and less able will multiply at the expense of the abler and more provident, bringing eventual ruin upon all who share in the commons. Besides any system of "sharing" that amounts to foreign aid from the rich nations to the poor nations will carry the taint of charity, which will contribute little to the world peace so devoutly desired by those who support the idea of a world food bank. . . .

Chinese Fish and Miracle Rice

The modern approach to foreign aid stresses the export of technology and advice, rather than money and food. As an ancient Chinese proverb goes: "Give a man a fish and he will eat for a day, teach him how to fish and he will eat for the rest of his days." Acting on this advice, the Rockefeller and Ford Foundations have financed a number of programs for improving agriculture in the hungry nations. Known as the "Green Revolution," these programs have led to the development of "miracle rice" and "miracle wheat," new strains that offer bigger harvests and greater resistance to crop damage. Norman

Borlaug, the Nobel Prize winning agronomist who, supported by the Rocke-feller Foundatin, developed "miracle wheat," is one of the most prominent advocates of a world food bank. . . .

Overloading the Environment

Every human born constitutes a draft on all aspects of the environment: food, air, water, forests, beaches, wildlife, scenery and solitude. Food can, perhaps, be significantly increased to meet a growing demand. But what about clean beaches, unspoiled forests, and solitude? If we satisfy a growing population's need for food, we necessarily decrease its per capita supply of the other resources needed by men.

India, for example, now has a population of 600 million, which increases 30 by 15 million a year. This population already puts a huge load on a relatively impoverished environment. The country's forests are now only a small fraction of what they were three centuries ago, and floods and erosion continually destroy the insufficient farmland that remains. Every one of the 15 million new lives added to India's population puts an additional burden on the environment, and increases the economic and social costs of crowding. However humanitarian our intent, every Indian life saved through medical or nutritional assistance from abroad diminishes the quality of life for those who remain, and for subsequent generations. If rich countries make it possible, through foreign aid, for 600 million Indians to swell to 1.2 billion in a mere twenty-eight years, as their current growth rate threatens, will future generations of Indians thank us for hastening the destruction of their environment? Will our good intentions be sufficient excuse for the consequences of our actions?

My final example of a commons in action is one for which the public has the least desire for rational discussion—immigration. Anyone who publicly questions the wisdom of current U.S. immigration policy is promptly charged with bigotry, prejudice, ethnocentrism, chauvinism, isolationism or selfishness. . . .

Immigration vs. Food Supply

World food banks move food to the people, hastening the exhaustion of the environment of poor countries. Unrestricted immigration, on the other hand, moves people to the food, thus speeding up the destruction of the environment of rich countries. We can easily understand why poor people should want to make this latter transfer, but why should rich hosts encourage it?

As in the case of foreign-aid programs, immigration receives support from selfish interests and humanitarian impulses. The primary selfish interest in unimpeded immigration is the desire of employers for cheap labor, particularly in industries and trades that offer degrading work. In the past, one wave of foreigners after another was brought into the U.S. to work at wretched jobs for wretched wages. In recent years the Cubans, Puerto Ricans and Mexicans have had this dubious honor. The interests of the employers of cheap labor mesh well with the guilty silence of the country's liberal intelligentsia. White Anglo-Saxon Protestants are particularly reluctant to call for a closing of the doors to immigration for fear of being called bigots.

But not all countries have such reluctant leadership. Most educated Hawaiians, for example, are keenly aware of the limits of their environment, particularly in terms of population growth. There is only so much room on the islands, and the islanders know it. To Hawaiians, immigrants from the other forty-nine states present as great a threat as those from other nations. At a recent meeting of Hawaiian government officials in Honolulu, I had the ironic delight of hearing a speaker, who like most of his audience was of Japanese ancestry, ask how the country might practically and constitutionally close its doors to further immigration. One member of the audience countered: "How can we shut the door now! We have many friends and relatives in Japan that we'd like to bring here some day so that they can enjoy Hawaii too." The Japanese-American speaker smiled sympathetically and answered: "Yes, but we have children now, and someday we'll have grandchildren too. We can bring more people here from Japan only by giving away some of the land that we hope to pass on to our grandchildren someday. What right do we have to do that?"

At this point, I can hear U.S. liberals asking: "How can you justify slamming the door once you're inside? You say that immigrants should be kept out. But aren't we all immigrants, or the descendants of immigrants? If we insist on staying, must we not admit all others?" Our craving for intellectual order leads us to seek and prefer symmetrical rules and morals: a single rule for me and everybody else; the same rule yesterday, today, and tomorrow. Justice, we feel, should not change with time and place. 35

We Americans of non-Indian ancestry look upon ourselves as the descendants of thieves who are guilty morally, if not legally, of stealing this land from its Indian owners. Should we then give back the land to the now living American descendants of these Indians? However morally or logically sound this proposal may be, I, for one, am unwilling to live by it and I know no one else who is. Besides, the logical consequence would be absurd. Suppose that, intoxicated with a sense of pure justice, we should decide to turn our land over to the Indians. Since all our wealth has also been derived from the land, wouldn't we be morally obliged to give that back to the Indians too?

Pure Justice vs. Reality

Clearly, the concept of pure justice produces an infinite regression to absurdity. Centuries ago, wise men invented statutes of limitations to justify the rejection of such pure justice, in the interest of preventing continual disorder. The law zealously defends property rights, but only relatively recent property rights. Drawing a line after an arbitrary time has elapsed may be unjust, but the alternatives are worse.

We are all the descendants of thieves, and the world's resources are inequitably distributed. But we must begin the journey to tomorrow from the point where we are today. We cannot remake the past.

Questions for Discussion

1. How accurate is Hardin's lifeboat metaphor?
2. What does Hardin see as the "tragedy of the commons"?
3. How does Hardin's view differ from that of Singer?
4. Is Hardin's approach to the problem morally justifiable? Why or why not?
5. Why might the issue that Singer and Hardin address be an emotionally charged one for many people?
6. Who makes a better case for his position, Singer or Hardin? Give a detailed response, and be sure to offer reasons in support of your view. Try your argument out on a classmate and see if he or she is persuaded.

Suggested Readings

Govier, Trudy. *God, the Devil and the Perfect Pizza*. Peterborough, Ontario: Broadview Press, 1989. A charming introduction, through the use of dialogues and stories, to ten philosophical issues that have challenged thinkers for centuries.

Harris, James F. *Philosophy at 33⅓ RPM*. Chicago: Open Court, 1993. An investigation of rock music and the philosophical themes that find their way into it.

Hirsch, E. D., Jr. *Cultural Literacy*. Boston: Houghton Mifflin, 1987. Argues that Americans need to know much more about the heritage, traditions, and culture of the United States. Though facts alone do not enable us to think better, thinking about important facts helps our thinking to be more worthwhile.

Lawhead, William. *The Philosophical Journey*. Mountain View, CA: Mayfield, 2000. An excellent interactive introduction to both the traditional problems and the leading thinkers of philosophy.

Martin, Robert M. *There Are Two Errors in the the Title of This Book*. Peterborough, Ontario: Broadview Press, 1992. An interesting discussion and analysis of a number of philosophical puzzles and paradoxes.

Postman, Neil. *Amusing Ourselves to Death*. New York: Penguin Books, 1985. A powerful critique of modern American culture and the influence of television on how we think about and look at the world.

Purtill, Richard. *A Logical Introduction to Philosophy*. Englewood Cliffs, NJ: Prentice-Hall, 1989. Combines an introduction to formal logic with a look at some of the arguments advanced by Plato, Aquinas, Kant, and other famous philosophers over the years.

Schick, Theodore, Jr., and Lewis Vaughn. *How to Think About Weird Things*. Mountain View, CA: Mayfield, 1995. A book designed to help students think more carefully about strange and exotic matters.

Sire, James. *The Universe Next Door*, Downers Grove, IL: InterVarsity Press, 1997. A helpful introduction to a number of leading worldviews, with a critical analysis of each of the views.

Weston, Anthony. *Toward Better Problems*. Philadelphia: Temple University Press, 1992. A highly readable approach to a number of challenging ethical issues, including abortion, animal rights, and the environment. Weston challenges readers to carefully frame the central issues and to think them through carefully and logically.

Answers to Selected Exercises

Chapter 1 Introduction to Critical Thinking

EXERCISE 1.1

1. An informed opinion involves having reasons (especially good ones) for one's belief.
4. A number of possibilities are appropriate here.
7. A number of possibilities exist here. Choices involving vocation, significant others, and lifestyle are three examples.
10. To be answered by the student.

EXERCISE 1.2

1. Mere disagreement
4. Mere agreement
7. Reasoned agreement
10. Reasoned disagreement

EXERCISE 1.4

1. *Female:* As stated
   Male: Addressing a different issue
4. *Raylene:* As stated
   Desiree: Addressing same issue
7. *Citizen 1:* As stated
   Citizen 2: Addressing a different issue (though he is also focusing on the candidates, he is not addressing the issue of whether they will be the two candidates in 2004.

10. *Metalhead:* As stated
    Non-metal Head: Addressing same issue

EXERCISE 1.5

1. b
4. c.

EXERCISE 1.7

1. a. As stated
   d. Extramarital affairs are not relevant for evaluating the president.
   g. Setting one's goals too high leads to despair.
2. a. Main point: Dr. Kevorkian acted immorally.
      Support: His behavior violated both the Hippocratic oath and the dignity of his patients.
   d. Main point: Violent crime is the biggest problem in the U.S. today.
      Support: It impacts the most people.
   g. Main point: Animals should have the same rights as human beings.
      Support: There is nothing special about humans (to distinguish them from other animals).

Chapter 2 *Obstacles to Thinking Well*

EXERCISE 2.3

1. a. All doctors are happy.
   d. The long delays in carrying out capital punishment undermine its deterrent effect.
2. a. Depression affects how we make our decisions.
3. a. All people on welfare are lazy and don't want to work.
   d. All feminists hate men.
   g. All country music songs are shallow.
   j. All politicians are dishonest.
   m. All blondes are dumb.

p. Faith and reason are mutually exclusive.
4. a. Friend claims Kennedy was a great president and clearly will not even consider any evidence to the contrary.

EXERCISE 2.4

2. a. More likely
   d. Bell bottom pants
   g. That it was flat
   j. Disco
   m. Significantly negative (one of betrayal)
   p. Much more likely

Chapter 3 *Definitions and the Importance of Language*

EXERCISE 3.3

3. a. Vague
   d. Vague and ambiguous
   g. Ambiguous and possibly vague

Chapter 4 *The Basic Elements of an Argument*

EXERCISE 4.1

1. Yes
4. Yes
7. Yes
10. No
13. Yes
16. Yes
19. Yes

EXERCISE 4.2

1. a. False
   d. False
   g. False
   j. True
   m. True

2. a. The probability of the conclusion being true is 60%.
   d. The conclusion has a 99% probability of being true.
   g. Again, this depends on the precise meaning of "most." I would suggest it means (all else equal) "at least 70%."
   j. "Almost all" suggests a very high probability—I would suggest at least 90% (if not 95).

One can make a pretty good case that the conclusions of d, h, and j are the three most probable conclusions.

EXERCISE 4.3

1. a. The third sentence is the conclusion.
   d. Third sentence
   g. Third sentence
   j. The conclusion is "the physical world is [ultimately] unreal."
2. a. What's missing is "If Ed does not pay his taxes, then he will get in trouble."
   d. All cheeseheads live in Wisconsin.
   g. We should vote for Senator Fussmire.
   j. All apple pie is [made of] a kind of fruit.
   m. What I did yesterday will crumble to the ground.

3. a. 1. All A's are B's
      2. Some m's are A's

      ∴ Some m's are B's
4. a. Ed is an unmarried male; Pattern 6.
   d. If I go south, then I will need a car; Pattern 1.
   g. Evil does exist; Pattern 2.
   j. You are a Manchester United fan; Pattern 5.
5. a. I will not see Sue.
      1. Either A or B
      2. If A, then C
      3. ~C   [Implicit]

      ∴ B

Chapter 5   *Distinguishing Good Arguments from Bad Ones*

EXERCISE 5.1

1. Valid and sound
4. Valid and sound
7. Valid but unsound (mammals and dogs are apolitical)
10. Valid and sound

EXERCISE 5.2

1. H → ~A
4. E & J
7. N & P
10. L ∨ H
13. T → D
16. G & H
19. T & R & C
22. ~C → (W ∨ U)

EXERCISE 5.3

1.

P	Q	P → Q	~Q	∴~P	
T	T	T	F	F	
T	F	F	T	F	
F	T	T	F	T	
F	F	T	T	T	*Valid*

4.

P	Q	R	P → Q	P ∨ R	∴P & R	
T	T	T	T	T	T	*
T	T	F	T	T	F	*Invalid by lines 2 and 5*
T	F	T	F	T	T	
T	F	F	F	T	F	
F	T	T	T	T	F	*
F	T	F	T	F	F	
F	F	T	T	T	F	
F	F	F	T	F	F	

5.

P	Q	P ∨ (P & ~Q)	~P ∨ Q	∴~Q	
T	T	T	T	F	*Invalid*
T	F	T	F	T	
F	T	F	T	F	
F	F	F	T	T	

10. Inconsistent, no relevant lines

P	Q	R	P ∨ Q ∨ R	R → (P & Q)	~P	∴Q ∨ R
T	T	T	T	T	F	T
T	T	F	T	T	F	T
T	F	T	T	F	F	T
T	F	F	T	T	F	F
F	T	T	T	F	T	T
F	T	F	T	T	T	T
F	F	T	T	F	T	T
F	F	F	F	T	T	F

EXERCISE 5.4

1.

A	B		A ∨ B	B	∴A	
F	T		T	T	F	*Invalid*

4.

A	B	C		A ∨ ~B	C → B	∴A → ~C	
T	T	T		T	T	F	*Invalid*

7.

A	B	C		(A & B) → C	~C	∴~A	
T	F	F		T	T	F	*Invalid*

10.

A	B	C	D		A ∨ (B & C)	~B ∨ D	B → (A ∨ D)	∴B & D	
T	F	T	T		T	T	T	F	*Invalid*

13.

A	B	C	D	E		(A & B) → (C ∨ D ∨ ~E)	B & (A ∨ D)	~C & B	∴B & C	
T	T	F	T	T		T	T	T	F	*Invalid*

EXERCISE 5.5

1. a. Contradictory
   d. Subcontrary
   g. Contradictory
   j. Contradictory
2. a. Converse: All wealthy people are politicians.
   Obverse: No politicians are nonwealthy.
   Contrapositive: All nonwealthy people are nonpoliticians.
   d. Converse: Some theists are historians.
   Obverse: Some historians are not nontheists.

Contrapositive: Some nontheists are nonhistorians.
   g. Converse: No vegetarians are snakes.
   Obverse: All snakes are nonvegetarians.
   Contrapositive: No nonvegetarians are nonsnakes.
   j. Converse: Some unjustified actions are wars.
   Obverse: Some wars are unjustified actions.
   Contrapositive: Some justified actions are not wars.

EXERCISE 5.6

1. a.

A	B	$A \rightarrow B$	A	$\therefore B$	
T	T	T	T	T	* Valid
T	F	F	T	F	
F	T	T	F	T	
F	F	T	F	F	

d.

A	B	$A \vee B$	~A	$\therefore B$	
T	T	T	F	T	
T	F	T	F	F	
F	T	T	T	T	* Valid
F	F	F	T	F	

g.

A	B	C	$A \vee B$	$A \rightarrow \sim C$	C	$\therefore B$	
T	T	T	T	F	T	T	
T	T	F	T	T	F	T	
T	F	T	T	F	T	F	
T	F	F	T	T	F	F	
F	T	T	T	T	T	T	* Valid
F	T	F	T	T	F	T	
F	F	T	F	T	T	F	
F	F	F	F	T	F	F	

j.

A	B	C	$A \vee (\sim B \& C)$	$B \rightarrow \sim A$	$\therefore \sim B$	
T	T	T	T	F	F	
T	T	F	T	F	F	
T	F	T	T	T	T	* Valid
T	F	F	T	T	T	*
F	T	T	F	T	F	
F	T	F	F	T	F	
F	F	T	T	T	T	*
F	F	F	F	T	T	

m.

A	B	C	$A \rightarrow B$	$B \rightarrow C$	C	$\therefore A$	
T	T	T	T	T	T	T	*
T	T	F	T	F	F	T	
T	F	T	F	T	T	T	
T	F	F	F	T	F	T	
F	T	T	T	T	T	F	*
F	T	F	T	F	F	F	
F	F	T	T	T	T	F	*
F	F	F	T	T	F	F	

Invalid by lines 5, 7

p. Inconsistent, no relevant lines

A	B	C	A → (B ∨ C)	A & ~C	~B & C	∴B
T	T	T	T	F	F	T
T	T	F	T	T	F	T
T	F	T	T	F	T	F
T	F	F	F	T	F	F
F	T	T	T	F	F	T
F	T	F	T	F	F	T
F	F	T	T	F	T	F
F	F	F	T	F	F	F

s. Invalid by line 8

A	B	C	D	(A → B) → (C ∨ D)	A & ~(C & ~D)	B → C	∴B ∨ D	
T	T	T	T	T	T	T	T	
T	T	T	F	T	F	T	T	
T	T	F	T	T	T	F	T	
T	T	F	F	F	T	F	T	
T	F	T	T	T	T	T	T	*
T	F	T	F	T	F	T	F	
T	F	F	T	T	T	T	T	*
T	F	F	F	T	T	T	F	*
F	T	T	T	T	F	T	T	
F	T	T	F	T	F	T	T	
F	T	F	T	T	F	F	T	
F	T	F	F	F	F	F	T	
F	F	T	T	T	F	T	T	
F	F	T	F	T	F	T	F	
F	F	F	T	T	F	T	T	
F	F	F	F	F	F	T	F	

2. Valid

a.

A	B	C	A ∨ B	B → C	∴~A → C	
T	T	T	T	T	T	*
T	T	F	T	F	T	
T	F	T	T	T	T	*
T	F	F	T	T	T	*
F	T	T	T	T	T	*
F	T	F	T	F	F	
F	F	T	F	T	T	
F	F	F	F	T	F	

d. Invalid by line 4

A	B	C	A → ~B	~B ∨ C	A	∴C	
T	T	T	F	T	T	T	
T	T	F	F	F	T	F	
T	F	T	T	T	T	T	*
T	F	F	T	T	T	F	*
F	T	T	T	T	F	T	
F	T	F	T	F	F	F	
F	F	T	T	T	F	T	
F	F	F	T	T	F	F	

g.   Valid

A	B	C	(A & B) → C	~C	∴~(A & B)	
T	T	T	T	F	F	
T	T	F	F	T	F	
T	F	T	T	F	T	
T	F	F	T	T	T	*
F	T	T	T	F	T	
F	T	F	T	T	T	*
F	F	T	T	F	T	
F	F	F	T	T	T	*

3. a. Valid

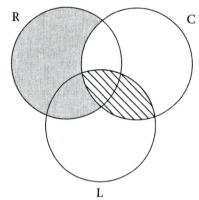

j. Valid

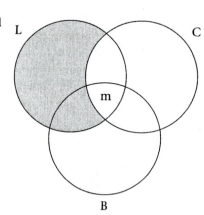

d. Invalid

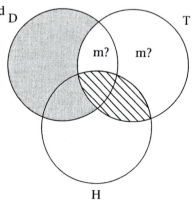

m. Invalid

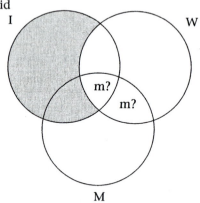

g. Valid

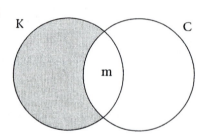

p. Invalid

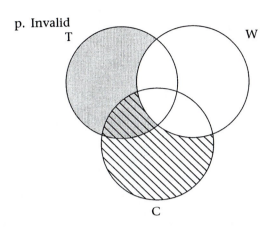

y. Invalid

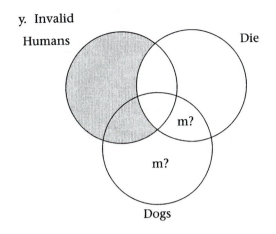

s. Invalid

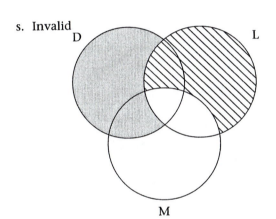

4. a. Valid

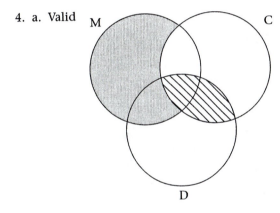

v. Invalid

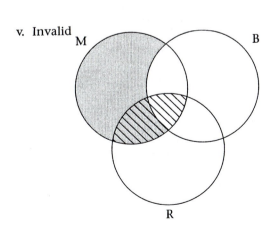

d. Invalid

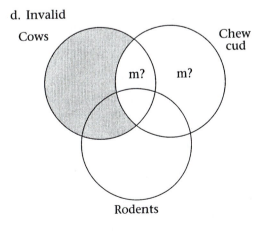

g. Invalid

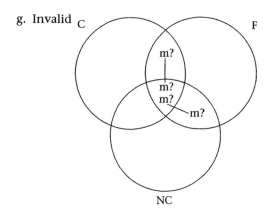

5. a. False
   d. True
   g. False

j. True
m. True
p. True
s. True
v. True
y. False

6. a. No
   d. No. Once one gets past poverty level, there is little correlation between wealth and happiness.
   g. Controversial (no consensus among philosophers)
   j. No. There exists much evidence to the contrary.
   m. No. Unfortunately, much evidence exists to the contrary.
   p. Controversial (my inclinations are yes)
   s. No—Boston is east.

Chapter 6 Fallacies

EXERCISE 6.1

1. Denying the antecedent
4. "You, too" ad hominem
7. Appeal to popular opinion
10. Abusive ad hominem
13. Appeal to popular opinion
16. Appeal to authority
19. Appeal to pity

EXERCISE 6.2

1. Equivocation
4. Appeal to ignorance
7. Appeal to ignorance
10. Two wrongs
13. Prejudicial language (and abusive ad hominem)
16. Prejudicial language

EXERCISE 6.3

1. Slippery slope
4. Complex question
7. Complex question
10. False dilemma
13. False dilemma
16. Complex question

EXERCISE 6.4

1. Hasty generalization
4. Incomplete statistic
7. Begging the question
10. Begging the question
13. Incomplete statistic
16. Common cause

EXERCISE 6.5

1. False dilemma
4. Denying the antecedent
7. Complex question
10. Appeal to authority
13. Appeal to pity
16. False confidence
19. False dilemma

EXERCISE 6.6

1. False dilemma
4. Straw man, prejudicial language
7. Appeal to pity
10. Prejudicial language
13. Equivocation (equal worth/rights ≠ equal circumstances)
16. Prejudicial language

EXERCISE 6.7

1. Prejudicial language
4. Abusive ad hominem
7. Common cause
10. Abusive ad hominem, prejudicial language
13. Affirming the consequent
16. Slippery slope

EXERCISE 6.8

1. Incomplete statistic
4. Prejudicial language
7. Prejudicial language
10. Prejudicial language
13. Abusive ad hominem, prejudicial language
16. "You, too" ad hominem

EXERCISE 6.9

1. Untestable claim
4. Incomplete statistic
7. Abusive ad hominem, prejudicial language
10. Hasty generalization
13. Prejudicial language
16. Appeal to popular opinion
19. Abusive ad hominem, prejudicial language

EXERCISE 6.10

1. Untestable claim
4. Appeal to popular opinion, prejudicial language

7. Prejudicial language (it also borders on being a positive slippery slope)
10. Abusive ad hominem, prejudicial language
13. Prejudicial language
16. Prejudicial language

EXERCISE 6.11

1. A lengthy example of an amazing and untestable claim
2. Abusive ad hominem, prejudicial language ("Well, . . . wacko)
   Abusive ad hominem ("From what egg . . . hatched?")
   Denying the antecedent ("I argue . . . any rights, period.")
   Equivocation (on "welfare")
   Abusive ad hominem ("The only reason . . . shelter")
   Abusive ad hominem ("an appropriate . . . her")
   Slippery slope ("If you grant . . . drain"), prejudicial language
   Appeal to popular opinion ('Everyone knows . . . seriously"), prejudicial language
   Prejudicial language, appeal to (economic) force
   Appeal to authority, prejudicial language
   False dilemma, prejudicial language
   Appeal to force (? political—"I conclude . . . hearts"), prejudicial language
   (Possible) appeal to force (physical)— "If Buford happens . . . sleep."

Chapter 7   *Knowledge and Worldview*

EXERCISE 7.2

1. A list of the most likely to be true (not in any particular order, given the degree of controversy surrounding many):
   1. C, n, and r all seem deserving of a high level of probability.
   2. E, h, k, l, p, q, r, and s all seem deserving of being in the "probable" range.
   3. A, m, and o all seem clearly false.
2. a. 1
   d. D, e, and f are all matters of great complexity and controversy.

EXERCISE 7.5

1. Material possessions (significantly) contribute to personal happiness.
4. A variation on #3
7. Personal preference matters.
10. Don't let others limit your horizons.
13. Hedonism with a dash of anti-establishment thrown in.
16. Life is good.
19. Material (physical) things are not what matter most in life.
22. Self-explanatory

25. Whether or not God exists is no longer relevant for modern humanity (many Nietzsche scholars reject the idea that he is an atheist in the traditional sense).

Chapter 8   *Thinking about Values*

EXERCISE 8.1

1. Descriptive
4. Descriptive
7. Descriptive

EXERCISE 8.2

1. Aesthetic
4. Aesthetic
7. Moral
10. Moral

Credits

TEXT CREDITS

Chapter 6   p. 147, from B. Herbert, "Separation Anxiety," *The New York Times,* January 19, 1996. Copyright © 1996 by the New York Times Co. Reprinted by permission.   **Chapter 9   p. 226,** from "Does the Death Penalty Work? Harris Hearing Revives Old Debate," April 1992. Reprinted with permission from Associated Press.   **Chapter 10   p. 238,** republished with permission of *Boston Globe,* from "Rutgers Senior Finds His $7 How-To Is in Demand Among College Students," 1992; permission conveyed through Copyright Clearance Center;   **p. 240,** reprinted with the permission of Scribner, a Division of Simon & Schuster from *The Woven Figure* by George F. Will. Copyright © 1997 by George F. Will;   **p. 242,** from B. Herbert, "Separation Anxiety," *The New York Times,* December 15, 1998. Copyright © 1998 by the New York Times Co. Reprinted by permission;   **p. 247,** from Mark Twain, *Devil's Race-Track: Mark Twain's Great Dark Writings,* translated/edited by John Tuckey, selection from Chapter 3, Little Bessie. Copyright © 1966, 1972, 1980 Mark Twain Co. Reprinted with permission from the Regents of the University of California and the University of California Press;   **p. 249,** from "Court Orders Treatment on Boy," March 18, 1999. Reprinted with permission from Associated Press;   **p. 251,** from Ralph Diaz, "Save African Children," *The New York Times,* January 6, 1985. Copyright © 1985 by the New York Times Co. Reprinted by permission;   **p. 252,** from "We Aren't the World," *National Review,* May 1985. Copyright © 1985 by National Review, Inc. Reprinted by permission; **p. 252,** from Peter Singer, *Practical Ethics,* Second Edition, Cambridge University Press, 1993. Reprinted with the permission of Cambridge University Press;   **p. 260,** from Garrett Hardin, "Lifeboat Ethics," *Psychology Today,* September 1974. Copyright © 1974 Sussex Publishers, Inc. Reprinted with permission from Psychology Today Magazine.

Index

Page references in **bold** type indicate glossary terms and definitions. Page references in *italics* indicate illustrations or boxed material.